JOURNAL FOR THE STUDY OF THE NEW TESTAMENT SUPPLEMENT SERIES
202

Executive Editor
Stanley E. Porter

Editorial Board
Elizabeth A. Castelli, David Catchpole, Kathleen E. Corley,
R. Alan Culpepper, James D.G. Dunn, Craig A. Evans,
Stephen Fowl, Robert Fowler, George H. Guthrie,
Robert Jewett, Robert W. Wall

STUDIES IN NEW TESTAMENT GREEK
8

Sheffield Academic Press

Transitivity-Based Foregrounding in the Acts of the Apostles

A Functional-Grammatical Approach to the Lukan Perspective

Gustavo Martín-Asensio

Journal for the Study of the New Testament
Supplement Series 202

Studies in New Testament Greek 8

Para mis padres

Published by
Sheffield Academic Press Ltd
Mansion House
19 Kingfield Road
Sheffield S11 9AS
England

http://www.SheffieldAcademicPress.com

Typeset by Sheffield Academic Press
and
Printed on acid-free paper in Great Britain
by Biddles Ltd
Guildford, Surrey

British Library Cataloguing in Publication Data

A catalogue record for this book is available
from the British Library

ISBN 1-84127-164-0

CONTENTS

PREFACE

In the early summer of 1995, Professor S.E. Porter began corresponding with me concerning the initial work into the doctoral thesis which has evolved into the present volume. His first words to me were 'Focus on your chosen linguistic method. Master that now, and you will save much precious time later.' During that summer in Vancouver, I read nothing but Halliday, and very soon began to share Porter's appreciation of Halliday's functional grammar, and its applicability to the Greek narrative of Acts soon became apparent. I wish, therefore, to express my gratitude to Professor Porter for his continued expert guidance and generous encouragement throughout the entire project. I also wish to thank two individuals without whose input into my life this work would never have been possible: Dr Ron Smith of University of the Nations, Hawaii, who first taught me to love the Greek New Testament. His commission and close supervision of my translation of the entire Greek New Testament, my last project as an undergraduate, was an example of his gift as an insightful motivator, always 'forcing' his students to reach just beyond what they think they are capable of. Last, but certainly not least, I give special thanks to Doug Kracht, my friend and teacher over critical years in Madrid. The love and encouragement I received from his family made that time a highly productive period of my life, excellent preparation for what was to come. As far as the present volume is concerned, my research cluster colleagues at University of Surrey Roehampton provided much needed sharpening and correction on a regular basis. Any remaining errors, however, are wholly my own.

ABBREVIATIONS

A1CS	The Book of Acts in its First Century Setting
AnBib	Analecta biblica
BDF	Friedrich Blass, A. Debrunner and Robert W. Funk, *A Greek Grammar of the New Testament and Other Early Christian Literature* (Cambridge: Cambridge University Press, 1961)
Bib	*Biblica*
BSOS	Bulletin of the School of Oriental Studies
BTB	*Biblical Theology Bulletin*
EstBíb	*Estudios bíblicos*
EvQ	*Evangelical Quarterly*
FN	*Filología neotestamentaria*
HTS	*Harvard Theological Studies*
ICC	International Critical Commentary
JBL	*Journal of Biblical Literature*
JETS	*Journal of the Evangelical Theological Society*
JSNT	*Journal for the Study of the New Testament*
JSNTSup	*Journal for the Study of the New Testament*, Supplement Series
Neot	*Neotestamentica*
NovT	*Novum Testamentum*
NovTSup	*Novum Testamentum*, Supplements
NTS	*New Testament Studies*
NTTS	New Testament Tools and Studies
SBG	Studies in Biblical Greek
SBLDS	SBL Dissertation Series
SBLMS	SBL Monograph Series
SBLSBS	SBL Sources for Biblical Study
SBT	Studies in Biblical Theology
SJLA	Studies in Judaism in Late Antiquity
SNTSMS	Society for New Testament Studies Monograph Series
ST	*Studia theologica*
TynBul	*Tyndale Bulletin*
WUNT	Wissenschaftliche Untersuchungen zum Neuen Testament
ZNW	*Zeitschrift für die neutestamentliche Wissenschaft*

INTRODUCTION

In his 1994 award-winning doctoral thesis at Harvard University, Daniel J. Goldhagen exploded upon the conscience of late twentieth-century Germany with what at first appeared to be yet another assessment of the horrors of the Holocaust.[1] it does not take long for most readers to realize, however, that there is a fundamental feature in Goldhagen's work which sets it apart from all previous discussions of the subject. *Hitler's Willing Executioners* is an attempt at much more than filling a specific lacuna within contemporary historical reseach: it represents a conscientious and thorough recasting of the familiar narratives of the Holocaust into a new, linguistically sharpened account of agents, their deeds and their victims:

> The first task in restoring the perpetrators to the center of our under-
> standing of the Holocaust is to restore to them their identities, gram-
> matically by using not the passive but the active voice, in order to ensure
> that they, the actors, are not absent from their own deeds... Any explana-
> tion that ignores either the particular nature of the perpetrators' actions
> or the identity of the victims is inadequate for a host of reasons... The
> proper description of the events under discussion, the re-creation of the
> phenomenological reality of the killers, is crucial for any explication.[2]

The result is not merely a gripping historical monograph, but, at least as importantly, a fascinating test case in narratology. Goldhagen is to be credited with—among other achievements—having demonstrated the intimate connexion that exists between specific language patterns (expressly, choices from the transitivity network of English, see below

---

1. Goldhagen's thesis was awarded the American Political Science Association's 1994 Gabriel A. Almond Award for best dissertation in the field of comparative politics. A somewhat abridged version of this dissertation (minus 100+ pages of 'methodology') has now become an international best-seller under the title of *Hitler's Willing Executioners: Ordinary Germans and the Holocaust* (London: Abacus, 1996).

2. Goldhagen, *Hitler's Willing Executioners*, pp. 6, 22.

for definition) and the effect that these patterns have upon readers.

In a recent *Washington Post* editorial, Richard Harwood discussed at some length the basic requirements of an effective newspaper story. While acknowledging the significant difficulties inherent in a journalist's attempt to reconstruct the complete chronologies, causes of events and roles various actors played, Harwood concurs with James Carey that

> [W]hen matters of fundamental importance surface in the news, they cannot be treated as secular mysteries and left unexplained... We insist that the economy and the polity be explicable: *a domain where someone is in control, natural laws are being obeyed, or events are significant and consequential* [my emphasis].[3]

In other words, Harwood argues that the intelligibility and effectiveness of a news story is inseparably bound up with the proper sequencing of processes and participants within the plot. Thus, Goldhagen the historian and Harwood the journalist draw attention to the fundamental role that the transitivity network plays in the composition of narratives within their respective fields.[4] The same applies to narrative plots of any type. Without a consistent depiction of the participants, their roles and actions, and, more specifically, the actions of those characters who in different ways advance or resolve the plot, a narrative will appear to lack a backbone and sense of direction. In fact, the question of 'who does what to whom' may be considered absolutely essential to the interpretation of all narrative texts.[5]

---

3.   Richard Harwood, 'The How and Why of it All', The *Washington Post* Thursday, 14 August 1997, A21.

4.   The term transitivity is here used by Halliday in the sense of 'the different types of processes that are recognized in [a] language, and the structures by which they are expressed'. A process consists potentially of three elements: the process itself, participants and circumstances. See M.A.K. Halliday, *An Introduction to Functional Grammar* (London: Edward Arnold, 1985), p. 101.

5.   See on this Vladímir Propp, *Morphology of the Folktale* (trans. L. Scott; Austin, TX: University of Texas Press, 1990), p. 20; A.J. Greimas, *Sémantique structurale* (Paris: Librairie Larousse, 1966), pp. 172-254; A.J. Greimas, *Les actants, les acteurs et les figures* (Paris: Librairie Larousse, 1973); Roger Fowler, *Linguistics and the Novel* (London: Methuen, 1977), pp. 29-30; Seymour Chatman, *Story and Discourse* (Ithaca, NY: Cornell University Press, 6th edn, 1993), p. 19; M.A.K. Halliday, *Language as Social Semiotic* (London: Edward Arnold, 1979); Halliday, *Introduction to Functional Grammar*, esp. 101-57; Ruqaiya Hasan, *Linguistics, Language and Verbal Art* (Oxford: Oxford University Press, 1985);

This important insight was first formulated in a systematic way in Vladímir Propp's ground-breaking *Morphology of the Folktale*, published originally in Russian in 1928.[6] In this greatly condensed summary of several years' research, Propp sets out to design a method capable of classifying Russian fairy tales from the Afanás'ev folktale collection. Rejecting criteria such as theme and motif as ultimately inadequate, Propp suggests the various functions of the 'dramatis personae', the actors in a story, as the most basic components of the fairy tale.[7] Conceived as 'act[s] of a character, defined from the point of view of [their] significance for the course of the action',[8] narrative functions are understood by Propp to be constant elements in a story, regardless of how and by whom they are fulfilled in the course of events. Propp discerned 31 of these functions, encoded in various verb forms, which included 'absentation', 'reconnaissance', 'trickery', 'departure', etc., and were capable of being carried out by actors such as 'hero', 'dispatcher', 'villain', donor', 'sought for person', and so on Propp's concern was to investigate the relationship of participant functions to each other and to the plot, as well as the degree to which these functions and their sequence are constant in the collections of tales he examined.

Useful as Propp's insights were, they did not become widely known outside of the former Soviet bloc until Roman Jakobson divulged Propp's work in the West.[9] Soon thereafter, however, and through the

---

Michael J. Toolan, *Narrative, a Critical Linguistic Introduction* (London: Routledge, 1988), pp. 238-41. Regarding causality in narrative, see also William Labov, 'Some Further Steps in Narrative Analysis' (only available online at: http://ling.upenn.edu/~labov/sfs.html). Though addressing primarily oral narratives of personal experience, Labov has developed a framework useful in interpreting narratives of many other types, including folktales and novels. One of the key theorems in Labov's framework is that 'narrative construction requires a personal theory of causality' (Labov, 'Further Steps', p. 11). William Labov's paper is available on his home page on the World Wide Web: http://www.ling.upenn.edu/-labov

6.   As Chatman points out, the subject was first raised in Aristotle's *Poetics*, but there it was merely delineated. Chatman, *Story*, p. 15. For a full bibliography on structuralist narratology see his p. 16.

7.   Propp, *Morphology*, p. 20. For a discussion of Propp's influence upon later narratology see Alan Dundes' introduction to the English edition cited, pp. xi-xvii; See also Pamela Milne, *Vladimir Propp and the Study of Structure in Hebrew Biblical Narrative* (Sheffield: Sheffield Academic Press, 1988), pp. 9-10.

8.   Propp, *Morphology*, p. 21.

9.   See on this Milne, *Vladimir Propp and the Study*, p. 30.

work of Greimas and other French structuralists, Propp's insights began to be understood and applied within a theoretical framework rather different from his own. Propp was in full agreement with the basic tenets of structuralism, that is, that narratives, like so many other human productions, are patterned and that this patterning or structuring may be understood. He did not, however, share its preoccupation with logic and its focus on a deep level (i.e. a psychologically-oriented level) of analysis that was of universal relevance and application, and expressed in highly complex terms and formulae. Propp's primary focus was rather on the text's narrative plot, that is, on the 'surface level' and the functional relationships discernible among its various elements. Further, his ultimate concern was description rather than theorizing, a fact that most structuralists perceive as a shortcoming.[10] The fundamental differences between Propp and his structuralist successors were made explicit in Claude Lévi-Strauss's essay entitled 'Structure and Form: Reflections on a Work by Vladimir Propp',[11] where Lévi-Strauss refuses to acknowledge the Russian as a true structuralist, and brands him instead—rather disparagingly—as a 'formalist'. Milne is, therefore, on target when she argues that, insofar as their ultimate aims, Propp and Lévi-Strauss represent opposite poles within narrative analysis.[12]

Yet, Propp's basic insights regarding actants and their functions in a narrative are useful regardless of one's larger theoretical persuasions. In discussing the necessary elements of a narrative text, Chatman refers to the standard structuralist view that a narrative is composed of the

---

10. Thus Ronald Schleifer writes: 'Propp [focuses] so closely on the manifested discourse that [he] sees "becoming" everywhere: his aim, as he says, is to "reveal the laws that govern the plot". Propp, that is, fails to develop a semiotics of plot, a "syntactic component" of the semio-narrative level of discourse... Actantial analysis, however, projects or "superimposes" a structure, conceived in spatial terms...upon discursive manifestation' (*A.J. Greimas and the Nature of Meaning* [London: Croom Helm, 1987], p. 93).

11. In V. Propp, *Theory and History of Folklore* (trans. Ariadna Martin; Minneapolis: University of Minnesota Press, 1984). See also Deborah Schiffrin's helpful chart of the differences between a 'structural' and a 'functional' approach to language, in her *Approaches to Discourse* (Oxford: Basil Blackwell, 1994), pp. 20-22; see also M.A.K. Halliday's chapter entitled 'Language in a Social Perspective', in his *Explorations in the Functions of Language* (London: Edward Arnold, 1973), pp. 48-71; the introduction to Halliday's *Introduction to Functional Grammar* (London: Edward Arnold, 1970), esp. pp. xxviii-xxix.

12. Milne, *Vladimir Propp and the Study*, p. 40.

elements of story and discourse, story being itself made up of 'events' ('actions' and 'happenings') and 'existents' ('characters' and 'setting').[13] Chatman acknowledges that the differentiation of these elements, regardless of the actual terms used to decribe them, transcends the boundaries of structuralism and is at least as old as Aristotle's *Poetics*. Thus, to the basic differentiation of these elements one might add, for example, as Chatman does, the superstructure of transformational grammar, or the functional and description-oriented linguistic theory of Halliday and other systemic functional grammarians, among other possible options.[14] It is my conviction that the latter provides a congruous framework for the development of Propp's basic ideas concerning dramatis personae and their functions in a narrative text. As I will attempt to show in Chapter 1, Halliday's functional grammar is, similarly to Propp's seminal work, focused primarily on the 'surface' level of text, and has a systemic and functional orientation that runs through all its parts. At the core of functional grammar is the network of transitivity, which specifies the various types of processes that are recognized in a language, together with the linguistic structures that encode those processes in texts. In non-technical terms, the transitivity network is ultimately concerned with the 'who does what to whom' set of questions.

In their provocative essay entitled 'On the Idea of Theory Neutral Descriptions',[15] Matthieson and Nesbitt discuss in some detail the manner in which applied linguists and others concerned with linguistic description have for some time expressed distaste for and suspicion of linguistic theorizing. Largely the result of an overreaction to the intricate and abstract notions of Chomsky's transformational grammar, Matthieson and Nesbitt argue, grammarians such as Huddleston or Quirk have attempted at various times to produce descriptions of language that are either free of perceived theoretical constraints, or borrow from several established frameworks in an eclectic approach to

---

13. Chatman, *Story*, p. 19.

14. The term 'systemic' refers to the notion, first put forth explicitly by Saussure, that language is a system of interelated elements. More on this in the following chapter.

15. Christian Matthiessen and Christopher Nesbitt, 'On the Idea of Theory-Neutral Descriptions', in R. Hasan, C. Cloran and D. Butt (eds.), *Functional Descriptions* (Amsterdam: John Benjamins, 1996), pp. 39-83.

theory.[16] Matthiessen and Nesbitt's response to this trend is twofold. First, the impossibility of 'theory-neutral' description is asserted,[17] and three different results of the sought-for neutrality are uncovered: Neutrality as common ancestry (i.e. the upholding of tradition), neutrality as domination (i.e. the upholding of the mainstream), and neutrality as commonality (i.e. the upholding of a common denominator). Secondly, a functional model of theory is put forth which is feature-rich, while at the same time being designed on the basis of description and with description in view:

> From a systemic functional point of view, the appropriate dimension [of theory] is realisation: theory is realised by description. In other words, particular descriptions of languages realise the general theory of language in a Token-Value relationship... This does not mean that description is a passive reflection of theory, on the contrary, description construes theory. Theories are semiotic systems and they are created semiotically in acts of description, just as these descriptions realize a higher-level theoretical semiotic.[18]

The disjunction between theory and description in modern linguistics is mirrored in a similar development in New Testament Greek since the publication of Blass's grammar.[19] The (explicit or not) aim of most New Testament Greek grammars has been primarily description, that is, these are grammars produced in order to equip individuals for the

---

16. Matthiessen and Nesbitt, 'On the Idea', p. 47.

17. Thus Halliday: 'The linguist who claims to be theory-free is like the conservative who claims to be non-political: they are both saying, to be impartial is to leave things as they are, only those who want to change them are taking sides'. Halliday cited in Matthiessen and Nesbitt, 'On the Idea', p. 64. On this, see also S.E. Porter, 'Studying Ancient Languages from a Modern Linguistics Perspective', *FN* 2 (1989), pp. 147-72.

18. Matthiessen and Nesbitt, 'On the Idea', p. 61. Yet, Robert de Beaugrande has criticized Hallidayan linguistics on the basis of his understanding that in Halliday's work 'the practical has run well ahead of the theoretical' ('"Register" in Discourse Studies: A Concept in Search of a Theory', in Mohsen Ghadessy [ed.], *Register Analysis: Theory and Practice* [London: Pinter, 1993], pp. 11-20 [14]).

19. Friedrich Blass, *Grammatik des neutestamentlichen Griechisch* (Göttingen: Vandenhoeck & Ruprecht, 1896); and its influential English translation of the 10th edition by Robert W. Funk incorporating supplementary notes by Albert Debrunner, *A Greek Grammar of the New Testament and Other Early Christian Literature* (Chicago: University of Chicago Press, 1961), hereafter BDF.

exegesis of the Greek New Testament.[20] Admirable as this aim may be, the nearly exclusive descriptive focus of New Testament Greek grammarians has led to some unintended deficiencies in their work. Chief among these is the uneasy relationship of most New Testament grammarians to linguistic theory, a relationship that is best described—to borrow Matthiessen's and Nesbitt's term—as 'neutrality as common ancestry', that is, the perpetuation of 100+ year-old linguistic principles found in Blass's work, such as a substantial dependence on comparative philology and historical grammar. This trend was expressed in no uncertain terms by Chamberlain when he wrote:

> There has been no attempt to be original. The one objective has been to condense, arrange or simplify the works of the great pioneers in the grammatical field, so as to give a convenient handbook to the seminary student.[21]

Even a casual perusal of the footnotes in both New Testament grammars and commentaries of our century reveals that, of all the 'great pioneers in the grammatical field', few if any are more revered and relied upon than Blass and Debrunner.[22] In the thirtieth anniversary of

20. At the introductory level, see for example J.G. Machen, who in his introduction asserts: 'Since [this] is an instruction book, everything in it is made subservient to the inparting of a reading acquaintance with the language' (*New Testament Greek for Beginners* [Toronto: Macmillan, 60th edn, 1989]); notice also the title of L. William Countryman, *The New Testament is in Greek: A Short Course for Exegetes* (Grand Rapids: Eerdmans, 1993). At the intermediate level, Chamberlain expresses similar concerns: 'This grammar has grown out of twelve years' experience in the classroom in presenting the facts of the grammar...and their bearing on the interpretation of the Greek New Testament' (W.D. Chamberlain, *An Exegetical Grammar of the Greek New Testament* [Grand Rapids: Baker Book House, 5th edn, 1988]), p. vii. At a more advanced advanced level, Moule writes: 'This book is an attempt to provide a syntactical companion to the interpretation of the New Testament: that is to say, it does not set out to be a systematic syntax... (C.F.D. Moule, *An Idiom Book of New Testament Greek* [Cambridge: Cambridge University Press, 1953]), p. vii.
21. Chamberlain, *An Exegetical Grammar*, p. vii. In his footnotes, Chamberlain cites Blass, Robertson and Moulton primarily, all of whom wrote in the same generation and share the same basic theoretical framework concerning the Greek of the New Testament. See below on Robertson.
22. See, for example, my comments on C.K. Barrett's dependence on Blass and Debrunner in his (1994!) Acts commentary (*The Acts of the Apostles*, I [ICC; Edinburgh: T. & T. Clark, 1994]), in Chapter 3. See also Ernst Haenchen, *The Acts of the Apostles* (trans. B. Noble and G. Shinn; Oxford: Basil Blackwell, 1971), pp. 72,

Funk's English translation of the German 10th edition, Porter and Reed issued a trenchant criticism of Blass's outdated theses concerning Koine Greek, with special reference to verbal aspect.[23] Of particular interest to me, given the subject of the present thesis, is the inadequate fashion in which transitivity is discussed in Blass and Debrunner, to wit, treating exclusively transitive or intransitive verbs in isolation from other elements in the clause, and, more importantly, lacking any reference to a system or network of transitivity (which includes much more than verb forms, as I will show throughout the present work), in light of which individual choices are to be understood.[24] These deficiencies are compounded by Blass's belief in the linguistic superiority of the 'classical standard' over the language of the New Testament, a belief reflected in his regular use of such adjectives as 'good' or 'true' when referring to the grammatical idiosyncrasies of the language of various Attic writers.[25] In contrast to Blass, a functional approach to language recognizes that the contexts of situation of, for example, a speech by Demosthenes and one attributed to Paul in the Acts of the Apostles are

76, 78, on the language and style of Acts. Among the grammars see A.T. Robertson, *A Grammar of the Greek New Testament in the Light of Historical Research* (Nashville: Broadman Press, 1934), pp. lxiv, 5. Robertson argues that Blass alone was comparable to the earlier epoch-making work by Winer. That Robertson's overall approach to the Greek of the New Testament is very similar to Blass's is made clear on p. viii: 'This grammar aims to keep in touch at salient points with the results of comparative philology and historical grammar *as the true linguistic science*' [my emphasis]. See also J.H. Moulton, *A Grammar of New Testament Greek*. I. *Prolegomena* (Edinburgh: T. & T. Clark, 1988), pp. 19, 40, 50, 60, etc.; James A. Brooks and Carlton L. Winbery, *Syntax of New Testament Greek* (Lanham, MD: University Press of America, 1979), p. ix.

23. Stanley E. Porter and Jeffrey T. Reed, 'Greek Grammar Since BDF: A Retrospective and Prospective Analysis', *FN* 4 (1991), pp. 143-64.

24. See, for example, the various entries under 'transitive verbs' in BDF's index of subjects; similarly, see Robertson's index in his *Grammar*; Nigel Turner, *Grammar of New Testament Greek*. III. *Syntax* (Edinburgh: T. & T. Clark, 1963), p. 400. Interestingly enough, Matthiessen and Nesbitt issue an identical complaint concerning grammarians they place under the 'neutrality as common ancestry' category: 'There is a sense of formal word systems—the paradigms of traditional grammar; but there is no theory of a multidimensional semantic space construed by the grammar's transitivity system. Semantic types are simply given as lists with no further semantic organization revealed by the interpretation' ('On the Idea', p. 65).

25. See, for example, the introduction entitled 'The New Testament and Hellenistic Greek', *passim*.

in fact quite different, and any comparison of the language of both must begin with a full recognition of this fact.[26]

As my title indicates, this work is an investigation of transitivity-based foregrounding in the Acts of the Apostles. Description, therefore, is my final aim, yet, this descriptive work (Chapters 3–5) is carried out after, on the basis of, and with regular reference to a detailed presentation of my chosen theoretical framework, namely, Halliday's functional grammar (Chapters 1–2). In Chapter 1, I enter into the ongoing discussion of New Testament rhetorical criticism in order to introduce functional grammar as a method of linguistic analysis that is rhetorically oriented at its core, and is, therefore, ideally suited to the task being pursued with, as I will argue, little success by the mainstream of rhetorical critics of the New Testament. In Chapter 2, I focus on a specific textual feature of great interest to rhetoricians and functional grammarians alike, that is, the textual device of foregrounding. Following Halliday, I define foregrounding as linguistic prominence which is consistent and motivated, and can be seen to cohere with the overall theme(s) of the text in which it is found. Further, I argue that in the narrative of Acts, the linguistic features upon which foregrounding is built by the author, belong, first and foremost, to the transitivity network of Greek, that is, the network that encodes processes, participants, and circumstances. Lastly, I present a detailed analysis of a transitivity-based foregrounding scheme in Acts 27 as a case study. That case study is then extended to other key episodes in Acts through my Chapters 3–5, rendering, it is hoped, a linguistically-based perspective on Luke's compositional and rhetorical agenda in producing his 'second treatise'.

It is further hoped that my work will become a contribution to biblical Greek scholarship's full engagement with modern linguistic theory, an agenda being pursued by Nida, Louw, Porter, Reed and others.[27] In response to my presentation of a paper at the Rhetoric and Scriptures conference, held at Pepperdine University, Malibu, California in July

---

26. See S.E. Porter, 'Dialect and Register in the Greek of the New Testament: Theory', in M. Daniel Carroll R. (ed.), *Rethinking Contexts, Rereading Texts: Contributions from the Social Sciences to Biblical Interpretation* (Sheffield: Sheffield Academic Press, 2000), pp. 190-208 where Porter points out that speeches in much of classical literature are 'not transcripts of conversation, as the Gospels purport to record, but a highly artificial literary variety of purported speech or written texts meant for public reading'.

27. See bibliography.

1996, one of the participants complained that if indeed linguistics was a science, its application to the language of the New Testament would destroy the intuitive element he valued so highly in his own work. This participant, a professor of New Testament at a medium-sized American university, was at least partially correct in his assessment. To wit, as Ronald Carter has done before me, I would argue that without analytic knowledge of and reference to the workings of the language system, any assertion concerning the meanings of words, clauses, pericopes or larger units of Greek text is bound to remain submerged in the murky waters of impressionism and untestability.[28] A classic example of this is the historical-theological debate which continues to swirl around the transitive or intransitive uses of ἐγείρει and ἀνιστάναι (see Chapter 5), where entire articles and monographs are written to argue for the alleged primitive or advanced Christology of various sections of Acts. This debate is carried out with little or no reference to the large and problematic issue of transitivity, the set of options that the transitivity system of Greek makes available to writers, the actual choices from that system made by Luke throughout Luke–Acts, the problem of deponency and restricted choice in the case of ἐγείρειν, and other issues. This is what Carter and others would call 'meaning without method'.[29] My aim in entering into that debate and others throughout this book is not to rule out other possible answers or dismiss more 'intuitive' approaches, but rather, to place the discussion of these matters within a linguistic framework, thus building my own argument in an accessible, principled manner, traceable and replicable by other scholars using the same method.

In my recent review of Egger's 'How to Read the New Testament'[30] I pointed out that the principal shortcoming of his introduction to linguistic methodology is the lack of cohesion and integration among the various linguistic methods he samples.[31] Egger offers, for example, a

28. Ronald Carter, 'Introduction', in Carter (ed.), *Language and Literature* (London: George Allen & Unwin, 1982), pp. 1-17.

29. Carter, 'Introduction', p. 3.

30. 'Review of Wilhelm Egger, "How to Read the New Testament: An Introduction to Linguistic and Historical-Critical Methodology" ', *Themelios* 23.2 (1998), pp. 61-62.

31. This assessment reveals how little progress has been made in most circles over the least decade or so. Seven years earlier, Cotterell and Turner lamented that, as far as discourse analysis is concerned, 'there are no firm conclusions, no

survey of how various narratologists, from Minguez to Greimas, have attempted to study the 'who does what to whom' questions. To begin with, Egger places narrative analysis and the study of the processes and participants in a narrative in a separate chapter from his discussion of the 'functions (intended purposes) of texts', a subject he places under 'pragmatic analysis'. Secondly, Egger's treatment takes for granted that the approaches of Propp, Greimas, Minguez, Theissen, Bremond and others are methodologically compatible and proceeds to utilize aspects from each without any serious attempt at justification. Lastly, Egger proceeds rather naively to defend the need for the 'transformation of the text', which, he argues, 'scarcely raises any difficulties'.[32] Such a presentation contributes to the impression among New Testament scholars that linguistic science is an obscure web of highly abstract and seemingly incongruous concepts, very unlikely to shed new light on the issues that occupy students of the New Testament. In view of this opinion, I will in the chapters that follow attempt to stress the potential of Halliday's functional grammar for integrating and making widely acccessible linguistic insights from various sources and theoretical persuasions. My discussion of foregrounding in Chapter 2 is a case in point, as I will show how Halliday's presentation of the subject in his seminal study, 'Linguistic Function and Literary Style',[33] effectively integrates into a workable linguistic framework insights from psycho-linguistics, literary criticism, and discourse analysis.

For the selection of the five major episodes of Acts for my analysis, two basic criteria have been operative. First, I have chosen to study episodes which contain both narrative and speeches and are sufficiently large in size to allow a meaningful analysis of such matters as variation in clause structure, cohesion and, particularly, foregrounding. Secondly, I have selected episodes which have received a significant amount of

generally accepted formulae, no fixed methodology, not even an agreed methodology'. Peter Cotterell and Max Turner, *Linguistics and Biblical Interpretation* (Downers Grove, IL: IVP, 1989), p. 233.

32. Wilhelm Egger, *How to Read the New Testament: An Introduction to Linguistic and Historical-Critical Methodology* (Peabody, MA: Hendrickson, 1996), p. 121. In stark contrast to Egger, Halliday's treatment of transitivity in, for example, his *Introduction to Functional Grammar*, is a functionally-based discussion of processes, participants and circumstances, requiring no transformation into 'homogeneous objects of investigation', but rather, a thorough analysis of the text with a primary focus on the rank of clause.

33. In Halliday, *Explorations in the Functions of Language*, pp. 103-40.

attention in recent scholarly discussion, with a view to engaging with and evaluating the conclusions of others and contrasting them with my own, linguistically based proposals. As I will show throughout my discussion of the various episodes, central to many of the arguments and theses I engage with is some theory, often unsubstantiated, concerning what is perceived to be the 'climax', or most emphatic point of the episode or speech in question. My contribution to these discussions centres upon my proposal of a linguistic framework for testing such claims. Halliday's functional grammatical approach to foregrounding stresses the need to ground any theory concerning what is 'emphatic' both in the language system from which the alleged foregrounded patterns emanate, and in a proposal concerning the text's overall literary/ rhetorical thrust(s). My research shows that the transitivity network, and the choices of process and participants in particular, that is, the 'who does what to whom' set of questions, is consistently central to Luke's foregrounding scheme in the Acts of the Apostles. I will attempt to show that the sum total of these choices, together with their distribution and arrangement throughout key episodes in Acts, reveals Luke's extraordinary concern to underline the overriding power of the divine purpose (βουλή) upon the stage of human affairs.

Chapter 1

HALLIDAYAN FUNCTIONAL GRAMMAR AS HEIR TO
NEW TESTAMENT RHETORICAL CRITICISM:
THE CASE OF FOREGROUNDING*

In his seminal work *New Testament Interpretation through Rhetorical Criticism*, George Kennedy defines rhetoric as 'that quality in discourse by which a speaker or writer seeks to accomplish his purposes'.[1] Although, as I will point out below, Kennedy's understanding of rhetoric turns out to be much narrower than this definition suggests, his statement serves as a suitable launching pad for what follows. Kennedy's agenda in this highly influential volume is none other than to provide students of the New Testament with an 'additional tool', which might complement the older and more established ones of form, redaction, literary and historical criticism.[2] Although the degree to which Kennedy has succeeded is a matter for debate, as I will show, his work and that of his many followers has brought about a methodological reorientation in New Testament study of significant proportions. It is to that reorientation that I now wish to turn. My aim in the present chapter is, first, to argue that, although the fundamental goals of rhetorical criticism of the New Testament seem both worthwhile and attainable, the approach in its most prevalent form has shown itself

* An earlier form of this chapter was presented at the 'Rhetoric and the Scriptures' Conference Pepperdine University Malibu, California, in July 1996, and is in Stanley E. Porter and Dennis L. Stamps (eds.), *The Rhetorical Interpretation of Scripture: Essays from the 1996 Malibu Conference* (JSNTSup, 180; Sheffield: Sheffield Academic Press, 1999), pp. 87-107.

1. George A. Kennedy, *New Testament Interpretation through Rhetorical Criticism* (Chapel Hill: University of North Carolina Press, 1984), p. 1.

2. Kennedy, *Rhetorical Criticism*, p. 1. One could easily argue, however, that Kennedy's rhetorical criticism is not entirely dissimilar from a rather strict brand of form criticism. See especially my discussion of Paul's apologetic speech in Acts 22 below.

incapable of reaching them. Secondly, I wish to present Michael Halliday's functional grammar as a sounder, better informed and more capable method of reaching these goals. Lastly, I will suggest that, understood within the Hallidayan linguistic framework, foregrounding is a fundamentally rhetorical device of far greater importance than has heretofore been recognized.

1. *Rhetoric and the New Testament*

The recently published collection of essays *Rhetoric and the New Testament*,[3] affords a rather complete view of the current *état du jeu* of New Testament rhetorical criticism, and provides sufficient evidence for an evaluation of that 'near volcanic eruption of rhetoric'[4] that New Testament scholarship has witnessed in recent years.

Even a cursory reading of this volume reveals that, while the various contributors share similar aims and use analogous terms to describe them, the actual methods employed by these writers are diverse, seem often incompatible, and reveal a field of study that is far from unified. This diversity becomes particularly evident in the many uses and understandings of the word 'rhetoric'. For several contributors to this volume, rhetoric is generally limited to the discipline taught in certain classical Graeco-Roman manuals such as Cicero's *De Inventione* or Quintilian's *Institutio Oratoria*,[5] while for other writers the same word or its

3.   Stanley E. Porter and Thomas H. Olbricht (eds.), *Rhetoric and the New Testament: Essays from the 1992 Heidelberg Conference* (JSNTSup, 90; Sheffield: JSOT Press, 1993).

4.   Wilhelm Wuellner, 'Biblical Exegesis in the Light of the History and Historicity of Rhetoric and the Nature of the Rhetoric of Religion', in Porter and Olbricht (eds.), *Rhetoric*, pp. 492-513 (493).

5.   Frank Hughes, 'The Parable of the Rich Man and Lazarus (Luke 16.19-31) and Graeco-Roman Rhetoric', pp. 29-41; Folker Siegert, 'Mass Communication and Prose Rhythm in Luke–Acts', pp. 42-58; J. Ian H. McDonald, 'Rhetorical Issue and Rhetorical Strategy in Luke 10.25-37 and Acts 10.1–11.18', pp. 59-73; Daniel Marguerat, 'The End of Acts (28.16-31) and the Rhetoric of Silence', pp. 74-89; David Hellholm, 'Amplificatio in the Macro-Structure of Romans', pp. 123-51; Marc Schoeni, 'The Hyperbolic Sublime as a Master Trope in Romans', pp. 171-91; Joop Smit, 'Argument and Genre of 1 Corinthians 12–14', pp. 211-30; Duane Watson, 'Paul's Rhetorical Strategy in 1 Corinthians 15', pp. 231-49; John W. Marshall, 'Paul's Ethical Appeal in Philippians', pp. 357-74; all in Porter and Olbricht (eds.), *Rhetoric*.

cognates is understood in far more generic terms. Thus Vorster prefers to define rhetoric in terms of social interaction;[6] Reed understands the term as the study and application of argumentation,[7] and speaks of 'persuasive units' rather than Watson's 'rhetorical units';[8] Marshall seems to use 'persuasive power' as synonymous with rhetoric;[9] Berger argues that 'everything that leads the reader's psyche towards a goal has to be regarded as a rhetorical element...';[10] Lategan, in addressing the meaning of 'rhetorical', prefers 'the broader sense of the word', which for him means 'pragmatic intent'.[11] Thurén, in short, concludes that 'rhetoric' 'is not a value-free term'.[12]

This heterogeneous understanding of the term 'rhetoric', and particularly the degree of dependence of the various writers upon the rhetorical manuals of Graeco-Roman antiquity, seem to reveal three distinguishable groups of scholars in this volume. The first group ('group A'), generally following the seminal works of George Kennedy and Hans Dieter Betz,[13] sees New Testament rhetorical criticism as the interpretation of the various New Testament documents in light of the conventions and rules of the classical rhetorical texts. The second group ('group B') sees some value in studying the Graeco-Roman manuals, while at the same time issuing words of caution in regard to a mechanical or slavish application of the classical rhetorical categories to the books of the New Testament. Lastly, 'group C' is highly critical of the Kennedy–Betz

6. Johannes Vorster, 'Strategies of Persuasion in Romans 1.16-17', in Porter and Olbricht (eds.), *Rhetoric*, pp. 152-70 (155, 167).

7. Jeffrey T. Reed, 'Using Ancient Rhetorical Categories to Interpret Paul's Letters: A Question of Genre', pp. 292-324 (295, 297). Yet, as Thurén points out, the term 'argumentation' is also subject to a variety of interpretations and uses! See Lauri Thurén, 'On Studying Ethical Argumentation and Persuasion in the New Testament', in Porter and Olbricht (eds.), *Rhetoric*, pp. 464-78 (66).

8. Reed, 'Using Ancient Rhetorical Categories', p. 319.

9. Marshall, 'Ethical Appeal', pp. 357, 371, though Marshall also relies on classical rhetoric as his 'guiding theory', p. 357.

10. Klaus Berger, 'Rhetorical Criticism, New Form Criticism, and New Testament Hermeneutics', in Porter and Olbricht (eds.), *Rhetoric*, pp. 390-96 (393).

11. Bernard Lategan, 'Textual Space as Rhetorical Device', in Porter and Olbricht (eds.), *Rhetoric*, pp. 397-408 (397).

12. Thurén, 'Ethical Argumentation', p. 467.

13. Hans Dieter Betz, *Galatians: A Commentary on Paul's Letter to the Churches in Galatia* (Philadelphia: Fortress Press, 1979); Kennedy, *Rhetorical Criticism*.

approach,[14] and argues for a much more inclusive notion of rhetoric that incorporates ancient as well as modern insights into human communication. A more detailed discussion of each group will clarify these differences.

Group A

One of the fundamental tenets of the exponents of this approach is the conviction that many of the writers of the New Testament were familiar with the categories and concepts of the classical rhetorical manuals. Whether Luke, for example, had been to rhetorical school,[15] or, more commonly, Paul and other New Testament writers 'picked up' these categories merely from living in a rhetoric-saturated culture,[16] the scholars in 'group A' believe that the New Testament writers knew and applied at least the three main genera of judicial, epideictic and deliberative rhetoric. Such confidence leads to statements like Hellholm's, who describes his interpretation of Romans as 'a *decoding* rhetorical process...' (emphasis mine),[17] or Smit's, who argues that 1 Cor. 14.33b-

---

14. As I will show below (see n. 19), Kennedy disagrees with Betz at significant points (see Kennedy, *Rhetorical Criticism*, pp. 144-48), yet due to their shared understanding of the significance of the classical manuals for the study of the New Testament, and the influence that both scholars have had on subsequent New Testament rhetorical critics, I am arguing that they together are representative of my group A type of rhetorical criticism.

15. An idea taken for granted by Hughes, who writes, 'If indeed a rather well educated writer, like the writer of Luke–Acts, had been assigned to make declamations in a genre of Rich Man versus Poor Man *when* he was in rhetorical school...' (emphasis mine, 'The Parable', pp. 37-38). Hughes adds later, 'Yet given some ability in *enthopoiïa*, which rhetorical instruction and practice would likely have developed in a person as well educated as the writer of Luke–Acts...' (38).

16. Thus, for example, Smit writes, '...these schoolish handbooks provide a good impression of the rhetoric that was generally practised in Paul's time and surroundings' ('Argument and Genre', p. 212); Siegert argues that anyone addressing an ancient audience 'as spoiled as that of the big assemblies in the theatres and basilicas' had to employ the particular rhythms taught by Quintilian *et al.* ('Mass Communication', pp. 48-49). Though he approaches the issue critically, and I have consequently placed him in group B, Classen argues in a similar manner: 'Anyone who could write Greek as effectively as St Paul did, must have read a good deal of works written in Greek and thus imbibed applied rhetoric from others...' (C. Joachim Classen, 'St Paul's Epistles and Ancient Graeco-Roman Rhetoric', in Porter and Olbricht [eds.], *Rhetoric*, pp. 265-91 [269]).

17. Hellholm, 'Amplificatio', p. 126.

36 is a non-Pauline addition, because it 'runs counter to the rhetorical rules concerning the completeness of the *partitio*…'[18] Unfortunately, however, these writers often end up disagreeing as to what exactly is epideictic or deliberative, and cite ancient authorities such as Quintilian or Seneca against each other, a practice that seems to call into question the plausibility of the entire approach.[19]

Group B
The writers I place in this group believe that classical rhetorical theory may render service for interpreting the New Testament, but are much less enthusiastic about the applicability of specific categories and structures.[20] For Classen, for example, Philip Melanchthon was a model rhetorical critic of the New Testament (though Kennedy ignores him entirely and Betz relegates him to one footnote), insofar as he made abundant use of the classical manuals when appropriate, while at the

---

18. Smit, 'Argument and Genre', p. 219. The author offers no *textual* backing for this assertion.

19. Thus Watson, like Bünker, is by his own admission 'heavily dependent upon the rhetorical handbooks', yet believes, unlike Bünker, that 1 Cor. 15 is deliberative, not judicial (Watson, 'Paul's Rhetorical Strategy', p. 232). The debate between Kennedy and Betz is perhaps the best known. Kennedy argues that Betz's commentary is 'misleading in important respects', because it sees Galatians as apologetic-judicial, rather than (with Kennedy) as deliberative. Kennedy cites Quintilian's *Inst. Orat.* 3.4.9 in support of his view (Kennedy, *Rhetorical Criticism*, pp. 144, 148). The late Angelico-Salvatore Di Marco seems to have been on target when he wrote, 'Indeed, in rhetoric, scholars do not agree how to name a phenomenon…' (Di Marco, 'Rhetoric and Hermeneutic—On a Rhetorical Pattern: Chiasmus and Circularity', in Porter and Olbricht [eds.] *Rhetoric*, pp. 479-91 [479]). The difficulties inherent in making clear-cut distinctions between deliberative and epideictic are evident in statements by McDonald, who writes that Peter's speech in Acts 10 'exemplifies *deliberative* rhetoric…*but it also has epideictic* features…' (emphasis mine) ('Rhetorical Issue', p. 68); or Marshall, who argues that passages in Phil. 2 and 3 'may be characterized as epideictic, [but] their ultimate purpose is deliberative' ('Ethical Appeal', p. 363); or Olbricht, who believes that Hebrews conforms to the epideictic genre in its superstructure, but 'the body of the argument may be conceived as deliberative' ('Hebrews as Amplification', in Porter and Olbricht [eds.], *Rhetoric*, pp. 375-88 [378]).

20. Classen, 'St Paul's Epistles', p. 289; A.H. Snyman, 'Persuasion in Philippians 4.1-20', in Porter and Olbricht (eds.), *Rhetotic*, pp. 325-37; Claudio Basevi and Juan Chapa, 'Philippians 2.6-11: The Rhetorical Function of a Pauline Hymn', pp. 338-57; Olbricht, 'Hebrews', p. 377; all in Porter and Olbricht (eds.), *Rhetoric*.

same time feeling free to alter and add to their categories and structures.[21] Basevi and Chapa follow Kennedy's method to a large extent,
yet warn against applying rhetorical patterns, 'sometimes rather stereo-
typed, to texts that do not fit a particular Graeco-Roman model'.[22]

Group C
The critique offered by the writers in this group has done, I wish to
argue, irreparable damage to the Kennedy–Betz approach to rhetorical
criticism. It is interesting to note that all the essays in part two of this
volume ('Rhetoric and Questions of Method') approach the issue from
this critical angle. It is the aim of these writers, first, to demonstrate the
inadequacy of the narrow, 'group A' style understanding of rhetoric.
The social contexts of ancient rhetoric and biblical rhetoric, it is argued,
were significantly different,[23] the rhetorical manuals were addressing
not epistolary literature but various types of speeches,[24] and finally, it

21. Classen, 'St. Paul's Epistles', pp. 273-75.
22. Basevi and Chapa, 'Philippians 2.6-11', p. 350. These two writers later add
'we think it is necessary to underline the flexibility of the three genera...' (p. 352).
23. Thurén, 'Ethical Argumentation', p. 470. Similarly Vorster writes, '...clas-
sical rhetorical categories are inextricably linked to the social situation...' ('Strategies of Persuasion', p. 153). See also Wuellner, 'Biblical Exegesis', p. 503.
24. This seems to be the most devastating criticism of the Kennedy–Betz school
and its followers in this volume. Porter deals with this issue in detail. Depending on
the previous work of A.J. Malherbe (*Ancient Epistolary Theorists* [SBLSBS, 19;
Atlanta, GA: Scholars Press, 1988]), Porter shows that there was in fact a clear line
of demarcation between written letters and anything oral. Secondly, the sporadic
discussion of letter writing was only a late addition to the study of ancient rhetoric
(Julius Victor's *Ars Retorica*, fourth century CE), and was limited to matters of style
(see Porter, 'The Theoretical Justification for Application of Rhetorical Categories
to Pauline Epistolary Literature', in Porter and Olbricht [eds.], *Rhetoric*, pp. 110-
22); similarly Classen writes, 'Most ancient handbooks of rhetoric do not deal with
letters, and where they do, they are content with a few remarks mostly on matters of
style' ('St. Paul's Epistles', p. 269); see also Reed, 'Ancient Rhetorical Categories',
pp. 309-11; and Lategan, 'Textual Space', p. 397. If indeed it is the case that all the
insights New Testament interpreters may draw from Graeco-Roman rhetoric are
limited to stylistic matters, Kennedy's approach may, by his own admission be said
to have failed. Thus, at the outset of his highly influential work, Kennedy states,
'To many biblical scholars rhetoric probably means style, and they may envision in
these pages discussion of figures of speech and metaphors not unlike that already to
be found in many literary studies of the Scriptures. The identification of rhetoric
with style—a feature of what I have elsewhere called *letteratirizzazione*—is a common phenomenon in the history of the study of rhetoric, but represents a limitation

cannot be demonstrated that the writers of the New Testament were familiar with and adopted (whether consciously or not) the complex structures taught in the rhetorical manuals.[25] Secondly, the group C writers 'plead for methodological expansion',[26] arguing that the term 'rhetoric' encompasses much more than Aristotle, Quintilian or Seneca ever envisioned. Thus, Wuellner wants to see rhetoric 'unrestrained', because

> So long as biblical scholars remain blind to the reality that there is more
> rhetoric to be experienced in one hour in the marketplace (or even in the
> nursery) than in one day in the academy, scholarship devoted to biblical
> rhetoric will remain in a quandary, in a prison self-made and self-
> imposed.[27]

In the light of the above discussion, it seems fair to say that the Kennedy–Betz approach to rhetorical criticism has run its course. While Kennedy expressed his aims in terms similar to those that Berger, Crafton and others used in the present volume,[28] his rigid dependence on Graeco-Roman manuals, together with the concomitant narrow understanding of the term 'rhetoric', has kept him and his followers from reaching their aims. Of the many important questions that *Rhetoric and the New Testament* has raised, perhaps the most fundamental is simply: what is rhetoric? If indeed rhetorical language is that language which is functional or purposeful, is it not the case that all human communication is rhetorical *in this sense*?[29] Does the usefulness

and to a certain extent a distortion of the discipline of rhetoric as understood and taught in antiquity' (*Rhetorical Criticism*, p. 1).

25. 'However, a close identification of ancient techniques is meaningful only if we can reasonably assume that the authors had learnt those techniques by name at school', Thurén, 'Ethical Argumentation', p. 470; See also Porter, 'Theoretical Justification', p. 105.

26. Vorster, 'Strategies of Persuasion', p. 153.

27. Wuellner, 'Biblical Exegesis', p. 500.

28. Thus, Kennedy writes, 'The ultimate goal of rhetorical analysis, briefly put, is the discovery of the author's intent and of how that is transmitted through a text to an audience' (*Rhetorical Criticism,* p. 12); 'The primary aim of rhetorical criticism is to understand the effect of the text', p. 33; '[the Bible is] rhetorical, again not in the sense of "false" or "deceitful", but in the sense of "purposeful"' (p. 158).

29. Thus, Michael Gregory and Susanne Carroll write in *Language and Situation: Language Varieties and their Social Context* (London: Routledge and Kegan Paul, 1978), p. 94: 'prescriptions for how to use language well and effectively...is

of the word 'rhetoric' outweigh the problems arising from its traditional association with the Graeco-Roman manuals?

A feature common to many of the essays in all three groups is an emphasis on the *function* of texts in their social contexts as central to rhetorical study. The writers in group A normally express this idea in terms of rhetorical situation (corresponding to the *Sitz im Leben* of form criticism), exigence (the need or problem arising from that situation and capable of being addressed or removed by discourse), and rhetorical strategy (the function intended for the text, in the form of Graeco-Roman deliberative, epideictic or judicial structures).[30] On the other hand, the contributors in groups B and C generally insist that New Testament texts, their functions and contexts be studied in the light of 'general human communication, and…be analysed with the best means available, whether ancient or modern'.[31] Dennis Stamps excepted,[32] the

what is meant here by a "rhetoric"'; also Berger, 'Rhetorical Criticism', p. 395 argues that 'Hermeneutics is based on rhetoric, because application does not merely rely on theoretical comprehension…but mainly on the pragmatic effect (function)'. Thus also Geoffrey N. Leech: 'The point about the term rhetoric, in this context, is the focus it places on a goal-oriented speech situation, in which speaker uses language in order to produce a particular effect in the mind of hearer. I shall also use the term rhetoric as a countable noun, for a set of conversational principles, which are related by their functions' (*Principles of Pragmatics* [London: Longman, 1983], p. 15). In this regard, Ruqaiya Hasan writes, '…the sharp division of rhetoric and grammar is itself a fairly recent phenomenon in the long history of the study of language and literature' (Hasan, 'Rhyme and Reason in Literature', in Seymour Chatman [ed.], *Literary Style: A Symposium* [London: Oxford University Press, 1971], pp. 287-99 (299). See also Gillian Brown and George Yule, *Discourse Analysis* (Cambridge Textbooks in Linguistics; Cambridge: Cambridge University Press, 1983), pp. 148-49; Halliday, *An Introduction to Functional Grammar*, pp. xxiii, xxviii. Speaking of the limited scope of linguistic theory, Van Dijk writes that 'rhetorical function [is] related to the EFFECT of the utterance on the hearer' (emphasis original), adding that 'we do not want to treat such structures within a linguistic theory of discourse because they are restricted to certain types of discourse or certain STYLISTIC USES of language, and because they cannot be accounted for in terms of a grammatical form-meaning-action rule system…' (Teun A. Van Dijk, *Text and Context* [London: Longman, 1977], p. 4). It must be asked, however, what type of discourse or what stylistic use of language can be said to have no effect on the hearer?

30. McDonald, 'Rhetorical Issue', pp. 60-70; Watson, 'Paul's Rhetorical Strategy', pp. 233-34.

31. Thurén, 'Ethical Argumentation', p. 471.

32. See his 'Rethinking the Rhetorical Situation: The Entextualization of the

writers in this volume share a certain degree of optimism as to the possibility that the careful, systematic analysis of a text (whether by means of classical or Burkean rhetoric, pragmatics or neo-form criticism) will yield insights into its intended function(s) and the situation it is designed to address. That is, the question can be answered 'what kind of effect was it intended to achieve and what does this tell us about the situation?'[33]

I wish to argue that rhetorical criticism in all its forms has done much to highlight the importance of *function in context* in the study of the

Situation in New Testament Epistles', in Porter and Olbricht (eds.), *Rhetoric*, pp. 193-210. Stamps is very critical of Bitzer and Kennedy's understanding of the concept of rhetorical situation, and denies a direct correspondence between rhetorical forms in the text and the actual historical context. His caveat seems reasonable. Stamps is right in pointing to the subjective nature of the rhetorical situation as 'inscribed in the text', since it necessarily reflects the author's perspective on the historical events that motivate his text, rather than those events pure and simple (p. 199). One may even agree that the author's representation of the rhetorical situation in his text is in fact part and parcel of his rhetorical strategy. Yet, Stamps also recognizes that 'it may be granted that any text, and an ancient New Testament epistle in particular, stems from certain historical and social contingencies...' (p. 199) and that, regarding 1 Cor., 'the sender must present the entextualized situation in such a manner that elicits correspondence with some, if not most of the audience' (p. 200). Thus, though it is certainly true that 'any textual presentation of historical reality represents a process which involves interpretation and narrativization...' (p. 199) this is equally true of any presentation of history, textual or otherwise. The selection and arrangement that this involves does not necessarily falsify or distort history. If true communication (in the widest sense of the word) is to take place between writer and reader/hearers, he must make reference to facts and ideas about the world that are commonly known and accepted. Though Stamps claims not to have slipped into formalism (p. 199 n. 17) his concluding statement seems to indicate otherwise: 'In more literary terms, the textuality of the rhetorical situation means that the speaker and audience as literary constructions themselves only meet in the "world-of-the-text". One aspect of the world-of-the-text which the text constructs is the rhetorical situation' (p. 210).

33. Berger, 'Rhetorical Criticism', p. 392. Similarly Crafton writes, 'Burke's concern with rhetorical strategy leads to a fascination with how people deal with life through language, how they attempt to "encompass" situations. Burke proposes that these ventures may be explored through a "sociological criticism of literature". Such a method would develop categories of genre which reveal author's tactics for handling circumstances, thereby connecting literature to real life...' ('The Dancing of an Attitude: Burkean Rhetorical Criticism and the Biblical Interpreter', in Porter and Olbricht [eds.], *Rhetoric*, p. 435).

New Testament documents. In addition, its emphasis on the analysis of the various letters and books *prout extant* ('as they exist today') is a welcome corrective to the recurrent speculation of some of the older critical methods. Yet, for these fundamental insights to be truly fruitful, a more 'productive match' must be sought between the biblical texts and a critical method. Such a method must, in the words of Crafton, 'develop categories of genre which reveal authors' tactics for handling circumstances, thereby connecting literature to real life…'[34] Such a method, in short, must be aimed at the study of language as a means, indeed the primary means, of social interaction. It is my contention that this method exists, and may be used with profit in the study of the New Testament. Michael Halliday's 'functional grammar' is, I will argue below, an ideally suited method for achieving the aims of rhetorical criticism as expressed by Crafton above.

2. *Background to Hallidayan Functional Grammar*

> [W]hen a savage learns to understand the meaning of a word, this pro-
> cess is not accomplished by explanations, by a series of acts of apper-
> ception, but by learning to handle it. A word means to a native the proper
> use of the thing for which it stands, exactly as an implement means
> something when it can be handled and means nothing when no active
> experience of it is at hand. The word therefore has a power of its own, it
> is a means of bringing things about, it is a handle to acts and objects and
> not a definition of them.[35]

Statements on language and culture such as the one above in the ethnographic papers of Bronislaw Malinowski represent the earliest expression of what has come to be known as functional grammar. Though the focus of Malinowski's study of the Trobriand culture in the 1920s was primarily anthropological, four of his treatises and articles from the period[36] include significant discussions of language as the primary means of cultural behavior.

---

34. Crafton, 'The Dancing', p. 435. See definition of 'register' below.
35. Bronislaw Malinowski in 'The Problem of Meaning in Primitive Languages', cited in Terence Langendoen, *The London School of Linguistics: A Study
of the Linguistic Theories of B. Malinowski and J.R. Firth* (Research Monograph,
46; Cambridge, MA: M.I.T. Press, 1968), p. 23. Langendoen's monograph is a revision of his doctoral dissertation produced at MIT under Noam Chomsky in 1964.
36. 'Classificatory Particles in the Language or Kiriwina', *BSOS* 1, part 4
(1920), pp. 33-78; *Argonauts of the Western Pacific* (London: Routledge, 1922);

Malinowski's early discovery of the raw instrumentality of much of the natives' language is summarized in some detail in 'Classicatory Particles'. In seeking to understand the meaning of certain words and formatives in the culture of Kiriwina, it was discovered that constant reference to ethnographic data was unavoidable. Thus, the use of bare numeral stems without a classicatory particle was reserved for the counting of baskets of yams, which in the local culture was felt to be 'counting *par excellence*'.[37] Several similar examples led Malinowski to issue a call for a semantic theory that would account for lexico-grammatical facts in light of the cultural constraints that motivate them.[38] Two years after the publication of 'Classicatory Particles', Malinowski's first substantial ethnographic treatise appeared under the title *Argonauts of the Western Pacific* (1922). Particularly significant in this work is the final chapter entitled 'The Power of Words in Magic', in which the author argues that 'magical style' in its pure instrumentality is different from ordinary narrative. Each word or formula is wielded as a tool or weapon to bring about specific effects in the world.

With 'The Problem of Meaning' (1923) we see a major shift in the sociolinguistic thought of Malinowski. In an attempt to spell out his ethnographic semantic theory, he concludes that words derive their meaning not from the physical qualities of their referents, but from the socio-cultural context in which they are uttered, from the function they are made to serve.[39] In this regard, Malinowski is forced to conclude that 'magical style', rather than being an exception, is in fact the rule, other types of language such as a scientic treatise being derivative and secondary. His argument in support of this assertion is twofold. (1) In primitive societies, where there is no written language, the only type of

'The Problem of Meaning in Primitive Languages', supplement to O.K. Odgen and I.A. Richards, *The Meaning of Meaning* (New York: Harcourt, 10th edn, 1923), pp. 296-336; and *Coral Gardens and their Magic* (New York: American Book Co., 1935), the latter being Malinowski's final word on his semantic theory. Key ideas from this work were soon taken over by John R. Firth who was by this time interacting with Malinowski in seminars led by the latter at the University of London.

37. See Langendoen, *The London School*, p. 11.

38. Thus, in 'Classicatory Particles' Malinowski writes of the need '...to show how necessary it is to give some ethnographic information if grammatical relations are to be fully understood'. Cited in Langendoen, *The London School*, p. 11.

39. Though he seems to have contradicted himself at other points in this same essay. See Langendoen, *The London School*, p. 19.

communication possible is that of the purely functional sort,[40] in which each utterance is inseparably tied to the context of situation. (2) Language acquisition by infants develops along strictly functional lines, indeed, '[t]he child *acts* by sound at this state...' (emphasis original).[41]

Malinowski's work *Coral Gardens and their Magic* (1935) has been by far the most influential, and represents the apex of his sociosemantic theory. In *Coral Gardens* Malinowski pursues his insights into language as a mode of cultural behavior to their logical conclusions:

> The sentence is at times a self-contained linguistic unit, but not even a sentence can be regarded as a full linguistic datum. To us, the real linguistic fact is the full utterance within its context of situation.[42]

By 1935, the isolated and germinal insights of 'Classificatory Particles' had been integrated into a fairly detailed theory of language as a mode of (societal) action, already including several of the essential tenets of functional grammar. By this time, Malinowski and John Firth were interacting regularly at University College, London, and the influences were mutual. It was Firth's vision to shape Malinowski's ideas about language in society, and that of context of situation in particular, into a consistently linguistic theory. While Malinowski had defined context of situation in rather concrete language, Firth came to realize that for the notion to become a truly valuable one, and capable of sufficiently wide application, it needed to be expressed in more abstract terms.[43] Thus, Firth suggested the following 'categories of context of situation': relevant features of participants, their verbal and non verbal actions, relevant objects, and the effect of the verbal action. In addition, the notion of 'typical' context of situation was introduced to account for

---

40. Thus also Oscar Uribe-Villegas: 'Among primitive peoples, language is purely an instrument' ('On the Social in Language and the Linguistic in Society', in Uribe-Villegas (ed.), *Issues in Sociolinguistics* (Contributions to the Society of Language, p. 15; The Hague: Mouton, 1977), pp. 60-85 (85).

41. Cited in Langendoen, *The London School*, p. 17. Michael Halliday's work *Learning How to Mean* is a thorough investigation of this idea. Halliday, *Learning How to Mean: Explorations in the Development of Language* (London: Edward Arnold, 1975).

42. Cited in Langendoen, *The London School*, p. 31. Not surprisingly, Langendoen is highly critical of this development in Malinowski's thought. See n. 36.

43. '[Context of situation is] a group of related categories at a different level from grammatical categories but rather of the same abstract nature' (J.R. Firth, *Papers in Linguistics, 1934–51* [London: Oxford University Press, 1957], p. 6).

the limited variety of social situations an individual encounters through-out his or her life. Once a patient, for example, begins to converse with his doctor on the nature of his ailment, the doctor is, in his response, bound by the social-linguistic conventions proper to the context of 'doctor–patient interviews', a context type familiar to most members of modern society. From this follows that just as there is a limited number of recognizable context types, there is in each case a context-specific language variety: 'The multiplicity of social roles we have to play... involves also a certain degree of linguistic specialization. Unity is the last concept that should be applied to language...'[44] Such variety of language according to use or function has come to be known as 'register'.[45]

It is what is perceived to be Firth's *sui generis* understanding of 'meaning' that has earned him (and many of his followers) the greatest criticism from several sources. Although Firth's use of the word 'mean-ing' may be 'highly idiosyncratic',[46] it cannot be branded as incon-sistent within his own theory of function in context. Firth's assertion (after Malinowski) that 'meaning is function in context' amounts in fact to a recognition of the impossibility of establishing a clear-cut distinc-tion between sense and reference,[47] semantics and pragmatics,[48] lin-

44. Firth, *Papers*, p. 29.

45. See Butler, *Systemic Linguistics: Theory ad Applications* (London: Bats-ford, 1985), p. 67; M.A.K. Halliday, *Language as Social Semiotic* (London: Edward Arnold: 2nd edn, 1979), pp. 31-35, 60-63; *idem, Learning How to Mean,* p. 126; Margaret Berry, *Introduction to Systemic Linguistics. I. Structures and Systems* (London: Batsford, 1977), pp. 2, 87-88; Jean Ure and Jeffrey Ellis, 'Register in Descriptive Linguistics and Linguistic Sociology', in Uribe-Villegas (ed.), *Issues in Sociolinguistics* (The Hague: Mouton, 1974, pp. 197-40; Gregory and Carroll, *Language and Situation*, pp. 27-74; Moshen Ghadessy (ed.), *Register Analysis: Theory and Practice* (London: Pinter, 1993); for a collection of essays on register in English, see Moshen Ghadessy (ed.), *Registers of Written English* (London: Pinter, 1988). For an application of the notion of register to the Greek of St Mark's Gospel see Porter, 'Dialect and Register', and 'Register in the Greek of the New Testament: Application with Reference to Mark's Gospel', in M. Daniel Carroll R. (ed.), *Rethinking Contexts, Rereading Texts: Contributions from the Social Sciences to Biblical Interpretation* (Sheffield: Sheffield Academic Press, 2000), pp. 209-29.

46. These are Butler's words in *Systemic Linguistics*, p. 67.

47. See F.R. Palmer, *Semantics: A New Outline* (Cambridge: Cambridge Uni-versity Press, 1976), pp. 30-34.

48. See Stephen Levinson's chapter entitled 'Defining Pragmatics', in his *Prag-*

guistic knowledge and knowledge of the world. Katz and Fodor not-withstanding,[49] it seems impossible to construct a semantic theory devoid of any reference to the contextual elements of words or sentences.[50] Instead, Firth proposed that meaning ought to be understood in terms of a multi-layered context theory, in which there are contexts of situation as well as grammatical and phonological contexts.[51] The function, and consequently the meaning of each linguistic element is understood in terms of its relationships with the other elements in its environment.

Lastly, Firth's maxim known by him as 'renewal of connection', insofar as it is followed, ensures that the entire model will remain firmly based on the data of real language in use. In the words of Monaghan, 'renewal of connection with language in situations requires a relativization of the linguist's metalanguage. It is not the theory that gives validity to the description, but rather the description has to be always tested against real language in use.'[52]

3. *Hallidayan Functional Grammar*

As I pointed out above, Malinowski coined the term 'context of situation' to account for the typical environments in which members of a society behave linguistically. Firth, in turn, attempted to convert what was essentially the former's sporadic collection of primarily anthropological insights into a coherent socio-linguistic theory. Firth's success was, however, only partial, and his theory has often been described as

---

matics (CSL; Cambridge: Cambridge University Press, 1983); Leech argues for the strong interdepencence of both disciplines in *Principles of Pragmatics* ; thus also John Lyons, *Language, Meaning and Context* (Suffolk: Fontana, 1981), pp. 71, 72, who warns against drawing this distinction too sharply.

49. J.J. Katz and J.A. Fodor, 'The Structure of a Semantic Theory', *Language* 39 (1963), pp. 170-210.

50. Deictic markers, such as 'he', 'then', or 'there', are perhaps the best example of this. 'The single most obvious way in which the relationship between language and context is reflected in the structures of languages themselves is through the phenomenon of deixis' (Levinson, *Pragmatics*, p. 54).

51. Firth, *Papers in Linguistics,* passim.

52. James Monaghan, *The Neo-Firthian Tradition and its Contribution to General Linguistics* (Linguistische Arbeiten, 73; Tübingen: Max Niemeyer, 1979), p. 185; see also pp. 36-40 in the same volume.

merely 'programmatic'.[53] Standing firmly in the tradition of his two predecessors of the London school, Halliday set out to investigate and expound 'the functional basis of language'. The indebtedness of Michael Halliday to John Firth, his teacher at University College, London, is readily admitted by Halliday, and becomes particularly evident in statements such as the following: 'Text is meaning and meaning is choice, an ongoing current of selections each in its paradigmatic environment of what might have been meant (but was not)'.[54] For Halliday, language is the primary attribute of social man ('homo grammaticus'), and the behavioral potential of a society (i.e. what it 'can do'), is primarily realized by its linguistic potential ('can mean', socio-semantics), which is itself realized in the lexico-grammar ('can say').[55] Language, then, is fundamentally functional, indeed, it is man's most effective means of 'doing'. This functional nature of language has in large measure—argues Halliday—determined its current form, and is reflected in its three major functional components or 'macro-functions': the ideational, the interpersonal and the textual.[56] Halliday's chief hypothesis in regard to these 'macro-functions' is that each tends to be determined and constrained by one element of the context of situation.[57] Thus, the 'field' (i.e. 'what is going on', for example a game of poker) tends to constrain the choices arising from the ideational macro-function. The element of 'tenor' (i.e. the participants), similarly, tends to constrain the interpersonal choices, while the 'mode' (the function of language in the situation, e.g., to warn) constrains the textual choices.[58]

53. Butler, *Systemic Linguistics*, p. 3.

54. Halliday, *Social Semiotic*, p. 137.

55. See Halliday, 'Language in a Social Perspective', in *idem*, *Explorations*, pp. 51-53 (51).

56. The independence and validity of Halliday's three functional components has been questioned by Fawcett, among others, who proposes a much greater number of these. See Robin Fawcett, *Cognitive Linguistics and Social Interaction* (Heidelberg: Julius Groos Verlag, 1980), p. 12.

57. Halliday, *Social Semiotic*, p. 68.

58. Halliday is unclear as to the degree of determination of macro-functions by elements of situation. Thus, his descriptions of this relation range from 'a general tendency' (*Social Semiotic*, p. 68), to 'A systematic correspondence' (p. 116); 'tends to determine' (p. 117); 'activates', 'determines' (p. 125); 'rule' (p. 142). For more on this problem, see Butler, *Systemic Linguistics*, p. 88; cf. George Kennedy: 'The situation controls the rhetorical response in the same sense that the question

Elements of Situation	'tends to determine…'	Meta-Functions	Functional Roles	Realizations in Text
Field ('what is going on')		Ideational>	Transitivity	
Tenor (participants)	**<REGISTER>** A context-specific, function-based language variety.	Interpersonal>	Mood, Modality	
Mode (medium and function)		Textual>	Theme/rheme, Information	
'Can mean' (semantics)				'Can say' (lexico-grammar)

Figure 1.1[59]

Hallidayan functional grammar can be approached from several angles. Given my present aim, namely, to demonstrate its methodological suitability for the rhetorical/functional study of the New Testament documents, I wish to emphasize the following points:

(1) The focus of functional grammar is on language as an 'inter-organism' phenomenon. This is perhaps one of Halliday's favorite terms, used often to contrast his linguistic approach with that of Noam Chomsky, who favoured an 'intra-organism' perspective. In other words, Halliday's theory is decidedly socio-linguistic,[60] rather than

controls the answer and the problem controls the solution' (*Rhetorical Criticism*, p. 34).

59. The chart is my own, based on my reading of Halliday's works, esp. *Social Semiotic* and *Explorations*.

60. Besides acknowledging his debt to Malinowski, Halliday has affirmed his dependence on the sociological theory of Basil Bernstein. See M.A.K. Halliday, 'The Significance of Bernstein's Work for Sociolinguistic Theory', in Halliday, *Social Semiotic*, pp. 101-107. For a discussion of the origin and significance of socio-linguistics, see Oscar Uribe-Villegas, 'Introduction: Sociolinguistics in Search of a Place among the Academic Disciplines', in Uribe-Villegas (ed.), *Issues in Sociolinguistics* (Contributions to the Sociology of Language, 15; The Hague: Mouton, 1977), pp. 21-35 (30-35).

psycho-linguistic. It focuses on language as the primary means of social behaviour, rather than as 'competence' stored in people's brains. Given the mentioned sociological focus, it is not surprising that the emphasis of linguistic analysis is placed on system and choice, that is, on the paradigmatic, rather than the syntagmatic axis (see Halliday quotation at the beginning of this section). In connection with this, Halliday argues that the failure of many text-descriptive theories is rooted in an inability or unwillingness to properly account for paradigmatic relations. If we are to relate a text to 'higher orders of meaning, whether social, literary or of some other semiotic universe',[61] we must—argues Halliday—move beyond the mere description of syntax to an account of the contextually determined networks of options from which particular textual choices emanate. Our knowledge of the language system(s) (e.g. the transitivity network) allows us to explain the various lexico-grammatical structures in a text as purposeful choices, indeed, as part and parcel of a larger rhetorical strategy of its author. Understood within this framework, the study of the linguistic/literary device of foregounding offers, as I will show below, a clear demonstration of the purposeful nature of linguistic choices made by a writer or speaker within a text.

(2) The aim of functional grammar is the study of texts,[62] 'which may be regarded as the basic unit of semantic structure'.[63] This is demonstrated in Halliday's analysis of William Golding's *The Inheritors*,[64] in which various linguistic means of foregrounding are discussed in light of the overall theme of the narrative. In a similar study, Halliday uses the text of James Thurber's fable, 'The Lover and his Lass', to illustrate the concept of situation in written narrative, as well as the links 'between the semantic configurations of the text and the situational description...'[65] Ruqaiya Hasan has produced similar analyses in *Linguistics, Language and Verbal Art*, using as sample texts a poem (Les Murray's *Widower in the Country*), and a short story (Angus Wilson's

61. Halliday, *Social Semiotic*, p. 137.
62. 'We are interested in what a particular writer has written, against the background of what he might have written...in what it is about the language of a particular work of literature that has its effect on us as readers...' (Halliday, *Social Semiotic*, pp. 56-57); See also Berry, *Introduction*, pp. 193-95; Butler, *Systemic Linguistics*, p. 25.
63. Halliday, *Social Semiotic*, p. 60.
64. 'Linguistic Function and Literary Style: An Inquiry into the Language of William Golding's *The Inheritors*', in *idem, Explorations*, pp. 103-35.
65. 'The Sociosemantic Nature of Discourse', in *idem, Social Semiotic*, p. 128.

Necessity's Child).[66] In the analysis of texts, Halliday argues, there are two possible levels of achievement. The first may be described as a contribution to the understanding of the text, and is reached by the study of lexis and grammar. This first level of analysis may help to answer the question of why a text means what it does. The second level represents a signicantly higher achievement, and focuses on whether or not the text in question is effective in encompassing the situation it is designed to address. It is the second level of achievement that Halliday's functional grammar aims for. Such an agenda seems well suited for the fulfillment of the aims of rhetorical criticism as expressed above. If rhetoric is the study of effective communication *(ars bene dicendi)*, a text may be considered rhetorically successful insofar as it is shown to be *functionally appropriate to the situation* that motivated it. It follows, then, that rhetorical theory must be equipped to encompass the fundamental elements of situation, the text, and the reciprocal relations between them. This leads to the third point I wish to make.

(3) Perhaps most importantly, the aim of Hallidayan functional grammar is to expose and exploit the links between text and its context of situation.

> [A] text is an instance of social meaning in a particular context of situation. We shall therefore expect to find the situation embodied or enshrined in the text, not piecemeal, but in a way which reflects the systematic relation between the semantic structure and the social environment.[67]

This is, I wish to argue, the facet of functional grammar that is most valuable for the task of interpreting the New Testament documents. In ancient texts such as these, where the context of situation is at best only partially understood, a functional analysis of their language may yield important clues for the recovery of that context.[68] An example offered

---

66. Hasan, *Linguistics, Language*.

67. Halliday, *Social Semiotic*, p. 141.

68. In this regard, Hasan writes, 'the relationship between text and context is two-fold for the acculturated reader: if we have access to the context, we can predict the essentials of the text; if we have access to the text, then we can infer the context from it', Hasan cited in Mohsen Ghadessy, 'The Language in Written Sports Commentary: Soccer—A Description', in Ghadessy (ed.), *Registers of Written English*, pp. 19-24 (21). Similarly, Brown and Yule affirm that 'Even in the absence of information about place and time of original utterance, even in the absence of information about the speaker/writer and his intended recipient, it is often pos-

by Halliday serves to illustrate this. In his analysis of 'The Lover and his Lass' mentioned above, Halliday finds that the three roles the writer wishes to adopt in relation to his readers (recounter, humorist, and moralist) are embodied respectively in his choices of mood (every clause in the narrative section of the story is declarative), 'vocabulary as attitude' (e.g. the expression inamoratus), and the 'special mood structure' characteristic of proverbial literature.[69] These are choices in the interpersonal network and relate to the situational element of tenor.

(4) Halliday's functional view of the clause. In the introduction to his *Introduction to Functional Grammar*, Halliday laments the long-standing divorce between rhetoric and grammar, a divorce he blames on Aristotle.[70] If, in studying a text (be it oral or written), the analyst fails to take into account its lexicogrammatical features, together with their nature as motivated choices within the language system, his or her study will have all the limitations of a mere running commentary of that text, with little or no explanatory value.[71] Halliday's functional grammar focuses on the lexicogrammatical system, understood as a network of options having a functional input (the set of social functions that language is called upon to serve), and a structural output (the set of linguistic items that together form a text). If rhetoric is the study of those

---

sible to reconstruct at least some part of the physical context and to arrive at some interpretation of the text. The more co-text there is, in general, the more secure the interpretation is' (Brown and Yule, *Discourse Analysis*, pp. 49-50). See also Halliday, *Social Semiotic*, p. 62; Porter, 'Register in the Greek'.

69. Halliday, *Social Semiotic*, p. 148.

70. Halliday points out that prior to Aristotle, syntax was always studied in connection to rhetoric, that is, in connection to an explanation of what makes discourse effective. Aristotle, however, took grammar and syntax away from rhetoric and into the realm of logic. See Halliday, *Introduction to Functional Grammar*. See also Hasan, 'Rhyme and Reason', p. 297. See also José S. Laso-De La Vega, *Sintaxis Griega I* (Enclopedia Clásica, 6; Madrid: Consejo Superior de Investigaciones Científicas, 1968), p. 15. Yet at the time of the early Roman Empire, a certain 'encroachment' of grammar upon rhetoric was still discernible by some of the rhetorical school-masters. See E. Patrick Parks, *The Roman Rhetorical Schools as a Preparation for the Courts under the Early Empire* (The Johns Hopkins University Studies in Historical and Political Science, 83.2; Baltimore: The Johns Hopkins University Press, 1945), p. 62.

71. Halliday, *Functional Grammar*, p. xvii; M.A.K. Halliday and R. Hasan, 'Text and Context: Aspects of Language in a Social-Semiotic Perspective', *Sophia Linguistica* 6 (1980), pp. 4-91 (11); see also Carter's 'Introduction', pp. 1-17.

features of language that make it effective in a specific situation, it seems clear that it is a linguistic method like Halliday's that is best suited for such a task.

The fundamental unit of organization in functional grammar is the clause, wherein we find the integrated expression of all the functionally distinct elements of language.[72] Thus in a Greek clause such as ὅς ταύτην τὴν ὁδὸν ἐδίωξα ἄχρι θανάτου (Acts 22.4) we discern grammatical elements that are the structural expression of the ideational, interpersonal and textual functions. The elements of theme[73] (that with which the clause is concerned, ταύτην τὴν ὁδὸν) and rheme (what is being said about the theme, ἐδίωξα ἄχρι θανάτου) are (among others) the structural realization of the *textual* function of language, in virtue of which a cohesive, unified message (as opposed to 'mumble jumble') is created. Secondly, the same clause may be analyzed in terms of subject (ὅς) and finite (ταύτην τὴν ὁδὸν ἐδίωξα). In this case we are looking at the clause not as message but as exchange, and our focus is upon the role(s) that a speaker may adopt in relation to his audience. In our sample clause, Paul's role is that of narrator-recounter, and this is expressed by means of a simple declarative statement in the indicative mood. The elements of subject and finite, choices in the mood system of Greek, are expressions of the *interpersonal* function of language. Lastly, and most importantly, we may also analyze the clause as the expression of a process. This is the cornerstone of Halliday's functional grammar:

> Our most powerful conception of reality is that it consists of 'goings-on': of doing, happening, feeling, being. These goings-on are sorted out in the semantic system of the language, and expressed through the grammar of the clause. Parallel with its evolution in the function of mood, expressing the active, interpersonal aspect of meaning, the clause evolved simultaneously in another grammatical function expressing the reflective, experiential aspect of meaning. This latter is the system of TRANSITIVITY.

72. M.A.K. Halliday, *Explorations in the Functions of Language* (London: Edward Arnold, 1976), p. 42.

73. Theme and rheme are terms Halliday borrows from the Prague school of linguistics. In English, theme is normally indicated by its position in the clause, where it precedes the rheme. In Greek its identification may have to be based on more complex criteria, including immediate context. Theme and rheme together make the clause a message, and express the textual function of language. See M.A.K. Halliday and R. Hasan, 'Notes on Transitivity and Theme in English, Part II', *Journal of Linguistics* 3 (1967), pp. 199-244.

Transitivity species the different types of process that are recognized in the language, and the structures by which they are expressed.[74]

Thus, our sample clause encodes a material process (i.e. a 'process of doing'), and contains the elements of agent (ὃς the non-explicit first person singular in ἐδίωξα), medium (ταύτην τὴν ὁδὸν) and process (ἐδίωξα), ἄχρι θανάτου being an adjunct. Other types of processes such as a relational process (i.e. a 'process of being') may lack the agent element: ἐγώ εἰμι ἀνὴρ Ἰουδαῖος, that is, they represent processes as lacking an external cause, or, more accurately, without reference to causation. The transitivity system, within which the elements of agent, medium, and process are possible choices, is the principal expression of the *ideational* function of language.

Within the framework of his functional grammar, Michael Halliday's register theory best illustrates the above mentioned aims.[75] Like George Kennedy and Dieter Betz, Halliday is concerned with 'language varieties according to use', yet, unlike these two scholars and their followers, he seems to have succeeded in constructing a model capable of wide application across temporal and geographical boundaries.[76] Starting from the Malinowskian insight that 'the language we speak or write varies according to the type of situation',[77] Halliday seeks to establish just what elements of situation determine what linguistic features in the text. As was briefly mentioned above, the element of field ('that which is going on', e.g., a game of poker), for example, determines choices arising from the ideational component of language, real-

74. Halliday, *Functional Grammar*, p. 101.

75. The term was first used by T.B.W. Reid in the context of a discussion of bilingualism ('Linguistics, Structuralism and Philology', *Archivum Linguisticum* 8.2 [1956]), pp. 28-37.

76. Unlike the culturally-bound categories of epideictic, judicial and deliberative genera, the notion of register (including that of the three macro-functions which constrain it) is flexible and sensitive enough to permit its widest application. Thus Halliday, 'it is postulated that in all languages the content systems are organized into ideational, interpersonal and textual components. This is presented as a universal feature of language. But the descriptive categories are treated as particular. So, while all languages are assumed to have a "textual" component, whereby discourse achieves a texture that relates it to its environment, it is not assumed that in any given language one of the ways of achieving texture will be by means of a thematic system...' (Halliday, *Functional Grammar*, p. xxxiv). See also Ure and Ellis, 'Register in Descriptive Linguistics', p. 201.

77. Halliday, *Social Semiotic*, p. 32.

ized in structures such as types of process, participant structures and so on. The sum total of the discernible lexico-grammatical and intonational (if dealing with a spoken text) features deriving from field, tenor and mode constitutes a context-specific variety of language, or register. While the usefulness of the notion of register is widely acknowledged, recent scholarly discussion of register analysis has raised several questions of importance. Robert de Beaugrande, for example, objects to 'making "social" categories [i.e. field, tenor, and mode] correspond to language forms',[78] and prefers to define register in essentially psychological terms. Whether register must ultimately be understood socio-semantically or lexico-grammatically, may well be merely a matter of point of view. I for one wish to argue, together with Matthiessen, that lexico-grammatical analysis may be used with profit, at least as a point of entry into the functional grammatical study of registers, and that at least from this angle 'registers can be described in the same way as languages'.[79]

4. Foregrounding as a Point of Entry into the Functional-Grammatical Analysis of New Testament Greek Texts

The complexity of some of the issues involved in recent discussion of register, together with the preliminary and pioneering nature of the conclusions thus far, must not be allowed to create too negative an impression of its real potential. The fruitful and insightful analyses of texts carried out by Halliday and Hasan, among others, are fair indicators of the results that further research along these lines may yield. Secondly, it must be noted that in New Testament studies, given the limited corpus of texts available, one cannot be concerned with several of the issues that most often occupy and divide register analysts, namely, register as a means of investigating idiolects (the sum total of the registers an individual controls) or sociolect (the sum total of registers discernible in a given society). The scantiness of the data clearly precludes such ambitious aims.

78. Robert de Beaugrande, '"Register" in Discourse Studies', pp. 13, 20. But see Christian Matthiessen, 'Register in the Round: Diversity in a Unified Theory of Register Analysis', who clarifies the matter by stating that while 'the semantic system is realized by the lexico-grammatical one…context of situation is realized not directly by the linguistic system but by *variation in* the linguistic system [his emphasis]', in Ghadessy (ed.), *Register Analysis*, p. 221-92 (236).
79. Matthiessen, 'Register in the Round', p. 275.

Discussing the complexity of register analysis in English, Matthiessen proposes that analysts must, first, 'be able to make principled selections' from all the evidence available, and, secondly, 'use such selections as a way into a comprehensive account'.[80] I wish to suggest that, in applying functional grammar to the Greek of the New Testament, the study of patterns of *foregrounding*[81] may be chosen with profit as that initial selection, with a view to an eventual comprehensive analysis. The need of writers to mark varying degrees of saliency in narrative seems to be a universal one. By investing the text with diverse viewpoints on the action, and highlighting key elements or episodes through lexico-grammatical means, the skilled narrator is able to impose an 'evaluative superstructure' upon the text, aimed at effecting the desired response(s) in the reader. The textual function of language, of which foregrounding strategies are a realization, enables the writer to organize his text into a coherent and cohesive whole, so that what he writes is appropriate to the context and fulfills its intended function.

80. Matthiessen, 'Register in the Round', p. 275.
81. The key works on the subject of foregrounding are: Jan Mukarovsky, 'Standard Language and Poetic Language', in Paul R. Garvin (ed.), *A Prague School Reader on Esthetic, Literary Structure and Style* (Washington DC: Georgetown University Press, 1964), pp. 17-30; Roman Jakobson, 'Linguistics and Poetics', in Thomas A. Sebeok (ed.), *Style in Language* (Cambridge, MA: MIT Press, 1960), pp. 350-68; Geoffrey N. Leech, 'Linguistics and the Figures of Rhetoric', in Roger Fowler (ed.), *Essays on Style and Language* (London: Routledge & Kegan Paul, 1970), pp. 135-56; Michael Halliday, 'Linguistic Function and Literary Style', pp. 103-38. See also Geoffrey N. Leech, 'Foregrounding and Interpretation', chapter 4 of his *A Linguistic Guide to English Poetry* (London: Longman, 1969); Stephen Wallace, 'Figure and Ground: The Interrelationships of Linguistic Categories', in Paul J. Hopper (ed.), *Tense-Aspect: Between Semantics and Pragmatics* (Amsterdam: John Benjamins, 1982), pp. 201-23; S. Fleischmann, 'Discourse Functions of Tense-Aspect Oppositions in Narrative: Toward a Theory of Grounding', *Linguistics* 23.6 (1985), pp. 851-82; Fleischmann, *Tense and Narrativity* (Austin: University of Texas Press, 1990); S. Fleischmann and L. Waugh (eds.), *Discourse Pragmatics and the Verb* (London: Routledge, 1991); (the last four works focus on tense-aspect); Willie van Peer, *Stylistics and Psychology: Investigations of Foregrounding* (Croom Helm Linguistics Series; London: Croom Helm, 1986), who provides a complete bibliography; Hasan, *Linguistics, Language*, especially pp. 29-106; Helen Dry, 'Foregrounding: An Assessment', in S.J.J. Hwang and W.R. Merrifield (eds.), *Language in Context: Essays for Robert E. Longacre* (Dallas: Summer Institute of Linguistics, 1992), pp. 435-50.

Before turning to transitivity-based foregrounding in my chosen text of Acts for the remainder of the present book, I wish to put forth an example of foregrounding in a non-narrative text to illustrate its fundamental importance as a rhetorical/literary device, and as indicative of an author's compositional intention. As I indicated in my above note concerning previous research into foregrounding, much of the work carried out in recent years has focused on tense-aspect morphology as a means of grounding in texts. As far as the New Testament texts are concerned, a study of Ephesians confirms that aspect is a common means of foregrounding in the epistolary literature of the New Testament.[82] A noteworthy linguistic feature of Ephesians is the uneven distribution of present and aorist tense forms through the epistle. Even a cursory analysis of these tense forms reveals that, regardless of mood, the first half of the epistle contains a similar amount of present and aorist tenses, while in the second half, the number of present tense forms is over double that of aorist forms.

DISTRIBUTION OF PRESENT AND AORIST FORMS IN EPHESIANS			
	TOTAL	CHAPTERS 1–3	CHAPTERS 4–6
AORIST	123	64	59
PRESENT	174	54	120

From a stylistic/rhetorical standpoint, the epistle is also evenly divided at chapter four. The first half is primarily expository, relating the events of God's election and call, as well as those of Christ's life, death and resurrection, with interspersed comments on the bearing of those events on the life and faith of the church. The second half is essentially hortatory, with an almost complete predominance of instruction and commands (the author uses only one imperative before 4.25 [2.11], and a staggering 40 from 4.25 to the end).

82. See Stanley Porter on 'planes of discourse', in *idem*, *Verbal Aspect in the Greek of the New Testament, with Reference to Tense and Mood* (New York: Peter Lang, 1989), p. 92; see also, following Porter, Thomas R. Hatina, 'The Perfect Tense-Form in Recent Debate: Galatians as a Case Study', *FN* 8 (1995), pp. 3-22. For several contrasting views on Porter's understanding of verbal aspect see S.E. Porter and D.A. Carson (eds.), *Biblical Greek Language and Linguistics: Open Questions in Current Research* (JSNTSup, 80; Sheffield: JSOT Press, 1993), pp. 14-82.

When Ephesians is analyzed, it can be seen that the present tense forms are used consistently by the author to communicate the verbal ideas that are most central to his purpose, or those related to the immediate experience or the behavior of his audience. In contrast to this, aorist tense forms are used when the author does not intend to signal immediacy or closeness to the experience of the audience, and is instead relating, for example, the acts of God or Christ on their behalf *without* a hortatory or paraenetic (exhortative) emphasis (see examples below). This consistent use of aorist and present forms may be illustrated by saying that the author has taken on the role of a teacher who is concerned with communicating to his audience the great acts of God and Christ on their behalf, as well as the significance of those acts. In pursuing this task, it is as though he were using an imaginary blackboard on which these events are recorded for the benefit of the audience. From time to time, however, he feels the point at hand has a specific bearing on the life of the church in its present situation and, leaving the blackboard behind, turns to the audience and addresses them eye to eye, as directly as he knows how.

In Ephesians 1 the present tense forms are used consistently to express either the purpose of the divine acts in the life of the believers (so that we may be holy, so that we may be for his praise, Eph. 1.4, 12 respectively), an explanation or application of a statement made in the aorist (in whom we have redemption [v. 7], which is the down-payment [v. 14], which is his body [v. 23]), or the writer's thanks for the Ephesians (v. 16). The aorist is used to narrate the events or acts of God or Christ on behalf of the believers, the events or conditions in the believers' life, *when* these lead to a conclusion or explanation in the present tense (we have been called having been predestined–aor–[v. 11], so as for us to be for the praise...-pres.-[v. 12]; you have been sealed with the Spirit,–aor–[13b], which is the down payment...–pres.–[v. 14]), and the one petition in the writer's prayer (that God may give you a spirit of wisdom [v. 17]). The central idea[83] in Ephesians 2 is the contrast between being once foreigners toward God and his people, being called 'the foreskin' by those who are circumcised and having no hope, and now having access and being fellow citizens with the saints and built

83. That this is his central idea is pointed out by the writer: διὸ μνημονεύετε ὅτι ποτὲ ὑμεῖς τὰ ἔθνη (the only imperative in the first half of the epistle)...ἄρα οὖν οὐκέτι ἐστὲ ξένοι καὶ πάροικοι, ἀλλὰ ἐστὲ συμπολῖται... (2.11, 19).

together into a house for God. This theme is carried by means of present tense forms. Of the 21 aorist forms in this chapter, 13 are used to indicate the gracious acts of God in behalf of the believers and the rest are used to describe the conduct of the believers aside from the central theme of 'from foreigners to fellow citizens'. The clearest example of this is perhaps the contrast between the two verbs ἐποικοδομηθέντες and συνοικοδομεῖσθε (vv. 20 and 22). Both are predicated of the believers, but only the latter uses the present tense, for it brings to conclusion the central idea as expressed above: the whole structure, being joined together grows into a holy temple in the Lord (v. 21), in whom *you too are being built together* (with the rest of God's people) into a spiritual dwelling of God. In Ephesians 3, aorist tenses are used consistently to communicate the events of the writer's calling and endowment with the gospel message and his petition in prayer. The present tenses, on the other hand, are used to convey the content of the gospel message (that the Gentiles are fellow heirs [v. 6], that we have freedom of access [v. 12]), the writer's direct request to his audience (I ask that you don't grow weary, v. 13]), and his statement to them that God is at work in them and will answer their prayers (v. 20).

In the second half of the epistle, as noted above, the present tense forms become dominant as the writer shifts into hortatory gear. Continuing with my analogy of the classroom, in Ephesians 4 the writer begins to move away from the board, and in Ephesians 5–6 (the climax of his paraenesis) he walks in the midst of his audience, forcefully bringing the previous expository material to bear upon the listeners (present tense usage), with only an occasional return to the board to remind them of the example of Christ or to convey events or facts that are not considered central (aorist usage).

Suzanne Fleischmann describes a phenomenon in mediaeval Romance languages she terms 'Tenses as indices of "narrating personae"'.[84]

---

84. 'Each of the four tenses at issue [in medieval Romance languages] can be correlated with a particular *mode of representation*, with a particular *activity* carried out by the narrator, and with what I refer to as a *narrating persona*... The narrator who speaks in the unmarked PRET adopts the perspective of the historian. With a shift to the IMP, we see events no longer from the perspective of the historian but from that of the painter, who depicts rather than narrates...the PC views events from the perspective of a memorialist whose report, unlike that of a historian, makes explicit reference to personal experienced...' [emphasis original] Fleischmann, *Tense and Narrativity*, pp. 63, 66.

The central notion behind this term is that in selecting one particular tense form instead of another, the writer is imposing a specific perspective or point of view upon the discourse, a perspective he or she expects the readers to discern. This notion agrees with the minimal definition of aspect (in all the moods) shared by Buist Fanning, S.E. Porter and J.P. Louw: that the central or invariant meaning of aspect is 'the viewpoint or perspective which the speaker takes in regard to the action'.[85] The author of Ephesians' use of these forms is purposeful and consistent, except in those few instances where the grammatical or syntactical constraints of the language system present a limitation to the writer's aspectual choice. Although this example from epistolary exposition illustrates only one means of foregrounding available to writers and speakers for text production, it serves to elucidate and highlight the essential role of foregrounding in discriminating between that which is central and that which is secondary to an author's overall rhetorical/literary agenda in a text. The phenomenon of foregrounding in its various forms, part of the textual functional component of language,[86] represents, to borrow George Kennedy's words, an important key to 'the discovery of the author's intent and of how that is transmitted through a text to an audience'.[87]

85. Buist Fanning, *Verbal Aspect in New Testament Greek* (Oxford: Clarendon Press, 1990), p. 83. See also Porter, *Verbal Aspect*, p. 86; J.P. Louw, 'Verbal Aspect in the First Letter of John', *Neot* 9 (1980), pp. 98-104 (99). Joseph Grimes calls this element of perspective on the action 'staging', and argues that the speaker of a language 'can no more dodge incorporating a staging component than the photographer can decide to take his picture from nowhere, or from everywhere'. Joseph E. Grimes, 'Signals of Discourse Structure in Koine', in *SBL 1975 Seminar Papers*, I (Atlanta, GA: Scholars Press, 1975), pp. 151-64 (153).

86. A distinction must be made here between the patterns that are foregrounded and the phenomenon of foregrounding itself. Though foregrounded patterns such as certain types of verbal groups and clauses are choices arising from the transitivity network, and therefore the ideational macrofunction, foregrounding itself in its various forms is something consistent throughout the text, contributing to its 'texture', and belongs in the textual macrofunction. On this point, see E.A. Nida, J.P. Louw, A.P. Snyman and W.V. Cronje (eds.), *Style and Discourse* (Cape Town: Bible Society of South Africa, 1983), p. 46; and Fleischmann, *Tense and Narrativity*, p. 168.

87. Kennedy, *Rhetorical Criticism*, p. 12.

5. *Conclusion*

In his contribution to *Rhetoric and the New Testament*, Jeffrey Reed acknowledges the existence of a *functional* correspondence between the writings of St Paul and the rhetorical manuals of Graeco-Roman antiquity, while at the same time denying any signicant *formal* correspondence between the two.[88] I am in fundamental agreement with Reed at this point, since it has been my argument in this chapter that the inability of the writers in 'Group A' to make this important distinction has rendered their approach largely ineffective, clearly illustrating that 'labels [such as 'rhetorical'] can obstruct, and not only help'.[89]

In suggesting that Michael Halliday's functional grammar is an ideally suited method for achieving the aims of rhetorical criticism as expressed by Crafton and others in *Rhetoric and the New Testament*, I do not wish to preclude other approaches to the same problem. I do, however, wish to argue with Hasan that if analyses of literary texts (be they ancient or modern) are to lead to something more than statements of personal preference they must be linguistically informed, for

> To arrive at the truth—the themes(s) of literature text [*sic*]—we must go
> through the time-demanding exercise of meticulous linguistic analysis; it
> is this alone that can show what is being achieved in the work and how.
> And until we can do this, it is meaningless to talk of evaluation, for what
> we are evaluating in the absence of such careful analysis is more likely
> to be our inexplicit impressions against our equally accidental precon-
> ceptions of what an artist should or should not do.[90]

As is the case with rhetorical criticism, functional grammar aims to uncover the function(s) of texts, and the effects that texts have upon readers and/or hearers. Unlike much of rhetorical criticism, however, functional grammar aims to achieve its aims not by imposing extraneous forms or structures upon the texts to be studied, but by carefully observing and interpreting the linguistic choices made by the author(s) throughout those texts. The functional grammatical analysis of foregrounding is, I wish to argue, the clearest illustration of this. In the next

88. Reed, 'Ancient Rhetorical Categories', pp. 300, 301, 307, 308, 317, 321-24.

89. Nils Erik Enkvist, 'Text and Discourse Linguistics, Rhetoric, and Stylistics', in Teun A. Van Dijk (ed.), *Discourse and Literature* (Amsterdam: John Benjamins, 1985), pp. 1-16 (11).

90. Hasan, *Linguistics, Language,* p. 106; See also Hasan, 'Linguistics and the Study of Literary Texts', *Etudes de linguistique appliquée* 5 (1967), pp. 106-109.

chapter, I will survey the concept of foregrounding from its origins in Russian formalism to the present work of narratologists such as Fleischmann and Carter. I will argue that Halliday's approach to foregrounding brings together key insights from several related disciplines into one coherent and cogent explanation, ideally suited for the study of foregounding in my chosen texts of the Acts of the Apostles.

Chapter 2

THE RELEVANCE OF FOREGROUNDING FOR INTERPRETATION
AND TRANSLATION: THE EPISODE OF PAUL'S SHIPWRECK
(ACTS 27) AS A CASE STUDY

Since its origin in the context of Russian formalism, the concept of linguistic foregrounding has motivated a large volume of work from a
variety of angles. As has already been pointed out,[1] the differing theoretical frameworks that have thus far been brought to the discussion,
together with the lack of agreement as to a basic definition have greatly
limited the fruitfulness of this notion. It is not surprising, therefore, that
New Testament Greek scholarship has only recently begun its own reti-
cent forays into this exciting area of linguistic reasearch, and this at a
fairly limited scale.[2] The basic structure of this chapter is as follows.
First, I shall attempt to summarize and assess various recent theories of
linguistic foregrounding within the framework of functional grammar.
Secondly, I shall turn my attention to the self-contained story of Paul's
shipwreck in Acts 27, exploring the significance of transitivity-based
foregrounded elements therein. Finally, in my appendix to the main
body of this chapter, I shall refer to the notion of functional equivalence
in the translation of foregrounding as discussed in the work of V. Pro-
chazka and E.A. Nida, and offer some suggestions for the translation of
foregrounding into the receptor language of Spanish, with reference to
the Reina-Valera translation. I will attempt to demonstrate that research

1. See Dry, 'Foregrounding', pp. 435-50.
2. See Grimes, 'Signals of Discourse Structure in Koine', pp. 151-64; Robert
D. Bergen, 'Text as a Guide to Authorial Intention: An Introduction to Discourse
Criticism', *JETS* 30.3 (1987), pp. 34-49 ; Porter, *Verbal Aspect*, pp. 92-93; Fanning,
Verbal Aspect, pp. 72-77; Jeffrey T. Reed, 'Identifying Theme in the New Testa-
ment: Insights from Discourse Analysis', in Stanley E. Porter and Donald A. Car-
son (eds.), *Discourse Analysis and Other Topics in Biblical Greek* (JSNTSup, 113;
Sheffield: Sheffield Academic Press, 1995), pp. 75-101.

into foregrounding in New Testament Greek, a largely neglected area of study, has significant potential for both New Testament interpretation and translation, and requires much further study, along the lines here proposed.

1. *Linguistic Foregrounding in Twentieth-Century Discussion: 1917–1990*

The phenomenon of foregrounding has been a focus of study in several decades of literary criticism and discourse analysis in a wide variety of genres and languages.[3] In producing a text, a writer finds himself under several constraints. He or she has a limited space and time for its composition; he or she must abide—if communication is to take place between himself and the readers—by the lexico-grammatical conventions of the receptor speech community; lastly, he must impose a particular perspective on the text, a 'patterning of patterns' that unifies the composition, investing it with at least a minimal amount of structure and direction.[4] Through linguistic means such as lexico-grammatical structures, tense-aspect morphology, or choices from the transitivity network the writer attempts to guide his readers through the text, highlighting various levels of meaning or drawing attention to the episodes or themes that matter most in light of his overall rhetorical strategy.[5]

An adequate understanding of the theory of foregrounding requires at least a basic acquaintance with a small number of works that have dealt with it from the 1920s to the present. The discussion that follows will concentrate on seminal essays by Mukarovsky, Jakobson, Leech, and Halliday (see below), all of whom have left their imprint upon the notion in somewhat predictable ways.

The notion of linguistic foregrounding can be traced to insights developed within Russian formalism in the second decade of this century. Formalism's concern for differentiating between non-poetic and poetic works led Viktor Slovskij and others to the conclusion that the

---

3.   For foregrounding bibliography, please turn to n. 81 in the previous chapter.

4.   In the words of Grimes, this can no more be avoided than a photographer can choose to 'take his picture from nowhere or from everywhere' (Grimes, 'Signals', p. 153).

5.   The term 'rhetorical' is used here in its widest sense of *ars bene dicendi*, the art of addressing a situation effectively by means of speech. See Enkvist, 'Text and Discourse Linguistics', p. 11.

distinguishing mark of the latter is their potential for defamiliarization (Russian *ostranenie*), for causing readers and hearers to perceive elements of the poem with heightened awareness. Consequently, much of the energy of the formalists was dedicated to the investigation of the linguistic devices that activate such defamiliarization. Thus began the tendency to see foregrounding fundamentally as the departure from an established norm, a figure against a ground, to use the terms of subsequent psychological investigation.

The discussion of foregrounding, however, reached a point of significant development in the early 1960s, primarily at the hands of two Prague structuralists, Jan Mukarovsky and Roman Jakobson. Their two highly influential essays[6] mentioned in the bibliography in the previous chapter have much in common, as well as significant differences at various points. Both scholars saw the primary aim of their respective papers as the definition of the '*differentia specifica*' of poetic language vis-à-vis ordinary, standard language.[7] Both emphasize that the poetic function is a concentration on the message 'for its own sake', while ordinary language points rather to the referent or the subject matter. Further, Jakobson and Mukarovsky seem to share a determination to distinguish between the purely aesthetic function of poetic language, and the pragmatic focus of non-poetic language. Lastly and most importantly, both Jakobson and Mukarovsky see some form of foregrounding as the essence of poetic language.[8] Their differences are no less considerable, however. While Mukarovsky insists on a strong dichotomy between poetic and standard language, arguing that the former cannot be considered a brand of the latter, Jakobson would tone down the differences by affirming that poetics is an integral part of linguistics, and that every speech event, poetic or not, fulfills not one but several functions. For Mukarovsky, the essence of the poetic function is foregrounding, understood as the opposite of 'automatization', that is, the

6.   Jakobson, 'Linguistics', and Mukarovsky 'Standard Language'. This is particularly true of Mukarovsky's 'Standard Language', as translated and edited by Garvin in 1960. To Garvin we owe the English word 'foregrounding', his rendering of Mukarovsky's Czech term *aktualisace*.

7.   Jakobson, 'Linguistics', p. 350; Mukarovsky 'Standard Language', p. 17.

8.   Though Jakobson does not use the term foregrounding or its Czech equivalent, he does rely on one of the common metaphors for the notion, that is, 'palpability' (Jakobson, 'Linguistics', p. 356).

departure from a norm.[9] Jakobson, however, sees parallelism as the fundamental element of poetic language, that is, repetition of the same elements where a departure would have been expected.[10] Parallelism, argues Jakobson, is the primary means of promoting the 'palpability of signs' in a text.

Though the contribution made by these two essays to the theory of foregrounding makes them veritable landmarks in the history of the discussion, at least two serious objections must be raised against their commonly held views. The difference between a focus on the message 'for its own sake' (the poetic function) and a focus on the referent or subject matter (non-poetic, referential function) seems very difficult to demonstrate, as van Peer has noted.[11] Does the aesthetic nature of poetic language necessarily make it non-pragmatic? Does poetic language not communicate in the manner that 'ordinary' language communicates? Hasan has argued convincingly for the pragmatic import of verbal art, showing through her analyses of several texts the highly effective ways in which a writer can produce the desired effects in his or her readers through foregrounding various linguistic choices in

9. Thus, for example, in his short introductory story to his trilogy *U.S.A.*, John Dos Passos seeks to underline that it is its peculiar language that is the essence of America. This effect is achieved syntactically by a departure from an established pattern at two points. One example will suffice. The author embarks upon an extended list of negative statements: 'It was not in the long walks through jostling crowds at night that he was less alone, or in the training camp at Allentown, or in the day at the docks at Seattle... [this continues for 12 lines] ...but in his mother's words...it was the speech that clung to the ears, the link that tingled in the blood, U.S.A'. In this short story, this device can be shown to be motivated and consistent in its two instances. John Dos Passos, *The Big Money* (New York: Signet, 1979), p. xix.

10. In the anonymous fifteenth-century Spanish poem 'Romance del Rey Moro que perdió Alhama', the author presents a poetic justification of the Moorish loss of Granada ('Bien se te emplea, buen rey' etc.). Throughout these 56 lines, the narrator depicts the last moments of Moorish occupation of southern Spain from his Christian perspective. However, his repetition of the Moorish king's lament '¡Ay de mi Alhama!' (11X) gives the whole poem the feel of a dirge, and its effect is that of evoking sympathy for the defeated. The device of foregrounding serves here to undermine what would otherwise be clearly seen as the theme of this poem. José Bergua (ed.), *Las mil mejores poesias de la lengua castellana* (Madrid: Ediciones Ibéricas, 30th edn, 1991), p. 108.

11. van Peer, *Stylistics*, p. 9.

narrative.[12] Secondly, both scholars fail to provide adequate criteria for determining what is *significant* parallelism (Jakobson) or departure from a norm (Mukarovsky). Mukarovsky is aware of the need to develop such criteria, affirming that foregrounding is not a capricious, random, breaking of norm(s), but must be systematic and consistent. However, he seems unclear as to whether the norms are set up locally by the text or poem in question, or whether they are derived from the standard language.[13]

The publication of Geoffrey Leech's essay 'Linguistics and the Figures of Rhetoric' (see n. 81 in previous chapter) represents the first of several key contributions to foregrounding theory by scholars of University College, London. The main thrust of Leech's essay is his proposal for an integration of the two types of foregrounding discussed above, namely, by parallelism (Jakobson) and by deviation from norm(s) (Mukarovsky). This integration is achieved by means of applying Saussure's dichotomy of the paradigmatic and syntagmatic axes: while paradigmatic foregrounding would involve the selection of an item not permitted or expected at a particular point, syntagmatic foregrounding is the repeated selection of an item where a single selection is expected. The unifying element is that of selection along the two axes.

Michael Halliday's essay entitled 'Linguistic Function and Literary Style'[14] represents the foremost contribution of the London school of linguistics[15] to the discussion of foregrounding. In what could be Halliday's most persuasive presentation of his functional grammar,[16] the author provides a thorough account and interpretation of foregrounded transitivity patterns in William Golding's novel *The Inheritors*. Following Leech, Halliday affirms that foregrounding need not be understood exclusively in terms of deviation, and that whether it is seen as the transgression or the establishment of a norm is only a matter of point of view. Two points make Halliday's contribution to the discussion particularly significant. The author sets out to discover not only fore-

12. Hasan, *Linguistics, Language*, p. 99.
13. See, especially, Mukarovsky, 'Standard Language', p. 21.
14. In Halliday, *Explorations*, pp. 103-138. See also Ruqaiya Hasan's analyses of a poem and a story in Hasan, *Linguistics, Language*, esp. pp. 29-106.
15. For a critical introduction to the London School, see Langendoen, *The London School*.
16. See Butler, *Systemic Linguistics*, p. 198.

grounded patterns of language in a specific text such as Golding's, but, more importantly, criteria for relevant prominence that may be applied to all manner of texts. In fundamental agreement with Mukarovsky, Halliday seeks to distinguish between mere linguistic prominence, and that prominence which can be shown to be motivated or relevant in light of the overall theme or purpose of the text. The author affirms that the terms 'foreground' and 'foregrounding' can only be properly predicated of the latter. In addition, Halliday establishes his criteria within the framework of 'a functional theory of language' capable of relating every item of lexico-grammar in a text to the specific functions it has in the language system.[17]

The Inheritors is a story of the contrasting worldviews and lifestyles of two tribes of primitive men, of their encounter and conflict, and of the eventual survival of the more advanced group. In his analysis of the text, Halliday shows that the differing perspectives on reality of both tribes are skillfully conveyed by means of choices in the transitivity network at the rank of clause. Stemming from the ideational 'macrofunction' of language, transitivity choices have to do with the representation of experience, and are realized by the functional elements of process, participants, and circumstances.[18] These elements together define the typical clause used by Golding to characterize the first tribe (clause type 'A'): only one participant, action in simple past tense, almost complete absence of complements, overabundance of adjuncts (i.e. circumstantial clauses). This clause type becomes the norm for the bulk of the narrative and has the effect of conveying the limited understanding and ability, indeed, the frustrated existence of the Neanderthal tribe. In stark contrast, the last 16 pages of the novel depict the superiority of the Homo Sapiens group by means of a vastly different clause type: human subjects predominate in transitive clauses of action, encoding a far more complex perception of reality. Halliday concludes that the unexpected frequency of clause type 'A' throughout the work is related to an interpretation of the text's overall theme and subject matter, and can therefore be considered relevant, motivated prominence.

17. The importance of relating individual elements of style to a 'higher level functional framework' has been acknowledged by linguists outside the London School. See Paul J. Hopper and Sandra A. Thompson, 'Transitivity in Grammar and Discourse', *Language* 56.2 (1980), pp. 251-99 (280).

18. See Halliday, *Introduction to Functional Grammar*, pp. 101-44.

That the foregrounded structures are choices arising from the transitivity network is not surprising to Halliday, who affirms that 'transitivity is really the cornerstone of the semantic organization of experience'.[19]

In her evaluative assessment of the state of the art in foregrounding research as of 1992, Helen Dry notes the difficulties presented by the seemingly incompatible assumptions brought into the discussion by the disciplines of psychology, literary criticism and discourse analysis. It is my contention that Halliday's functional grammar is capable of integrating insights from these three approaches into one coherent theory of foregrounding which is widely applicable. Halliday's analysis of *The Inheritors* bears this point out. First, functional grammar enables us to recognize and study foregrounding in all kinds of texts, the only necessary condition for its identification being foregrounding's demonstrable motivation and consistency, in light of an interpretation of the theme or purpose of the text in question. According to Halliday's theory, and on the basis of extensive work carried out by himself and others, the three 'macro-functions' known by him as ideational, interpersonal, and textual are a universal of language.[20] The qualities that make a text what it is, for example, include cohesiveness and coherence, and these, whether exhibited by a poem or a newspaper article, are the product of the *textual* macro-function. Likewise, consistent, motivated prominence of the sort discernible, for example, in Golding's novel or Dos Passos's story (n. 9 above) is fundamentally contributive to the *texture* of those works, that is, it plays an essential role in their semantic organization. Functional grammar shows us, therefore, that the famous distinction between 'standard' and 'poetic' language is in fact much more tenuous than has been traditionally believed.[21] Secondly, Halliday's framework demon-

19. Halliday, *Functional Grammar*, p. 134.

20. Halliday, *Functional Grammar*, p. xxxiv. Cf. Jakobson, 'Linguistics', p. 353, and Jan De Waard and Eugene A. Nida, *From one Language to Another* (Nashville: Thomas Nelson, 1986), pp. 26, 43, 119. But Halliday adds that the particular realizations of these macrofunctions are language relative (*Functional Grammar*, p. xxxiv).

21. 'The search for the language of literature is misguided; we should look instead at language in literature' (Hasan, *Linguistics, Language*, p. 94). See also pp. 92-100. Though Hasan maintains a distinction between non-poetic and poetic language, this is strictly on the basis of the motivated nature of foregrounding in the latter. Furthermore, she calls for the 'demystification' of linguistic analysis of literature (p. 92), and affirms the potential for the widest use of foregrounding: 'once a novel patterning of patterns is introduced, it can become a currency…something

strates that insights from discourse analysis and psychology need not be incompatible. Since the seminal ethnolinguistic work of Bronislaw Malinowski, functional grammarians[22] have been profoundly aware that the meaning of every utterance is inseparably tied to its function in a specific context of situation. In light of this, Halliday's model aims to relate linguistic patterns of texts (the domain of discourse analysis) to the effects they have in their readers (the province of psycholinguistics).[23] 'Meaning, therefore, is function in context', not primarily the function of the individual elements of a text, but that of their strategically structured sum total. The implications of this insight for translation will be dealt with in the excursus following this chapter.

3. *Modern Luke–Acts Study: From Source to Literary Criticism*

Of the immense amount of scholarly work dedicated to the study of Luke–Acts[24] over the last 200 years, the question of purpose may well be the most important to have been asked.[25] As Gasque has pointed out, though the conclusions of the Tübingen school have long been rejected inside and outside of Germany, it must be recognized that it was Ferdinand Christian Baur who first pointed to the significance of the 'why question' in the study of Luke–Acts. Since Baur first presented his theory of the Paulinist–Jewish feud as the fundamental polemic behind the composition of Acts, the question of purpose has been pursued primarily along the lines of source-criticism and *tendenz*-criticism.[26]

that is available to the community for use in other textual environments' (p. 100).

22. Though the term is Halliday's, it is equally applicable to his teacher and predecessor at University College, John Rupert Firth, who first defined meaning as 'function in context'.

23. Halliday, 'Linguistic Function', p. 112.

24. Since H.J. Cadbury coined this designation and argued convincingly for it, the unity of the two volumes has not often been challenged. See Robert Maddox, *The Purpose of Luke–Acts* (Studies in the New Testament and its World; Edinburgh: T. & T. Clark, 2nd edn, 1985), pp. 3-6. A thorough recent attack on the unity of Luke–Acts, however, is M. Parsons and R.I. Pervo, *Rethinking the Unity of Luke–Acts* (Minneapolis: Fortress Press, 1990).

25. Thus Ward Gasque, *A History of the Criticism of the Acts of the Apostles* (Beiträge zur Geschichte der Biblischen Exegese, 17; Tübingen: J.C.B. Mohr, 1975), p. 50. This is also true of works published subsequently to 1975; see below.

26. Haenchen provided a memorable summary of this development: '...either

With the establishment of form and redaction criticism as widely accepted methods in the second half of this century, greater attention began to be paid to the text of Luke–Acts as a two-volumed literary unit, and to its final form as composed by the author with specific aim(s) in mind. Though this development often came at an unacceptable price, namely, the strong disjunction between history and literature,[27] the shift in focus from speculation about sources[28] to the text of Luke–Acts as a literary unit is a welcome and healthy turn of events in the investigation of the purpose of this work. Few scholars have done more to bring this shift about than Henry Joel Cadbury. In his celebrated monograph, *The Making of Luke–Acts*, Cadbury distances his new approach from that of previous scholars whose

> ...ultimate interest is not the author and his times, but the subject matter of his history. His own interests are considered merely as they color or adulterate his story. He is someone to be allowed for, eliminated and dis-counted, not someone to be studied and appreciated for his own sake. His literary methods are examined in order that we may discover the

the author of Acts was *unwilling*, or he was *unable*, to say more. The latter possibility led to source criticism, the former...to so-called tendency-criticism' (*The Acts of the Apostles*, p. 15).

27. Martin Dibelius was very much a pioneer of this new thrust in Luke–Acts scholarship, primarily through his essays 'Style Criticism of the Book of Acts' (1923) and 'The Acts of the Apostles in the Setting of Early Christian Literature' (1926). Dibelius's focus on Acts as a literary work was primarily due to his belief that: (1) the author lacked any significant source materials, and (2) the early Christians expected an immediate eschaton and were therefore uninterested in recording history. Consequently, Dibelius believed that '...we cannot, in the first place, consider this work from the aspect of *Formgeschichte* but only from that of its style'. Dibelius, 'Style Criticism of the Book of Acts', in *Studies in the Acts of the Apostles* (trans. Mary Ling; 1st English edn; London: SCM Press, 1956), pp. 1-13 (4). Following Dibelius, Haenchen has embraced a strong dichotomy between that which is historical and that which is literary. See Haenchen, *The Acts of the Apostles*, p. 44. Disputing Haenchen's belief in the absence of traditions behind Acts, Max Wilcox points out that all we are entitled to say is that if these existed, 'they are no longer extant as separate entities' (Wilcox, 'A Foreword to the Study of the Speeches in Acts', *SJLA* 12.1 [1975], p. 210). On the issue of the false dichotomy of history and literature, see also Gasque, *History*, p. 266; Colin J. Hemer, *The Book of Acts in the Setting of Hellenistic History* (ed. C. Gempf; WUNT, 44; Tübingen: J. C. B. Mohr, 1989), pp. 34-35.

28. See Dibelius 'Style Criticism', p. 1.

earlier sources behind them, or the facts and personalities behind the sources.[29]

In the early 1970s literary critics, primarily American, began arguing that redaction criticism had not gone far enough in its appreciation of the compositional artistry of the New Testament writings.[30] Though several scholars within this new stream have dealt with various aspects of the language of Luke–Acts,[31] only one has, to my knowledge,

29. Henry J. Cadbury, *The Making of Luke–Acts* (3rd British edn; London: SPCK, 1968), p. 7. Cadbury has rightly been called the 'patron of the literary approach to Luke', Richard I. Pervo, 'On Perilous Things: A Response to Beverly Gaventa', in Mikeal Parsons and Joseph Tyson, *Cadbury, Knox and Talbert: American Contributions to the Study of Acts* (SBL Centennial Publications; Atlanta, GA: Scholars Press, 1992), pp. 30-41 (39). Pervo adds that Cadbury was a 'forerunner of redaction criticism', and one who 'prepared the ground for its natural heir: literary criticism' ('On Perilous Things', p. 41).

30. See Charles H. Talbert, *Literary Patterns, Theological Themes, and the Genre of Luke–Acts* (SBLMS, 20; Missoula: Scholars Press, 1974), p. 5; W.A. Beardslee, *Literary Criticism of the New Testament* (Philadelphia: Fortress Press, 1970); F. Scott Spencer, 'Acts and Modern Literary Approaches', in Bruce Winter and Andrew Clarke (eds.), *The Book of Acts in its Ancient Literary Setting* (A1CS, 1; Grand Rapids: Eerdmans; Carlisle: Paternoster Press, 1994), pp. 381-414 (385-86). Other works that have approached Luke–Acts from a literary standpoint are Paul Schubert, 'The Final Cycle of Speeches in the Book of Acts', *JBL* 87.1 (1968), pp. 1-16; J. Kilgallen, 'Acts: Literary and Theological Turning Points', *BTB* 7 (1977), pp. 177-80; Maddox, *The Purpose of Luke–Acts*; Robert C. Tannehill, *The Narrative Unity of Luke–Acts: A Literary Interpretation* (2 vols.; Minneapolis: Fortress Press, 1990); Mark A. Powell, 'Reading Acts as Literature', in his *What are they Saying about Acts?* (Mahwah, NJ: Paulist Press, 1991), pp. 96-107; Philip E. Satterthwaite, 'Acts against the Background of Classical Rhetoric', in Winter and Clarke (eds.), *The Book of Acts in its Ancient Literary Setting*, pp. 337-79; Stephen M. Sheeley, *Narrative Asides in Luke–Acts* (JSNTSup, 72; Sheffield: Sheffield Academic Press, 1992); see also the essays in the section entitled 'Issues of Literary Criticism' in Ben Witherington III (ed.), *History, Literature and Society in the Book of Acts* (Cambridge: Cambridge University Press, 1996), pp. 283-362; Stanley E. Porter, *The Paul of Acts: Essays in Literary Criticism, Rhetoric and Theology* (WUNT, 115; Tübingen: J.C.B. Mohr [Paul Siebeck], 1999), esp. Chapters 2, 6, 7.

31. Paul Schubert, 'The Place of the Areopagus Speech in the Composition of Acts', in J.C. Rylaarsdam (ed.), *Transitions in Biblical Scholarship* (Essays in Divinity, 6; Chicago: University of Chicago Press, 1968); A.W. Argyle, 'The Greek of Luke–Acts', *NTS* 20 (1974), pp. 441-45; John Kilgallen, *The Stephen Speech: A Literary and Redactional Study of Acts 7:2-53* (AnBib, 67; Rome: Biblical Institute

pursued consistently a study of its literary composition from a modern linguistic perspective.[32] It remains to be seen, therefore, whether linguistic analysis has any contribution to make to the study of Luke–Acts as literature, and to the investigation of its purpose in particular. It is hoped that the following exploration of foregrounding in Acts 27 will confirm that the answer is affirmative on both counts.

4. *Foregrounded Syntax in Acts 27:*
Its Nature and Meaning

The account of Paul's shipwreck off the coast of Malta has rightly been described as being 'among the most literary sections of Acts'.[33] A self-contained narrative at a crucial point of Luke's depiction of Paul in Roman custody, it commences with the decision to set sail for Rome (27.1), and ends with the colophon-like statement: καὶ οὕτως ἐγένετο πάντας διασωθῆναι ἐπὶ τὴν γῆν ('and thus it occurred that everyone was rescued on ground'; 27.44). A first reading of this story may yield the following further observations: the 'we' subject[34] continues from

Press, 1976); Nigel Turner, 'The Quality of the Greek of Luke–Acts', in J.K. Elliott (ed.), *Studies in New Testament Language and Text* (NovTSup, 44; Leiden: E.J. Brill, 1976); Dionisio Minguez, *Pentecostes: Ensayo de Semiotica Narrativa en Hechos 2* (Rome: Biblical Institute Press, 1976); Earl Richard, *Acts 6:1–8:4, The Author's Method of Composition* (SBLDS, 41; Missoula, MT: Scholars Press, 1978); Stephen H. Levinsohn, *Textual Connections in Acts* (SBLMS, 31; Atlanta, GA: Scholars Press, 1987); C.M. Tuckett (ed.), *Luke's Literary Achievement* (JSNTSup, 116; Sheffield: Sheffield Academic Press, 1995).

    32. Levinsohn, *Textual Connections in Acts*.

    33. Martin Dibelius, *Studies in the Acts of the Apostles* (London: SCM Press, 1956), p. 205; see also 'Style Criticism', p. 7, though see my caveat concerning literature and history in n. 27; Haenchen, *The Acts of the Apostles*, p. 710, though I disagree that 'it is precisely the Pauline speeches…which give this section its literary character', as I shall attempt to show.

    34. For a recent discussion of the 'we' sections see Stanley E. Porter, 'Excursus: The "We" Passages', in D. Gill and C. Gempf (eds.), *The Book of Acts in its Graeco-Roman Setting* (A1CS, 2; Grand Rapids: Eerdmans; Carlisle: Paternoster Press, 1994), pp. 545-74. See also A.J. Mattill Jr, 'The Value of Acts as a Source for the Study of Paul', in Charles H. Talbert (ed.), *Perspectives on Luke–Acts* (Danville, VA; Association of Baptist Professors of Religion, 1978), pp. 76-98, who shows how one's evaluation of Acts as a source for the study of Paul is directly related to one's assessment of the 'we' sections; Vernon K. Robbins, 'By Land and by Sea: The We-Passages and Ancient Sea-Voyages', in Talbert (ed.), *Perspectives*,

previous material, beginning at v. 1 and being discontinued after v. 37, where the referent is the totality of the crew and passengers; there are four brief speeches attributed to Paul, of which the second is by far the longest; Paul's speeches appear in the 'I style';[35] the writer has been particularly detailed in his description of both nautical equipment and its (ineffective) use to overcome the elements; besides 'we' and Paul, other subjects in the narrative are Julius the centurion, the soldiers and the sailors. These preliminary observations suggest several possible themes for this narrative: the survival of the crew and passengers through Paul's (or Julius's) intervention; the perils of first-century navigation during the winter months; the condition of prisoners in Roman custody, and so on. Unless, however, these intuitions can be grounded in more precise linguistic criteria, we are bound to be influenced primarily by historical or theological preconceptions of what the author 'could' or 'could not' be saying. This was the bane of much of German Luke–Acts scholarship in the nineteenth century.[36]

The analysis that follows is a search for motivated prominence in this narrative, that is, an investigation of the author's foregrounding strategy and of how it has shaped the raw elements of lexico-grammar at his disposal into what Hasan has termed 'a second order semiosis',[37] a 'larger' meaning that transcends that of the individual elements. Following the pioneering works of Porter and Fanning in the discourse-pragmatic use of verbal aspect in the New Testament,[38] I shall first turn to the use of the present and aorist tense forms in this passage. Secondly, and using Porter's method for clause-structure analysis,[39] I shall investigate the possible use of contrasting clause types as a means of grounding in Acts 27. Last of all I shall turn to the author's use of transitivity patterns and provide an interpretation of my findings.

pp. 215-42; Colin J. Hemer, 'First Person Narrative in Acts 27–28', *TynBul* 36 (1985), pp. 79-109.

35. On the 'I style', see Schubert, 'The Final Cycle', p. 4. Schubert's conclusion is that the 'I style' is characteristic of his 'cycle III' of speeches in Acts 22–28.22, and that this is motivated by the judicial nature of the situation.

36. See Gasque, *History*, p. 106.

37. Hasan, *Linguistics, Language*, p. 8.

38. Porter, *Verbal Aspect*, pp. 92-93, 98-107; Fanning, *Verbal Aspect*, pp. 72-77.

39. Porter, 'Word Order and Clause Structure in New Testament Greek', *FN* 6 (1993), pp. 177-206. See also Berry, *Introduction*, esp. pp. 62-90.

(a) *The Discourse Use of the Aorist and Present Tense Forms in Acts 27*
As I pointed out in Chapter 1, the use of tense-aspect morphology to
indicate foregrounding has been a subject of recent study in a variety of
languages and genres.[40] Fleischmann, for example, has noted that the
work that verbal forms perform in language use is by no means
exhausted by their 'basic grammatical functions', and suggests that
discourse-pragmatic considerations are essential for an adequate understanding of tense forms.[41] Stanley Porter's and Buist Fanning's volumes
on verbal aspect in the Greek of the New Testament both include a brief
discussion of the discourse function(s) of aspect, based largely on
Stephen Wallace's 1982 essay 'Figure and Ground'.[42] It seems appro-

40. See for example the study of the *pretérito imperfecto de subjuntivo* in jour-
nalistic Spanish by Patricia Lunn and Thomas Cravens, 'A Contextual Reconsideration of the Spanish -ra "Indicative" ', in Fleischmann and Waugh (eds.), *Discourse
Pragmatics*, pp. 147-78; Giulia Centineo, 'Tense Switching in Italian: The Alteration between *Passato Prossimo* and *Passato Remoto* in Oral Narratives', in
Fleischmann and Waugh (eds.), *Discourse Pragmatics*, pp. 55-85; Robert E. Longacre, *The Grammar of Discourse* (New York: Plennum, 1983), p. 27, for a discussion of the use of Hebrew tenses in the Genesis flood narrative.
41. Fleischmann and Waugh, 'Introduction', in Fleischmann and Waugh (eds.),
Discourse Pragmatics, p. 2.
42. Wallace, 'Figure and Ground', pp. 201-23. It must be said that Fanning's
wholesale adoption of Wallace's scheme is ill-informed given that Fanning's subject is New Testament Greek. Wallace's argument is that '...part of the meaning of
the perfective aspect, at least in narration, is to specify major, sequential, foregrounded events, while part of the meaning of the contrasting non-perfective
aspects, particularly an imperfective, is to give supportive, background information'
(Wallace, 'Figure and Ground', p. 209). But in the Mark passage we could also
argue that the aorist is used to set the scene for the two dialogues between the
demonized man and Jesus (5.7-10, 18-19) in both of which the present and
imperfects dominate. Another climactic point in this passage is 5.15, again built
upon the present tense: καὶ ἔρχονται πρὸς τὸν Ἰησοῦν καὶ θεωροῦσιν τὸν
δαιμονιζόμενον καθήμενον ἱματισμένον καὶ σωφρονοῦντα, τὸν ἐσχηκότα τὸν
λεγιῶνα, καὶ ἐφοβήθησαν. These events can hardly be said to be 'subsidiary'. In
contrast to Fanning, Porter argues that, in New Testament Greek, it is the aorist
(perfective aspect) that is the 'background tense'; see Porter, *Verbal Aspect*, p. 92;
idem, *Idioms of the Greek New Testament* (Sheffield: Sheffield Academic Press,
1992), p. 23. Among the examples offered by Porter in support of his view is Acts
16.1-5. Porter writes that in this passage, 'aorist tense-forms are used for the narrative events, present tense-forms are used for selected or highlighted events, and
the perfect tense-form is reserved for selective mention of a few significant
items...' (*Idioms*, p. 23). Even if we accept Porter's interpretation of vv. 1-5,

priate, then, to begin my search for relevant prominence in Acts 27 with a look at what has been designated 'the core of aspect',[43] the aorist-present opposition.

As is the case in the New Testament as a whole, aorist forms predominate over present forms in the shipwreck narrative (88 to 60, or 59.4% to 40.5% of present tense forms). This distribution, however, is reversed in the speeches attributed to Paul, where present tense forms predominate by a 69 per cent to a 31 per cent margin. Before suggesting a possible interpretation of this variation in terms of foregrounding, it is important to note the likely possibility that present tense forms naturally predominate in direct speech. If this possibility was to be confirmed as a result of studying the rest of the speeches in Acts, the mentioned variation in distribution would require no further explanation.[44] As for

consistency becomes very near impossible in the following verses. In the brief account of Paul's vision of the 'man of Macedonia', Porter's hypothesis would require us to understand 'a certain Macedonian man was standing [ἐστώς]' as 'significant', and, immediately following, 'and urging [παρακαλῶν] him and saying [λέγων]', as 'selected or highlighted' (16.9); further, the words of the Macedonian 'come to Macedonia and help [βοήθησον] us!' (16.9b) would be merely a 'narrative event', that is, a backgrounded event. A further difficulty with the application of Porter's theory to Acts 27 lies in the use of the imperfect tense forms in this story, a use which appears to be indistinguishable from that of the aorist forms. Haenchen called upon A. Debrunner to solve this problem, but the latter was unable to do so. See E. Haenchen, ' "We" in Acts and the Itinerary', *Journal for Theology and the Church* 1 (1965), pp. 65-99 (93). Porter's and Fanning's treatments of the discourse use of aspect in the Greek of the New Testament are both helpful and draw attention to a function of verb forms that is consistent in many languages (see above). However, the question may be raised: On what basis can we argue (besides the presence of a present or imperfect verb form!) that a clause is foregrounded or 'highlighted'? If we wish to argue that this is an intentional literary strategy by the author, how does this alleged choice(s) relate to his overall theme or aim? How does one instance of foregrounded morphology or syntax cohere with others throughout the text? Without a serious attempt at answering these questions, arguing for various degrees of grounding based on contrasting tense-aspects leads inevitably to a distressing circularity.

43. Daryl Schmidt, 'Verbal Aspect in Greek: Two Approaches', in Porter and Carson (eds.), *Biblical Greek Language and Linguistics*, p. 72.

44. A comprehensive analysis of aspectual contrasts in Acts cannot, however, be undertaken as part of the present book, and must remain a subject for future work. In regard to the significance of linguistic choice, Halliday writes: 'prominence...is not significant if the linguistically unpredicted configuration is predictable on other grounds' ('Linguistic Function and Literary Style', p. 118).

the use of the aorist and present tense forms elsewhere in the narrative, it seems clear that the lines between those which are 'narrative events', 'highlighted' and 'significant', to borrow terms used in Porter's works I have referred to (if indeed, such lines exist), cannot be drawn *on the basis of these tense forms alone.*[45]

(b) *Clause Structure in Acts 27*
As has been noted by Robert Longacre among others, contrasting clause structures are frequently used to mark grounding in a variety of languages.[46] Nevertheless, and in spite of the insights yielded by recent research into foregrounding as discussed above, the studies of clause structure from this angle have been relatively few. Among the possible reasons for this, I venture to suggest, is the strong interest in 'language universals' that Joseph Greenberg's work has created among linguists since 1963.[47] To the degree that one focuses on postulating linguistic 'laws' of universal application across languages, careful attention to linguistic usage in individual texts must probably recede to the background. In light of this unfortunate development in linguistic thought, students of New Testament Greek have grounds for a measured opti-

---

45. A few examples are sufficient to bear this out. In Acts 27.15-16 there are five aorist forms (bold) and three present forms (underlined): **συναρπασθέντος** δὲ τοῦ πλοίου καὶ μὴ <u>δυναμένου</u> <u>ἀντοφθαλμεῖν</u> τῷ ἀνέμῳ **ἐπιδόντες** ἐφερόμεθα. νησίον δέ τι **ὑποδραμόντες** <u>καλούμενον</u> Καῦδα **ἰσχύσαμεν** μόλις περικρατεῖς **γενέσθαι** τῆς σκάφης. My question is, simply, on what basis (apart from the tense-forms themselves) can we argue that 'being seized' is a narrative event, while 'not being able to face the wind' is highlighted? or that 'we were hardly able to control the dinghy' is a narrative event, but '[the ship] was not able to face the wind' is highlighted? See also, e.g., v. 35.

46. Longacre, *The Grammar*, p. 17, who cites examples in Anglo-Saxon, Biblical Hebrew and Trique; Hopper and Thompson, 'Transitivity in Grammar', pp. 280-86.

47. Joseph H. Greenberg, 'Some Universals of Grammar, with Particular Reference to the Order of Meaningful Elements', in *idem*, (ed.), *Universals of Language* (Cambridge, MA: MIT Press, 1963), pp. 49-57. Greenberg's 45 universals were based on samples of 30 languages with which the author had 'some previous acquaintance or for which a reasonably adequate grammar was available to [him]' (p. 59). Yet, attempts have been made to focus on language typology as a corrective to Greenberg's universals. See for example B. Comrie, *Language Universals and Linguistic Typology: Syntax and Morphology* (Chicago: University of Chicago Press, 1981).

mism. Stanley E. Porter's essay, 'Word Order and Clause Structure in New Testament Greek' (see n. 39 above),[48] must be considered a success on at least two counts. First, it has achieved its stated purpose, namely, to 'clear the ground' for further specialized projects on the subject. Secondly, it has made a significant contribution to the necessary correction of Greenberg's overemphasis on 'universals'.[49]

Three of Porter's conclusions seem particularly insightful. First, given the fact that Greek need not grammaticalize all of the clause constituents (including subject, object and verb), the structure of the Greek clause must be formulated on the basis of the elements that are explicit in each instance.[50] This fundamental fact has been largely ignored, with predictable results, in many of the older Greek grammars.[51] Secondly, the predicate is the fundamental or basic element of the Greek clause.[52]

---

48. See also Carlos Hernández-Lara, 'El Orden de las Palabras en Caritón de Afrodisias', *Myrtia* 2 (1987), pp. 83-89; M.E. Davison, 'New Testament Greek Word Order', *Literary and Linguistic Computing* 4(1) (1989), pp. 19-28, esp. pp. 24-28; Iver Larsen, 'Word Order and Relative Prominence in New Testament Greek', *Notes on Translation* 5/1 (1991), pp. 29-34. Davison's essay is of very limited usefulness, due to the very limited data incorporated into his study. Davison includes only main clauses with an indicative verb which have an explicit subject other than a pronoun. In the two pages that Larsen dedicates to clause structure, the writer limits himself to rather generic comments on the findings of other scholars.

49. See, e.g., Porter, 'Word Order', n. 22 in regard to universals 18 and 19. Greenberg affirmed that, given the six possible permutations of clause order, the three which never occur or at least are extremely rare are VOS, OVS and OSV. Further, Greenberg's universal 1 asserted that 'in declarative sentences with nominal subject and object, the dominant order is almost always one in which the subject precedes the object' (Greenberg, *Universals*, p. 61). This has been refuted with convincing evidence from several languages. See Andrés Romero-Figueroa, 'OSV as the Basic Word Order in Warao', *Linguistics* 23.1 (1985), pp. 105-21; Desmond C. Derbyshire and Geoffrey K. Pullum, 'Object Initial Languages', *International Journal of American Linguistics* 47.3 (1981), pp. 192-214. Both these essays explicitly address and refute Greenberg in regard to his first 'universal', Derbyshire and Pullum arguing that the geographical spread of SVO order is due first and foremost to the colonial expansion of speakers of European languages, rather than to the alleged 'naturalness' of such an order (p. 193).

50. Porter, 'Word Order', pp. 187, 190.

51. See, for example, BDF, p. 248.

52. Porter, 'Word Order', p. 192. However, Porter's data may need to be revised. On page 193, for example, speaking of participial clauses with a predicate structure, he cites Phil. 3.4, **καίπερ ἐγὼ ἔχων πεποίθησιν** καὶ ἐν σαρκί. εἴ τις

Thirdly, Porter notes that in Philippians, the subject is the most significant element that can be introduced in order to mark or highlight a clause.[53]

My study of clause structure in Acts 27 strongly confirms the first and second points above. In the shipwreck narrative, the predicate element (i.e. a verb form) is the only clause constituent that is present in every instance, in both independent and dependent clauses. When the object constituent is grammaticalized, it follows the predicate in a majority of instances.[54] My findings in regard to the subject constituent in Acts 27 (see Fig. 2.1, overleaf), however, are at variance with the (mostly) Philippians data as presented in Porter's essay (see below). This confirms Porter's expressed suspicion,[55] and is likely a result of the characteristics of the narrative genre. Among these characteristics is the high priority given to the distinction of participants, a factor that acquires particular relevance in Acts 27, as I will show below.

δοκεῖ ἄλλος πεποιθέναι ἐν σαρκί, ἐγὼ μᾶλλον, which is actually a subject–predicate–object structure; Phil. 3.18 is likewise cited as an example of participial clause with predicate structure: πολλοὶ γὰρ περιπατοῦσιν οὓς πολλάκις ἔλεγον ὑμῖν, νῦν δὲ καὶ **κλαίων λέγω**, τοὺς ἐχθροὺς τοῦ σταυροῦ τοῦ Χριστοῦ, where κλαίων is not a predicate but an adjunct qualifying the predicate (λέγω) adverbially. See Porter p. 193 n. 65.

53. Porter, 'Word Order', pp. 200-201.

54. Independent clauses: P–C (19x) as in 27.10, θεωρῶ ὅτι μετὰ ὕβρεως καὶ πολλῆς ζημίας...'; C–P (5×, though 39b is split construction) as in 27.18b, τῇ ἑξῆς ἐκβολὴν ἐποιοῦντο; dependent clauses: (i) Infinitival: P–C (6×) as in 27.21, κερδῆσαί τε τὴν ὕβριν ταύτην καὶ τὴν ζημίαν; C–P (3×) as in 27.3, ἐπιμελείας τυχεῖν; (ii) Participial: P–C (20×) as in 27.17, χαλάσαντες τὸ σκεῦος; C–P (8×) as in 27.33, τεσσαρεσκαιδεκάτην σήμερον ἡμέραν προσδοκῶντες; (iii) other (dependent clauses with finite verbs) P–C (1×), 27.25 λελάληταί μοι; C–P (2×) as in 27.42 ἵνα τοὺς δεσμώτας ἀποκτείνωσιν.

55. Porter, 'Word Order', p. 203. Unfortunately, Porter's essay gives no exact figures in regard to the subject constituent in his text, and states only that 'the subject constituent is apparently not used in the majority of clauses' (p. 194). If one is to argue that 'the subject is the most important element that an author can introduce to mark a given structure' (p. 200), a more precise summary of the data is required. Longacre also points to the likely possibility that word order and clause structure differ from genre to genre within a language (*The Grammar*, pp. 1, 17); see also Nida, *et al.* (eds.), *Style and Discourse*, p. 137.

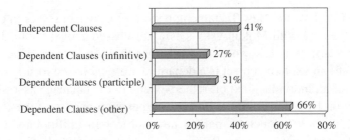

Figure 2.1. *Distribution of grammaticalized subjects*
within various clause types in Acts 27

Besides the greater number of grammaticalized subjects in the shipwreck narrative, my findings for Acts 27 differ from Porter's Philippians
data in other related respects. When the subject is explicit in Philippians, Porter notes that the strong tendency is for it to be placed first in
the cause,[56] and that its placement in second or third place (after predicate and/or object) seems to indicate a proportionate decrease in emphasis.[57] In the shipwreck story, however, explicit subjects at initial and
non-initial positions are nearly equal in number, in both dependent and
independent clauses (see Fig. 2.2):

	Subject Initial	Non-Subject Initial
Independent Clauses	13	12
Dependent Clauses (infinitive)	3	3
Dependent Clauses (participle)	10	10
Dependent Clauses (other)	6	2

Figure 2.2. *Placement of explicit subjects within the clause in Acts 27*

If these findings are shown to be consistent throughout Luke–Acts and
other narrative texts, Greenberg's universal 1 would be brought further
into question (see n. 49).

In summary, both the number of explicit subjects and their even
placement in initial and non-initial positions within the clause make any
interpretation of their possible 'highlighting' role difficult to prove in
the shipwreck narrative. Though Porter's essay has done much to encourage and lay the foundation for further research into clause structure

56. 'Word Order', p. 188.
57. 'Word Order', p. 201.

in the Greek of the New Testament, a word of criticism seems in order. As is the case with Mukarovsky's essay discussed above, the reader of Porter's article is left wondering whether the norms from which (for instance) an explicit subject is a departure are established locally by the writer of an individual text or, rather, extend to the language as a whole. In section III.2, for example, Porter comments on the use of the clause-initial explicit subject to mark a new subject in Philippians 2 or a 'heightened' statement by Paul in 3.13. Yet, the overall aim that is apparently being pursued by Porter is to discover 'marked' structures in the language of the New Testament as a whole.[58] It seems to me that the fundamental problem at this point is one of vague usage of a difficult term. The word 'marked' is apparently being used by Porter as synonymous with highlighted, emphasized, and other related terms, all akin to 'foregrounded'. But to make such 'markedness'[59] claims for the language of the New Testament as a whole without an exhaustive analysis of the features that one claims as 'marked', seems at best extremely difficult to prove. Further, if an exegete wishes to argue that a particular linguistic item (e.g. an explicit, fronted subject) is being used in Philippians to highlight a key protagonist, such an argument must be

58. See 'Word Order', pp. 190, 203.

59. Though markedness theory is beyond the scope of the present work, a word of clarification is in order. Markedness theory was pioneered by N. Trubetzkoy and R. Jakobson in the 1920s. The central notion behind this method of phonological and grammatical analysis is based on the observation that phonemes, cases, or verbal aspects have what are known as distinctive features (in the case of phonemes) or conceptual features (in the case of cases or verbal aspects, for example), that define their minimal semantic content. This semantic content is gleaned from all the uses of the item in question, which is then said to be 'marked' or 'unmarked' in relation to the particular feature that defines it. See Roman Jakobson, 'Shifters, Verbal Categories and the Russian Verb', in S. Rudy, *Roman Jakobson: Selected Writings*, II (10 vols.; The Hague: Mouton, 1971), pp. 130-47; Edwin Battistella, *Markedness: The Evaluative Superstructure of Language* (Albany: State University of New York Press, 1990), p. 33; Edna Andrews, *Markedness Theory: The Union of Asymmetry and Semiosis in Language* (Durham: Duke University Press, 1990), p. 137. A significant departure from previous work in markedness theory was brought about by Greenberg and Comrie, who defined 'marked' not in terms of a feature, but on the basis of such 'criteria' or 'characteristics' (Greenberg uses these words interchangeably) as being less frequent, or having greater morphological bulk. Joseph H. Greenberg, *Language Universals* (The Hague: Mouton, 1966), esp. pp. 26-29; Bernard Comrie, *Aspect* (Cambridge: Cambridge University Press, 1976), pp. 111-22. Porter follows the latter model of markedness theory.

supported by a discussion of the author's 'highlighting strategy' else-where *in that text*, and of how that strategy relates to his aim(s) in writing. This is, as I pointed out above, Halliday's central thesis in his analysis of Golding's *The Inheritors*.

(c) *Foregrounded Transitivity Patterns in the Shipwreck Narrative of Acts 27*

Hopper and Thompson's essay 'Transitivity in Grammar and Discourse', did much to highlight the crucial role that transitivity systems play in many of the world's languages. Seeking to refine the classic notion of transitivity in western linguistics, the authors present a scale of transitivity features such as 'participants', 'volitionality', and agency', as a means of gauging clauses in terms of their high or low transitivity. Secondly, Hopper and Thompson argue convincingly that it is at the discourse level, rather than at the sentence or clause level, that the main function of transitivity is found. Their data point to high transitivity clauses being used consistently to foreground material in texts, while low transitivity clauses carry out the backgrounding function.[60]

For Halliday, however, the term transitivity has two distinct interpretations. According to the first and more generic interpretation, the system of transitivity includes the various types of processes that exist in a language, together with the structures that realize these processes. A process consists of three basic elements: the process itself, participants and circumstances. The second and narrower interpretation of transitivity is roughly equivalent to the classic notion as presented by Hopper and Thompson, though in Halliday's scheme it is limited to his 'material processes'.[61] In this process type, the elements of actor (subject) and process (predicate) are obligatory, and that of goal (object) is optional. When the element of goal is present (i.e. A is doing something to G) the transitive interpretation applies.

Of particular relevance for my present purpose, however, is Halliday's notion of *ergativity*, a somewhat more abstract explanation of the transitive/intransitive concept. In the classic notion of transitivity, the

---

60. Hopper and Thompson, 'Transitivity in Grammar', p. 284.

61. Halliday, *Introduction to Functional Grammar*, pp. 101-105. Halliday affirms that the traditional understanding of transitivity is an accurate interpretation, so long as it is understood: (1) that the concept applies to clauses rather than to individual verb forms, and (2) that it is only applicable to certain clauses, namely, material process clauses.

question being asked of a clause is 'does the process in question extend beyond the actor to a goal?' Here the variable is *extension*. In Halliday's ergativity model, however, the question being asked is, 'is the process in question being brought about from within or from outside?' The variable in this case is *causation*. In the ergative analysis, the nucleus of the clause is made up of process and medium:

Non-Ergative Clause:

Ergativity-Based Interpretation	Transitivity-Based Interpretation
τὸ πλοῖον ἀνήχθη The ship (medium) sailed (process)	τὸ πλοῖον ἀνήχθη The ship (actor) sailed (process)

In the ergativity-based interpretation the medium is the key element, that is, the entity through the medium of which the process occurs. In addition to the medium, there is in this case another participant functioning as a cause external to the medium, which Halliday calls the agent, as in

Ergative Clause:

Ergativity-Based Interpretation	Transitivity-Based Interpretation
ἀνήχθημεν τὸ πλοῖον we (**agent**) sailed (process) the ship (medium)	ἀνήχθημεν τὸ πλοῖον The ship (actor) sailed (process) we (actor) sailed (process) the ship (goal)

Within the ergativity-based interpretation, the process may, then, be represented either as self-engendering, in which case there is no external agent (non-ergative clause), or as brought about from the outside, in which case the presence of an agent is obligatory (ergative clause). It is important to note that, in reality, there may well have been an external agent in such processes as *the plant withered* (e.g. the sun's rays), or *the window broke* (e.g. a football); nevertheless, non-ergative clauses represent these processes as self-engendered, or, more accurately, make no reference to causation.[62] With this framework in place, we now return to the shipwreck narrative.

62. In Jakobsonian markedness theory, we would say that non-ergative clauses are unmarked as to the feature [causation], or [Ø causation], while ergative clauses are marked as to the same feature, or [+ causation]. For further discussion of erga-

In the analysis of narrative, the number of, means of introduction of, and roles assigned to participants acquire an importance unparalleled in the study of other genres. In Acts 27, human participants may be divided into two groups: (1) primary: the 'we' participant and Paul; and (2) secondary: Julius, and the soldiers and ship's crew, often referred to simply by means of third person plural verb suffixes.

One of the most striking features of this story is the peculiar use made of the 'we' participant. Beginning at the start of the narrative, it appears regularly through to Acts 27.8, reappearing at vv. 15 through 29, and surfacing one last time at v. 37. Its referent in the beginning clauses could be the captive group of Paul's companions (esp. vv. 2 and 6). However, from v. 7 on, 'we' seems to include the totality of the ship's passengers and crew, for it is the whole ship which 'the wind does not allow to move forward' (v. 7), 'pass[es] Crete with difficulty' (v. 8), '[is] being carried along' (v. 15), '[is] violently storm-tossed' (v. 18), etc. A close reading of all the 'we' clauses reveals that the fundamental feature they have in common is not primarily their referent,[63] but rather, the sense of powerlessness created by their non-ergative structures. That is, the processes depicted in these clauses are represented without reference to an external agent, and therefore the 'we' participant is consistently perceived as a passive medium, who is literally carried along by the course of events, rather than affecting them in any way. The cumulative effect of these clauses may be accurately summarized by 27.15b: ἐπιδόντες ἐφερόμεθα, having given way, we were being carried. This cumulative effect is best appreciated as a result of a continuous reading of these clauses:

Ὡς δὲ ἐκρίθη τοῦ ἀποπλεῖν ἡμᾶς (27.1)...ἀνήχθημεν (2)...κατήχθημεν (3)...ἀναχθέντες ὑπεπλεύσαμεν τὴν Κύπρον (4)...διαπλεύσαντες κατήλθομεν εἰς Μύρα (5)...βραδυπλοοῦντες καὶ μόλις γενόμενοι κατὰ τὴν Κνίδον...ὑπεπλεύσαμεν τὴν Κρήτην (7)...μόλις τε παραλεγόμενοι αὐτὴν ἤλθομεν εἰς τόπον τινὰ (8)...ἐπιδόντες ἐφερόμεθα. (15)...νησίον δέ τι ὑποδραμόντες...ἰσχύσαμεν μόλις περικρατεῖς γενέσθαι τῆς σκάφης (16)...σφοδρῶς δὲ χειμαζομένων ἡμῶν (18)...τοῦ σῴζεσθαι ἡμᾶς (20)...διαφερομένων ἡμῶν...(27)...φοβούμενοί τε μή που κατὰ τραχεῖς τόπους ἐκπέσωμεν (29)...ἤμεθα δὲ αἱ πᾶσαι ψυχαὶ (37).

tivity, see also John W. Du Bois, 'The Discourse Basis of Ergativity', *Language* 63 (1987), pp. 805-55.

63. Haenchen expressed uncertainty as to the referent of 'we:' 'is it Paul's group or all the passengers?' ' "We" in Acts', p. 93.

> When it was decided that we set sail...we sailed...we sailed down to...
> we sailed under the shelter of Cyprus...having sailed through (Cilicia
> and Pamphilia) we came to Myra...navigating slowly and passing with
> difficulty in front of Knidos...we sailed under the shelter of Crete...
> passing by it with difficulty, we came to a certain place...having given
> way, we were being carried...running under the shelter of a certain
> island...we were hardly able to exercise control...being violently storm-
> tossed...(all hope was abandoned) that we be saved...being carried
> through...fearing lest we may run aground in a rocky coast...we were in
> all 276 souls.

It is important to note that the consistent non-ergativity of the 'we'
clauses is not due to the prisoner status of their referent. I have already
shown that the referent of 'we' in the story is for the most part the
totality of the ship's passengers and crew (as in v. 37); secondly, v. 16
has 'we' being 'unable to maintain control of the dinghy', an unnecessary statement, if prisoners on a ship were always inactive; thirdly, one
should note the variant reading for v. 19 attested in the Byzantine text,
which has the 'we' participant doing the jettisoning. In connection with
this textual variant, William Ramsay pointed out that such an action by
prisoners on a ship was by no means unthinkable.[64]

In stark contrast, soldiers and crew (often simply 'they'), appear from
beginning to end involved in unflagging and assiduous activity, that is,
as agents, beginning immediately after Paul advises them not to sail
from 'Beautiful Havens' (27.10). Paul's warning notwithstanding, 'the
majority' made the decision to set sail from there (v. 12), and appear
from that point on enmeshed in a struggle that spirals downward from
sailing in rough weather (vv. 13-17), to seeking to save the ship at the
expense of the ship's gear (v. 18), to attempting to escape (v. 30), to
seeking to save the ship at the expense of the grain cargo (v. 38), to
finally trying to run the ship aground onto a beach (v. 39). It is interesting to note, first, that the actions of 'they' are the result of their 'sup-
posing to have achieved *their* purpose' (v. 13); secondly, that although
the vast majority of these clauses are ergative, with 'they' playing the
role of a highly dynamic agent, all their actions lead eventually to
failure:

---

64. William Ramsay, *Saint Paul the Traveller and the Roman Citizen* (London:
Hodder & Stoghton, 1896), p. 332; see also Brian Rapske, 'Acts, Travel and Ship-
wreck', in David Gill and Conrad Gempf (eds.), *The Book of Acts in its Graeco-
Roman Setting*, pp. 32-33.

ἄραντες (13) ...ἦν ἄραντες βοηθείαις ἐχρῶντο ὑποζωννύντες τὸ
πλοῖον...χαλάσαντες τὸ σκεῦος (17) ...τῇ ἑξῆς ἐκβολὴν ἐποιοῦντο
(18) ...αὐτόχειρες τὴν σκευὴν τοῦ πλοίου ἔρριψαν (19) ...βολίσαντες
(26, 28) ...ἐκ πρύμνης ῥίψαντες ἀγκύρας τέσσαρας (29) ...χαλα-
σάντων τὴν σκάφην (30) ...ἀπέκοψαν οἱ στρατιῶται τὰ σχοινία τῆς
σκάφης καὶ εἴασαν αὐτὴν ἐκπεσεῖν (32) ...καὶ αὐτοὶ προσελάβοντο
τροφῆς (36) ...ἐκούζον τὸ πλοῖον ἐκβαλλόμενοι τὸν σῖτον εἰς τὴν
θάλασσαν. (38) ...καὶ τὰς ἀγκύρας περιελόντες εἴων εἰς τὴν θάλασσαν, ἅμα ἀνέντες τὰς ζευκτηρίας τῶν πηδαλίων, καὶ ἐπάραντες τὸν
ἀρτέμωνα τῇ πνεούσῃ κατεῖχον εἰς τὸν αἰγιαλόν.(40) ...ἐπέκειλαν
τὴν ναῦν (41).

Having lifted [the anchor] (13)...which having lifted with ropes they
were using to undergird the ship...having lowered the gear (17) the following day they began to do a jettisoning (18) they cast out the ship's
gear with their own hands (19) having taken soundings (28) ...having
cast four anchors from the stern (29) having lowered the dinghy (30) the
soldiers cut the dinghy's ropes and allowed it to run aground they themselves also took food (36) they began to lighten the ship casting out the
grain into the sea (38) and having cast off the anchors they allowed
[them to fall] into the sea, at the same time loosening the rudder's straps,
and having hoisted the foresail to the blowing wind, they headed for the
shore (40) they ran the ship ashore (41).

It is interesting to note that vv. 15b and 17 contain respectively a clause
typical of each participant: ἐπιδόντες... 'having given way', v. 15b)
predicated of 'we', and χαλάσαντες τὸ σκεῦος... ('having lowered the
gear', v. 17b) with 'they' as agent. Yet, the same is concluded about
each: we/they *were being carried*.

The role of Julius in the shipwreck narrative is a somewhat ambiguous one. From the outset, he is inclined to act kindly toward Paul,
allowing him the privilege of obtaining assistance from friends while at
Sidon (27.3). At a crucial juncture, however, Julius is swayed by the
resoluteness of the ship's captain and navigator to set sail, ignoring
Paul's warning about the approaching winter season (v. 11). From that
point on, the focus of the story is placed squarely on the ship's crew,
and Julius disappears from the scene for 22 verses, appearing again
only at the very end (v. 43) when he prevents the killing of the prisoners, and commands all who are able to swim to safety (vv. 43-44).
While several of the nine clauses in which Julius appears as participant
are largely ergative in their structures, the 'affectedness' of the mediums (that is, the degree to which the recipients of Julius's actions are

affected by them), is rather low in most instances.[65] As Hopper and Thompson point out, low affectedness of the mediums diminishes proportionately the overall transitivity coefficient of the clause. This is the case with the clauses in which Julius appears as participant:

> φιλανθρώπως τε ὁ Ἰούλιος τῷ Παύλῳ χρησάμενος (27.3a) ...ἐπέτρεψεν πρὸς τοὺς φίλους πορευθέντι ἐπιμελείας τυχεῖν (27.3b) ...κἀκεῖ εὑρὼν ὁ ἑκατοντάρχης πλοῖον Ἀλεξανδρῖνον (6a) ...ἐνεβίβασεν ἡμᾶς εἰς αὐτό (6b) ...ὁ δὲ ἑκατοντάρχης τῷ κυβερνήτῃ καὶ τῷ ναυκλήρῳ μᾶλλον ἐπείθετο (11) ...ὁ δὲ ἑκατοντάρχης βουλόμενος διασῶσαι τὸν Παῦλον (43a) ...ἐκώλυσεν αὐτοὺς τοῦ βουλήματος (43b) ...ἐκέλευσέν τε τοὺς δυναμένους κολυμβᾶν... (43c).

> Julius having dealt kindly with Paul (27.3a) he allowed him to obtain assistance after going to his friends (27.3b) and after the centurion found there an Alexandrian ship (6a) he placed us on board (6b) but the centurion was more persuaded by (what was said by) the navigator and the captain (11) but the centurion, wanting to save Paul (43a) he thwarted their purpose (43b) and he commanded that those who could swim... (43c).

Before addressing the nature and significance of Paul's role in the story, brief reference must be made to a set of participants that is notable in terms of the amount of space they occupy in the narrative. I am referring to the 24 inanimate participants that range from the ship and the port of Beautiful Havens, to various natural elements such as the wind (3 times) and the waves.[66] Except for one (μὴ προσεῶντος ἡμᾶς

---

65. This is one of Hopper and Thompson's parameters that are applicable to Halliday's model. Thus, the affectedness of Paul in 27b above ([Julius] allowed [him] to obtain help) is much lower than the affectedness of the 'we' participant in 6b ([Julius] placed us on board). It seems clear to me that other parameters suggested in Hopper and Thompson's essay (e.g. kinesis) may be used with profit to refine Halliday's ergative/non-ergative distinction. A comparison of the ergativity of the clauses in the previous paragraph ('they' clauses) with that of the clauses in which Julius participates points to the need for such a refinement. See also Hasan, *Linguistics, Language,* pp. 45-46; Halliday, 'Linguistic Function and Literary Style', pp. 127-28, where Halliday discusses a notion akin to affectedness.

66. πλοίῳ (v. 2); τοὺς ἀνέμους (4); πλοῖον (6); τοῦ ἀνέμου (7); Ἱκανοῦ δὲ χρόνου (9); τοῦ πλοός (9); τὴν νηστείαν (9); τὸν πλοῦν (10); τοῦ λιμένος (12); νότου (13); ἄνεμος τυφωνικὸς (14); τοῦ πλοίου (15); μήτε δὲ ἡλίου μήτε ἄστρων (20); χειμῶνός τε οὐκ ὀλίγου (20); ἐλπὶς πᾶσα (20); Πολλῆς τε ἀσιτίας (21); ἀποβολὴ γὰρ ψυχῆς (22); τεσσαρεσκαιδεκάτη νὺξ (27); ἡμέρα (33); ἡμέρα (39); ἡ μὲν πρῷρα (41); ἡ δὲ πρύμνα (41); βουλὴ (42).

τοῦ ἀνέμου, v. 7), all these clauses are clearly non-ergative and encode for the most part processes of being.[67]

Lastly, the role of Paul must be considered. Though from Acts 13 onwards Paul is clearly *the* protagonist of Acts, his role clearly reaches its climactic point in the final section of the book (Acts 21–28), where his arrest and imprisonment are related in detail. In what amounts to nearly one fourth of Acts (23.5%),[68] the writer recounts Paul's seizure and appearance before a Roman tribune and the Jewish council (21.22–23.11), his escape from a Jewish conspiracy to kill him (23.12-35), the trial before Felix (24.1-26), his appearance before Festus and appeal to Caesar (25.1-12), and his defense before Herod Agrippa (25.13–26.32). The shipwreck story represents the last great episode before Paul's arrival in Rome, where he will appear before the emperor and fulfill the Lord's last commission to him: ὁ κύριος εἶπεν, Θάρσει, ὡς γὰρ διεμαρτύρω τὰ περὶ ἐμοῦ εἰς Ἰερουσαλήμ οὕτω σε δεῖ καὶ εἰς Ῥώμην μαρτυρῆσαι (23.11) ('Courage! For just as you testified about me in Jerusalem, it is necessary that you testify in Rome').

Paul's participation in the shipwreck narrative is essentially limited to four separate addresses, all of which offer direction to the ship's crew and passengers for the safe completion of the journey.[69] The nature and significance of Paul's role, however, becomes clear when we look at the clauses wherein he himself is a participant, that is, a subject in the traditional sense, or an agent or medium in Halliday's ergative/non-ergative model. In these 12 clauses Paul's activity centers on communicating to the ship's crew the necessary conditions for a safe journey, and encouraging all aboard the ship with the thought of God's protection.[70] Of particular significance is Paul's second and longest address in

---

67. That is, clauses the central meaning of which is 'that something is'. See Halliday, *Introduction to Functional Grammar*, pp. 112-15.

68. Maddox, *The Purpose of Luke–Acts*, p. 66. Maddox notes that the section dedicated to 'Paul the prisoner' is slightly longer than that dedicated to 'Paul the missionary'.

69. Vv. 10; 21-26; 31; 33-34.

70. παρῄνει ὁ Παῦλος λέγων αὐτοῖς (v. 9b-10a); θεωρῶ ὅτι μετὰ ὕβρεως καὶ πολλῆς ζημίας... (10); σταθεὶς ὁ Παῦλος ἐν μέσῳ αὐτῶν εἶπεν (21); παραινῶ ὑμᾶς εὐθυμεῖν (22); πιστεύω γὰρ τῷ θεῷ (25); εἶπεν ὁ Παῦλος τῷ ἑκατοντάρχῃ (31); παρεκάλει ὁ Παῦλος ἅπαντας (33) παρακαλῶ ὑμᾶς μεταλαβεῖν τροφῆς (34); εἴπας δὲ ταῦτα (35a); καὶ λαβὼν ἄρτον (35b); εὐχαρίστησεν τῷ θεῷ (35c); κλάσας ἤρξατο ἐσθίειν (35d).

vv. 21-26, which comes immediately after 'all hope of salvation was abandoned':

Ἔδει μέν, ὦ ἄνδρες, πειθαρχήσαντάς μοι μὴ ἀνάγεσθαι ἀπὸ τῆς Κρήτης κερδῆσαί τε τὴν ὕβριν ταύτην καὶ τὴν ζημίαν. (22) καὶ τὰ νῦν παραινῶ ὑμᾶς εὐθυμεῖν, ἀποβολὴ γὰρ ψυχῆς οὐδεμία ἔσται ἐξ ὑμῶν πλὴν τοῦ πλοίου. (23) παρέστη γάρ μοι ταύτῃ τῇ νυκτὶ τοῦ θεοῦ οὗ εἰμι [ἐγώ], ᾧ καὶ λατρεύω, ἄγγελος (24) λέγων, Μὴ φοβοῦ, Παῦλε· Καίσαρί σε δεῖ παραστῆναι, καὶ ἰδοὺ κεχάρισταί σοι ὁ θεὸς πάντας τοὺς πλέοντας μετὰ σοῦ. (25) διὸ εὐθυμεῖτε, ἄνδρες· πιστεύω γὰρ τῷ θεῷ ὅτι οὕτως ἔσται καθ᾽ ὃν τρόπον λελάληταί μοι. (26) εἰς νῆσον δέ τινα δεῖ ἡμᾶς ἐκπεσεῖν.

Men! in order to have avoided the present damage and loss it would have been necessary (ἔδει) to listen to me and not have sailed from Crete. Now I urge you to take courage, for there shall be no loss of life, though the ship itself will be lost. For this night appeared to me an angel of the God to whom I belong and whom I worship, who said to me: 'Do not be afraid Paul! It is necessary (δεῖ) that you appear before Caesar, and God has graciously given you all those who sail with you'. Therefore, cheer up men! for I believe God, and that it shall be just as he said to me. It is necessary (δεῖ) that we run aground on some island.

Three points made in this speech are essential for an adequate understanding of the shipwreck story. First, the angelic oracle affirms that 'it is necessary' for Paul to stand before Caesar (cf. Acts 23.11), one of three instances of the impersonal verb δεῖν in these five verses alone. While in the first instance, ἔδει refers to a past event in which the right course was not followed and serious trouble ensued, in the last two, the reference is to events as yet unfulfilled. The fondness of the author of Luke–Acts for this verb has been a subject of specialized study in recent years, and has often been explained in light of what appears to be one of his favorite themes in the work, namely, the unstoppable unfolding of God's sovereign plan.[71] Secondly, because of Paul's presence on

71. Luke–Acts has 65.5% of the instances of δεῖ in the New Testament. On the theme of 'necessity' in Luke–Acts, John Squires writes, 'Inherent in the life and passion of Jesus and in the missionary deeds of the apostles, there is a necessity which had been foreordained by Jesus. Juxtaposed along this theme of necessity is the role of human agents in carrying out the plan of God; some may oppose this plan, but those who are obedient to the will of God play key roles in God's plan.' John T. Squires, *The Plan of God in Luke-Acts* (SNTSMS, 76; Cambridge: Cambridge University Press, 1993), p. 3; see also pp 4-6; Cadbury, *The Making*, p. 303; Haenchen, *The Acts of the Apostles*, p. 159 n. 8; C.H. Cosgrove 'The Divine ΔΕΙ in

the vessel, the lives of all his fellow travelers will be spared. Lastly, Paul's response to the oracle is simply to believe God, and to encourage all to do likewise, perhaps understanding that no other avenue is in fact open to them.

In light of the above, it seems fair to say that the literary function of Paul's role in the shipwreck narrative is not that of an agent in the ergative sense of the word as used above (his only action in Acts 27 is that of breaking bread!),[72] but rather, that of an interpreter, a Hermes-like figure (cf. Acts 14.12) who understands (θεωρῶ, v. 10) and elucidates events from a divine perspective. In light of God's plan as revealed in vv. 21-26, certain things are 'necessary', and the only proper human response is to believe and await their unfolding. Human attempts to resist God's plan are, therefore, irrevocably bound to fail.

It is my contention that this theme is embodied in the author's foregrounding scheme in the shipwreck narrative. In their seminal essay referred to above, Hopper and Thompson noted that narrative story lines are usually carried by people who intentionally initiate events.[73] In Halliday's terms, it is agents who are represented as bringing about events in ergative clauses, while their absence in non-ergative clauses leaves the question of causation unanswered. In the shipwreck story, against the background of the non-agentive participants ('we', Paul, and the 24 inanimate participants), the author foregrounds the highly dynamic 'they' agent who appears to be actively involved in the shaping of events. The resolve of the ship's crew and captain to sail is strong enough to sway Julius, who from that point until the end of the narrative fades into the background. As the story progresses, however, the utter futility of the sailors' efforts is revealed, as the ship begins to drift, helplessly carried by wind and waves. One might say that the powerful effect of this narrative upon the reader is partly due to the subverting of the natural expectation that is created by the feverish activity of the crew, as those who appeared throughout to be moving events forward are in the end shown to be moved by events, much like the rest of the ship's passengers. The reader is thus powerfully drawn to consider the final, if partially hidden cause of these events. The conclusion of the narrative sees the safe rescue of all the ship's passengers and crew at the expense of the ship and its cargo, in strict fulfillment of the

Luke–Acts', *NovT* 26 (1984), pp. 168-90.
    72. But see his more active role after landing in Malta.
    73. Hopper and Thompson, 'Transitivity', p. 286.

divine message conveyed to Paul. Thus the writer utilizes the syntax of Greek to work out the theme of the supremacy of divine will and necessity as revealed in vv. 21-25.

Although the shipwreck narrative is, admittedly, a very small fragment of the vast work that is Luke–Acts, I believe it is large and stylistically varied enough to begin to show the relevance of foregrounding for the full appreciation *and* appraisal of a literary work. Without grounding our claims regarding such issues as the 'theme' of Luke–Acts on a careful study of the language system and the author's choices in that system, one scholar's guess may be as good as that of the next.[74] The linguistic analysis of foregrounding may or may not add new theories to the long and prolific discussion of the purpose of Acts. Its primary value resides, rather, in its role as a relatively objective test of the plausibility of such theories. If we accept that the meaning of such clauses as δόξαντες τῆς προθέσεως κεκρατηκέναι (27.13) ('thinking they had achieved their purpose'), or διαφερομένων ἡμῶν ἐν τῷ Ἀδρίᾳ (27.27) ('while we were being driven in the Adriatic'), is determined by their function in the larger context of Acts 27, and that the story as a whole has been shaped artfully and intentionally by the writer to produce a specific effect in his readers, then any theory of the purpose of this work must be tied, in one way or another, to a type of linguistic analysis similar to the one I have proposed above. Thus, if my conclusions in regard to foregrounding in the shipwreck narrative are accepted and are found confirmed in my analysis of other Act episodes below, Squires's proposal in regard to the purpose of Luke–Acts[75] would find fresh support from a new angle, while Haenchen's would certainly become more difficult to accept.[76]

6. *Conclusion*

I began this chapter with a reference to Helen Dry's recent evaluation of the state of the art in foregrounding theory as of 1992. Though a helpful summary in more than one way, Dry's article tended to emphasize some of the perceived problems in this complex and multi-faceted

---

74. See on this Hasan, 'Linguistics', p. 107.

75. Namely, the edification of Christian believers through an exposition of God's providence in the face of human opposition. Squires, *The Plan*, pp. 191-92.

76. Haenchen's proposal was essentially a rehashing of the 'apology before the Roman power' thesis. Haenchen, *The Acts of the Apostles*, pp. 90-110.

area of linguistic research. The author's conclusion, not surprisingly, was an attempt at a minimal definition of foregrounding that would be flexible and generic enough to encompass insights from the various disciplines that have contributed to its study:

> In the absence of an agreed upon definition of the central concept, we may identify as foreground whatever textual feature strike as as prominent.[77]

It is hoped that this chapter has shown the inadequacy of such a definition. Beginning with a full discussion of the multi-faceted theoretical background of foregrounding, I have argued that Michael Halliday's functional grammar is a method capable of integrating the most fruitful insights from literary criticism, psycholinguistics and discourse analysis into one coherent theory of foregrounding, as presented in Halliday's analysis of *The Inheritors*. My study of the shipwreck narrative is intended as a demonstration of Halliday's central claim in that seminal work, namely, that foregrounding is linguistic prominence that can be shown to be consistent and motivated in light of the overall theme(s) of the work in question. Given the specific nature of the narrative genre, transitivity choices are shown to play an essential role in foregrounding, a role played in non-narrative texts by other elements of the language system, such as contrasting tense-aspect morphology. In the chapters that follow, my analysis of transitivity-based foregrounding will be extended to other key episodes of Acts.

EXCURSUS

THE RELEVANCE OF FOREGROUNDING FOR FUNCTIONALLY
EQUIVALENT TRANSLATION: ACTS 27 AS A CASE STUDY

1. *Foregrounding: 'A Hard Nut for the Translator'*[78]

In his stimulating and ground-breaking essay on the translation of foregrounding, Vladimir Procházka suggests three essential qualifications of a 'good translator': (1) 'Understand the original work thematically

77. Dry, 'Foregrounding', p. 447.

78. This is Vladimir Procházka's translation of the Czech title of Rene Wellek's article 'Prekladatelsky Orisek', published in 1935; cited in Procházka, 'Notes on Translating Technique', in Garvin, *A Prague School Reader*, pp. 93-112.

and stylistically'; (2) 'Overcome by his own means of expression the differences between the two linguistic structures', and (3) 'Reconstruct the stylistic structure of the original work in translation'. The last qualification is considered by the writer 'the center of gravity of the translator's work'.[79] Consequently, argues Procházka, it is unhelpful to define translations in terms such as 'free', 'literal', or 'halting', for these designations fail to address the fundamental problem, namely, whether or not words, clauses and larger units in the source text are translated adequately in the light of the total stylistic structure of the work. The final aim of a translation, continues Procházka, is not the literal rendering of words, clauses and sentences (that is, the formal elements of language) from source into receptor language, but rather, the search for linguistic elements in the receptor that are functionally analogous to those of the source.[80] This principle is illustrated by means of the example of Procházka's translation of a German novel into Czech:

> First of all, I had to face the basic problem: whether, and to what extent, it is necessary to preserve Scholz's complicated compound sentences and in general the baroque qualities of his style. After long reflection, I came to the conclusion that this complexity, baroqueness, almost lack of clarity, belongs to the basic structure and therefore must be preserved. It could, of course, not be done mechanically; Scholz's sentences and entire passages had to be, as it were, melted down in my mind, and then recreated in Czech. I have the impression that my reconstruction has been relatively successful, and that *the Czech reader gathers a similar impression from the translation to that of the German reader from the original.*[81]

Procházka's notion of functional analogy makes his 1942 essay a significant precursor of the work of Eugene Nida, the dean of modern Bible translators. Though Nida recently admitted to me that he was not aware of Procházka's essay, he openly confessed his indebtedness to Prague functionalism as a whole.[82] Nida's approach to translation may

79. Procházka, 'Notes on Translating', p. 97.
80. Procházka, 'Notes on Translating', pp. 97, 99, 104.
81. Procházka, 'Notes on Translating', p. 104. Emphasis mine.
82. Telephone conversation held on 17 April 1996. I wish to express my thanks to Dr Nida for his phone call, fax, and letter shortly thereafter in response to my questions to him. That two linguists with similar interests arrive at strikingly similar notions independently of each other is not as surprising as some may think. A classic example of this is the nearly simultaneous and wholly independent founding of semiotics by Charles S. Peirce (who used the term 'semeiotics') and Ferdinand de

be summarized by reference to three fundamental points made in his recent work on translation, *From One Language to Another*. First, Nida's is a socio-semiotic approach. In essence, this means that linguistic signs such as verb forms or relative clauses are understood within a larger framework of signs, linguistic (e.g. other verb forms and clauses), para-linguistic (e.g. punctuation), and extra-linguistic (e.g. the symbolic meaning of eating a meal in the ancient Mediterranean world).[83] Secondly, his is a functional approach. Nida posits eight distinct universal functions in language: expressive, cognitive, interpersonal, informative, imperative, performative, emotive, and aesthetic, arguing that their universality across languages is what makes the translator's task possible.[84] Lastly, the work of translation involves for Nida not primarily a transfer of forms from one language to another, but rather a process of searching for functional equivalents between languages at the lexical, grammatical, and rhetorical levels.[85]

Though De Waard and Nida make only a brief specific reference to foregrounding in their book,[86] the authors pay due attention to what they call 'rhetorical functions', that is, the varying degrees of selection and arrangement in a text together with the effects these have upon the reader. The writers affirm that the rhetorical level is 'more inclusive' than the syntactical level, and that the meaning of rhetorical patterns cannot be fully appreciated without reference to the total context. Foregrounding is, thus, subsumed by the authors within the rhetorical level of linguistic structure.[87]

The theory of functional equivalence as presented by Nida seems to represent a confirmation of the seminal insights of Vladimir Procházka referred to above, and provides translators with an ideally suited conceptual framework for the translation of foregrounding schemes in texts

Saussure (who coined the term 'sémiologie').

83. De Waard and Nida, *From One Language*, pp. 73-77. Cf. Halliday, *Language as Social Semiotic*.

84. De Waard and Nida, *From one Language*, pp. 26, 43, 119; Nida *et al.*, *Style and Discourse*, p. 168. Though Nida is generally very appreciative of Halliday's work, he adamantly rejects the latter's reduction of functional components to three. Telephone conversation, see above.

85. De Waard and Nida, *From One Language*, p. 68.

86. De Waard and Nida, *From One Language*, p. 84.

87. De Waard and Nida, *From One Language*, pp. 78-85. The specific rhetorical functions discussed by the authors are 'wholeness', 'aesthetic appeal', 'impact', 'appropriateness', 'coherence', 'cohesion', 'focus', and 'emphasis'.

such as the Acts of the Apostles. In order to test this hypothesis, I shall now return to Acts 27 and offer some suggestions for the translation of transitivity-based foregrounding into the receptor language of Spanish.

2. *Some Suggestions for the Translation of Transitivity-Based Foregrounding: From Hellenistic Greek to Modern Castillian Spanish*

In a very recent study of transitivity in Spanish, José María García-Miguel offers the following criticism of Hopper and Thompson's essay discussed above:

> It must be recognized that transitivity cannot be determined by means of a mere counting of properties on a scale (whichever scale that may be), that the various parameters each have different 'weight', and that that relative 'weight' may vary from one language to another.[88]

Of the three objections to Hopper and Thompson's thesis raised by García-Miguel, the last two seem particularly well founded. Although many of their insights are extremely valuable, the reader of Hopper and Thompson's essay is certainly left with the impression that all that is involved in gauging the transitivity of a clause is counting the number of 'parameters' present within it, without discriminating, for example, between 'kinesis' and 'punctuality'. García-Miguel does well, therefore, to point us to the unequal 'weight' that the various properties carry within a language, as well as to the fact that the relative value of individual parameters varies from one language to another. This last point must be extended to foregrounding as a whole, whether it be realized by transitivity patterns as is the case in the shipwreck narrative, or contrasting tense–aspect morphology. Having studied the nature and function of foregrounded structures in the Greek of Acts, the translator must turn his attention to the receptor language system, and determine which linguistic structures therein (if any) are functionally analogous to those in the original. Thus Nida writes,

---

88. 'Habra que admitir que la transitividad no puede determinarse mediante un simple recuento de rasgos en una serie (sea cual sea ésta), que los diferentes parámetros tienen distinto "peso", *y que este "peso" relativo puede variar de una lengua a otra*' [emphasis mine]. José María García-Miguel, *Transitividad y Complementación Preposicional en Español* (Verba, 40; Santiago: Universidade de Santiago de Compostela, 1995), p. 57 (my emphasis).

> In view of the fact that we cannot match rhetorical forms, it is essential
> that careful consideration be given to the equivalent rhetorical functions,
> for these functions can in large measure be matched if one bears in mind
> carefully the respective degree of impact and appeal in the source and
> receptor texts. The question is basically 'what is the function of the
> rhetorical feature or features?... Though the features may not be univer-
> sal, the functions are, for all languages have devices for such functions
> as emphasis, marking similarities and contrasts, foregrounding and back-
> grounding...[89]

The presence of foregrounding schemes in Spanish texts of various
genres has been the subject of several recent studies.[90] The focus of the
translator's work may, therefore, be that of narrowing down the particular elements within the Spanish language system that may best
'promote the palpability' of the foregrounding scheme in a text. As I
mentioned in the previous section, the core of foregrounding in Acts 27
is the contrast between the ergativity of the 'they' clauses and the comparatively passive role of the rest of the participants in the story. With
the Reina-Valera[91] translation as a reference point, I shall now highlight
several features of both Spanish and Greek that may be profitably
exploited in the translation task.

(1) As with Greek, Spanish verb forms are, for the most part, person
and number specific. Consequently, the subject constituent is normally
absent from the clause, and appears grammaticalized as an explicit
subject only when its presence is felt to be required, for example, for
the introduction of a new participant. A degree of ambiguity is introduced in both languages when non-finite verbs such as participles are
used. Such forms as χειμαζομένων and (Reina-Valera's rendering)
siendo combatidos ('being violently resisted', 27.18), for example, are
number but not person specific. In vv. 18 and 27, however, the author
of Acts wishes to distinguish the 'we' and 'they' participants which
appear in the same clauses, and does so by means of an explicit first
person plural subject. The Reina-Valera translators have missed this
entirely, and by their choice of the ambiguous participial forms *siendo
combatidos* (v. 18) and *siendo llevados* ('being carried', v. 27) without

89. Nida *et al.*, *Style and Discourse*, p. 168.
90. See the bibliography offered by García-Miguel in *Transitividad y Complementación*.
91. *Sagrada Biblia* (trans. Reina-Valera; Buenos Aires: Sociedades Bíblicas
Unidas, 1960).

explicit subjects, the 'they' participant is in effect made the subject of the entire clause in each instance:

Reina-Valera	UBS GNT4
27.18. Pero siendo combatidos por una furiosa tempestad, al siguiente dia empezaron a alijar.	σφοδρῶς δὲ χειμαζομένων **ἡμῶν** τῇ ἑξῆς ἐκβολὴν ἐποιοῦ**ντο**,
But being besieged by a mighty storm, the following day they began to make a jettisoning.	
27.27. Venida la decimocuarta noche, y siendo llevados a través del mar Adriático, a la medianoche los marineros sospecharon que estaban cerca de tierra.	ὡς δὲ τεσσαρεσκαιδεκάτη νὺξ ἐγένετο διαφερομένων **ἡμῶν** ἐν τῷ Ἀδρίᾳ, κατὰ μέσον τῆς νυκτὸς ὑπενόουν οἱ ναῦται προσάγειν τινὰ αὐτοῖς χώραν.
After the fourteenth night came, being carried through the Adriatic sea, at midnight the sailors suspected they were near land.	

Participant distinction in the Greek text is further obscured by Reina-Valera at v. 29, where the aorist subjunctive form ἐκπέσωμεν is translated by means of the Spanish infinitive *dar en escollos* ('hit the rocks'), with the same result as above. Lastly, Reina-Valera has made a very poor textual choice at v. 19, and introduced a first-person plural subject where the best available witnesses have none.[92] The end result of these poor choices by Reina-Valera is the partial defusing of the foregrounding scheme employed by the author in the source language, as the strong contrast between the activity of the 'we' subject and that of the crew is no longer as apparent as it is in the original.

(2) The wide semantic range of the Greek conjunctions δὲ and καὶ may be exploited with a view to highlighting the contrast between the ergative and non-ergative clauses in the story. Here too the work of the Reina-Valera translators stands in need of improvement. The overabundance of the *y* conjunction in the Spanish text creates at best a highly unnatural style and tends to obscure the logical and temporal relations in the story. In light of the strong contrast between the 'they' agent and the rest of the participants in the narrative, the translator

92. On this issue see n. 64 above.

would be well advised to reserve the rather colorless *y* conjunction for the backgrounded 'we' participant as much as possible, while using disjunctive conjunctions or temporal adverbs to highlight the role of 'they' at key points. Verse 13 is a case in point:

> **Y** (Gk. δὲ) soplando una brisa del sur, pareciendoles que ya tenían lo que deseaban, levaron anclas e iban costeando Creta.
>
> And, a south wind blowing, supposing they had what they wanted, they raised the anchors and were sailing along Crete.

Having also begun vv. 12, 15, 16 and 17 with *y*, the translators are failing to mark an important transition in the story, and have created a highly artificial Spanish. Instead, I suggest the following:

> Entonces,[93] soplando una brisa del sur, y cuando ellos suponían que habían logrado su propósito, levaron anclas e iban costeando Creta.
>
> Then, a south wind blowing, when they thought they had achieved their purpose, they raised the anchors and were sailing along Crete.

(3) Once the translator has decided that transitivity is an issue of particular significance in the shipwreck narrative, the transitivity system in the receptor language must be carefully considered. For Spanish, the recent work of García-Miguel proves invaluable at this point. He noted, for example, that processes that include two participants may be realized in Spanish by any of the following clause structures: Subj.–Pred.–Direct Object (*María compró lotería*), Subj.–Pred.–Indirect Object (*el premio le tocó a María*), and Subj.–Pred.–Prepositional Phrase (*María disfrutó del premio*).[94] García-Miguel notes, furthermore, that although these three clause types may all be considered 'transitive' insofar as each makes reference to two participants, the first (that is, Subj.–Pred.–Direct Object) is by far the most frequent in Spanish. On the basis of his data,[95] García-Miguel argues that the two less frequent constructions often present 'some kind of semantic "deviation" from the transitivity

---

93. The adverb *entonces* ('then') seems amply justified here in light of both the contrastive role of δέ and the likely adverbial function of the genitive absolute. See also Reina-Valera at Acts 27.42, where δε is also translated by *entonces*.

94. García-Miguel, *Transitividad y Complementación*, p. 10.

95. Data taken from 'Archivo de Textos Hispanicos de la Universidad de Santiago' (ARTHUS): narrative: 37%; Essay 18%; Plays/Theater 15%; oral speech 19%; newspapers 11%.

prototype'.[96] García-Miguel then proposes a transitivity continuum for Spanish in which the three clause types mentioned are given values ranging from high to low transitivity, with the Subj.–Pred.–Prep. standing in a middle position. On the basis of the data presented in this important essay, the translator must carefully consider the choices that the Spanish transitivity system offers when translating a clause such as βοηθείαις ἐχρῶντο ὑποζωννύντες τὸ πλοῖον (27.17), together with the various semantic nuances attached to each choice. In translating the clause just cited, Reina-Valera has chosen a Pred.–Prepositional Phrase rather than a Pred.–Direct Object structure, where either option was equally valid, though, according to García-Miguel, not equal in its transitivity.[97] Such choices must be justified in light of the use made of transitivity patterns in the source text, and, insofar as this is possible, the relative degree of transitivity discernible in various clauses within the source text must be preserved in the translation.

During the telephone conversation referred to above, Eugene Nida mentioned to me that although the translation of foregrounding is an issue of 'extreme importance', modern translations generally ignore it because they are too strongly tied to previous versions of the biblical text to make stylistic innovations of this nature. Nida's assessment holds true for the Reina-Valera translation. Analyses of the biblical text such as the one carried out in this book will hopefully encourage new translation projects that aim to be lexically, grammatically, and stylistically faithful renderings of the source text. Insofar as foregrounding is part and parcel of the meaning of a text, translators cannot escape its careful consideration without a loss to the receptor language readers. In the following chapters, foregrounding schemes in other key episodes of Acts will be examined with a view to gaining an understanding of Luke's overall narrative focus.

---

96. 'Algun tipo de "desviacion" semantica respecto al prototipo de transitividad', García-Miguel, *Transitividad y Complementación*, p. 96.

97. Thus Reina-Valera, 'usaron de refuerzos para ceñir la nave', instead of 'usaron refuerzos'. García-Miguel has this to say in regard to the semantic value of the Subj.–Pred.–D.O. structure: 'la relación entre el verbo y la frase nominal que le sirve de argumento deja de der directa para ser mediatizada por la preposicion. La consecuencia en el plano de contenido es que las denotaciones de verbo y complemento se presentan como relativamente mas independientes, obedeciendo a un principio de iconicidad en la sintaxis' (p. 97).

Chapter 3

PARTICIPANT REFERENCE AND FOREGROUNDED TRANSITIVITY
PATTERNS IN THE STEPHEN EPISODE (ACTS 6–7)

Ever since Dibelius's influential work on Acts, it has been customary to assume a radical disjunction between compositional artistry and cohesiveness on the one hand, and historicity on the other. It was Dibelius's argument that the author of Acts could not possibly have had sources for his 'second treatise', because the first-century church was wholly uninterested in recording events.[1] Consequently, he argued, the vast majority of the material in Acts is the result of the author's 'new literary freedom'.[2] A decade before Dibelius inaugurated the age of form criticism, the last of the great source critics, Adolf Harnack, had already affirmed that the possibility of the writer having rewritten a 'we' source to conform it to his own style was to him 'absolutely unimaginable'.[3] His conclusion was a foretaste of Dibelius's: what is stylistically polished and consistent with the rest of the work cannot have been grafted in from a source, and must, therefore, be considered to be the author's own creation. The same assumption has since then been held by scholars who, unlike Dibelius and his many modern followers, argue for the existence of sources behind most, if not all, of Acts. Max

1. Dibelius, 'Style Criticism', p. 4. But see Martin Hengel's 'The Earliest Christian Histories as Sources for a History of Earliest Christianity and the Unity of Kerygma and Historical Narrative', in his *Acts and the History of Earliest Christianity* (trans. John Bowden; London: SCM Press, 1979), esp. pp. 43-44.

2. Dibelius, 'Style Criticism', p. 196; see also the classic essay by H.J. Cadbury, 'The Speeches in Acts', in F.J. Foakes Jackson and Kirsopp Lake (eds.), *The Beginnings of Christianity I*, V (London: Macmillan, 1933), esp. pp. 406-407.

3. Adolf von Harnack, *Luke the Physician* (trans. J.R. Wilkinson; London: Williams & Norgate, 2nd edn, 1909), p. 53. In regard to the 'we' sections, Harnack denies adamantly that Luke had 'short notes which refreshed his memory', concluding that the material is all Luke's (p. 53). E. Haenchen feels that Harnack was rash in reaching this conclusion (*The Acts of the Apostles*, p. 32).

Wilcox is a case in point. His 'Foreword to the Study of the Speeches in Acts'[4] offers convincing arguments for the existence of sources behind the speeches. Yet, Wilcox relies on the familiar criteria for identifying the source-based material, namely, the alleged awkwardness of style, lack of adequate links, and unusual vocabulary or turns of phrase.[5]

The literary analysis of the speeches has been further complicated by the debate over the meaning and relevance for Acts of the famous programmatic statement found in Thucydides's *History of the Peloponnesian War*.[6] In his classic essay mentioned above, Cadbury affirmed that the speeches in Acts amounted to 'purely literary artifices', a feature Cadbury discerned in most Hellenic and Graeco-Roman historians, including Thucydides.[7] But Cadbury seems to have ignored that in the classical historiographical tradition of Thucydides and Polybius, two essential elements were given similar consideration, namely, *narratio*, or fidelity to real history, and *exornatio*, or perfection of style, the

4.   *Studies in Judaism in Late Antiquity* 12.1 (1975), pp. 207-24.

5.   Wilcox, 'Foreword', p. 213; see also Javier Colmenero-Atienza, 'Hechos 7, 17-43 y las Corrientes Cristológicas Dentro de la Primitiva Comunidad Cristiana', *EstBib* 33 (1974), pp. 31-62, esp. pp. 43, 50.

6.   For an excellent and up to date discussion of this issue see W.F. McCoy, 'In the Shadow of Thucydides', in Witherington (ed.), *History*, pp. 3-23; see also S.E. Porter, 'Thucydides 1.22.1 and Speeches in Acts: Is there a Thucydidean View?', *NovT* 32 (1990), pp. 121-42 (121-24).

7.   Cadbury, 'The Speeches', pp. 402, 405. According to Cadbury, Thucydides frankly admitted that in composing speeches, ancient historians 'probably rarely relied on any real knowledge of what was actually said' (p. 405). Yet, this is in fact the opposite of what Thucydides himself seems to assert: 'ἐχμένῳ ὅτι ἐγγύτατα τῆς ξυμπάσεως γνώμης τῶν ἀληθῶς λεχθέντων, οὕτως εἴρηται'. Thucydides, *History of the Peloponnesian War* 1.22.1. Furthermore, Cadbury may have contradicted himself. On p. 402 he affirms the conformity of the book of Acts to the ancient practice of 'adorning historical works with imaginative speeches', while on p. 425 he states that although for classical historians speeches were the 'most prized parts' of their works and they composed them most carefully, Luke did not follow their model. In an earlier essay (H.J. Cadbury, 'The Style and Literary Method of Luke. Part II: The Treatment of Sources in the Gospel of Luke', *HTS* 6 [1919], pp. 73-92 [73]) Cadbury had expressed great confidence in the accuracy with which Luke follows his Markan source. In light of this, Cadbury's radically different assessment of Acts seems at best difficult to accept. For a convincing study of Luke's editorial activity in *both* the Gospel and Acts, see Ben Witherington III, 'Editing the Good News: Some Synoptic Lessons for the Study of Acts', in *idem*, (ed.), *History*, pp. 324-47.

two being considered by no means mutually exclusive.[8]

In more recent years, the discussion of Acts as literature has moved forward, as various proposals concerning the genre of Luke's second treatise have been put forth. Perhaps the most influential of these works has been R. Pervo's *Profit with Delight*.[9] According to Pervo, Acts belongs to a complex genre he calls the 'historical novel', and which involves the teaching of historical and theological truths in an entertaining fashion. His argument is largely based on alleged parallel features in both Acts and a number of Graeco-Roman novels, including their largely fictional character, though some sources were relied upon, Pervo argues, to a limited extent. In two recent works, Stanley Porter has thoroughly refuted Pervo's thesis.[10] First, Porter shows that although Pervo's aim was to relate Acts to existing literary genres in the literature of the ancient world, his analysis creates a category clearly 'at odds with the ancient literature that Pervo cites as parallel'.[11] Further, Porter argues convincingly that Pervo's thesis is plagued by a serious case of parallelomania, presenting as parallel texts that are at best only partially so, and often dismissing passages in Acts (e.g. the shipwreck narrative of Acts 27) as unhistorical on the basis of alleged literary parallels in ancient Graeco-Roman novels.[12]

It seems to me that the mentioned dichotomy between that which is 'literary' and that which is 'historical', between compositional dexterity and reliance upon sources, makes the author of Luke–Acts look far less skilled than he actually was, and is ultimately both unwarranted and unnecessary. Several recent works have demonstrated that Luke–Acts is the product of a writer who was both a faithful editor *and* a skilled *littérateur*.[13] In the study that follows I shall focus on the Stephen story

8.   See Helen. F. North, 'Rhetoric and Historigraphy', *Quarterly Journal of Speech* 42 (1956), pp. 234-42, esp. pp. 237, 242.

9.   *Profit with Delight: The Literary Genre of the Acts of the Apostles* (Philadelphia: Fortress Press, 1987).

10.   See Brook W.R. Pearson and Stanley E. Porter, 'The Genres of the New Testament', in Porter (ed.), *Handbook to Exegesis of the New Testament* (NTTS, 26; Leiden: E.J. Brill, 1997), pp. 131-66; Porter, *The Paul of Acts*. See also R. Bauckham, 'The Acts of Paul as a Sequel to Acts', in Bruce Winter and Andrew Clarke (eds.), *The Book of Acts in its Ancient Literary Setting* (A1CS, 1; Grand Rapids: Eerdmans; Carlisle: Paternoster Press, 1994), pp. 105-52.

11.   Porter, *The Paul of Acts*, p. 15.

12.   Porter, *The Paul of Acts*, p. 19.

13.   Marion L. Soards, *The Speeches in Acts* (Louisville: Westminster/John

as an episode within the larger work of Acts. My method of analysis is
linguistic and literary rather than historical, not because I oppose the
two, but because I believe any study of a New Testament document
must begin by allowing the author himself to tell his story, focusing not
only on his literary style as an indicator of the presence or absence of
sources, but on the various functions that his language and style are
made to serve in that text. The notion of linguistic foregrounding,
defined as that prominence that can be shown to be consistent and motivated in light of the overall theme(s) of a text,[14] provides a link between
stylistic and functional analysis and is capable of revealing important
insights into the writer's agenda in producing this ancient text.[15]

1. *The Language of the Stephen Episode in Recent Study*

Of the considerable amount of scholarship dedicated to the Stephen
episode (Acts 6–7) in recent years,[16] the question of the relation of
Stephen's speech (Acts 7.2-53) to the charges brought against him has

Knox Press, 1994), pp. 12-17 (12); Porter 'The "we" Passages', esp. pp. 567-70;
Bill T. Arnold, 'Luke's Characterizing Use of the Old Testament in the Book of
Acts', in Witherington (ed.), *History*, pp. 300-23 (300); see also Johannes Munck,
The Book of Acts (AB; Garden City, NY: Doubleday, 1981), pp. xxv, xxxix-xli.
This is, however, by no means a novel view on the subject. Seventy years ago,
E. Jacquier affirmed: 'L'examen linguistique de Actes tend à prouver que toutes les
parties du livre ont été écrites par le même auteur, *quoiqu'il ne soit pas impossible
qu'un éditeur habile ait utilisé des sources diverses, soit dans la première partie,
soit dans la seconde, et n'ait retravaillé ces diverses parties en leur imprimant une
certaine conformité de style...*' [emphasis mine]. E. Jacquier, *Les Actes des Apôtres*
(Paris: Librairie Victor Lecoffre, 2nd edn, 1926), p. clviii.

14. See Halliday, 'Linguistic Function and Literary Style', pp. 103-138.

15. An agenda he has, at least partially, revealed in his prologues of Lk. 1.1-4
and Acts 1.1.

16. A.F.J. Klijn, 'Stephen's Speech—Acts VII. 2-53', *NTS* 4 (1957–58), pp. 25-
31; Colmenero-Atienza, 'Hechos'; Kilgallen, *The Stephen Speech*; Richard, *Acts
6:1–8:4*; Earl Richard, 'The Polemical Character of the Joseph Episode in Acts 7',
JBL 98.2 (1979), p. 255-67 (257); Jacques Steyn, 'Some Psycholinguistic Factors
Involved in the Discourse Analysis of Ancient Texts', *Theologia Evangelica* 17.2
(1984), pp. 51-65 esp. p. 59; J. Dupont, 'La structure oratoire du discours d'Etienne
[Actes 7]', *Bib* 66 (1985), pp. 153-67; Dennis D. Sylva, 'The Meaning and
Function of Acts 7:46-50', *JBL* 106.2 (1987), pp. 261-75; Craig C. Hill, 'Acts 6.1–
8.4: Division or Diversity?', in Witherington (ed.), *History*, pp. 129-53.

often stimulated the most heated debate.[17] In arguing for or against the speech as response to the charges of Acts 6.13-14, or for or against the uniformity of its style with previous and later material, scholars often make reference to items of the language used that are seen by them as indicators of emphasis or of major turning points in the narrative or speech. Thus, for example, Kilgallen argues that direct speech is used by Luke when he wishes to mark climactic elements in his story;[18] Soards affirms that the phrase καὶ νῦν ('and now') indicates 'major moments' in speeches,[19] and, following Conzelmann, asserts that relative clauses are indicative of 'kerygmatic style' and are, therefore, of central importance;[20] Richard writes that by means of the repetition of a term, phrase or theme, the writer 'draws particular attention to the components central to his views';[21] Colmenero-Atienza offers a stylistically-based proposal as to who the *figuras centrales* may be in Stephen's speech;[22] and lastly, Barrett affirms that οὗτος is 'emphatic' in 7.35-38 and that τοῦτον τὸν Μωϋσῆν in 7.35 is 'brought to the beginning of the sentence for emphasis'.[23] Though these statements are all valid as working hypotheses, the unsystematic and haphazard way in which they are presented raises important questions that remain unanswered. Of these, none is more crucial than the question of criteria: how exactly is a 'major moment' or a 'central figure' to be determined? In relation to what are these items major or central? Without an answer to these questions, potentially fruitful insights such as the ones just mentioned will always suffer from a condition we could term 'untestable impressionism', that is, they are statements of opinion, rather than systematic and linguistically principled analyses that are open to evaluation by all.[24]

17. For a summary of the discussion see Kilgallen, 'The Stephen Speech', pp. 6-10.

18. Kilgallen, 'The Stephen Speech', pp. 37, 39. One wonders, however, whether direct speech may be considered, in and of itself, climactic, without studying the several ways in which the writer may introduce direct speech when he deems it necessary: 'and he said...' (7.2); 'Paul stood up...and said...' (17.22), etc.

19 Soards, *The Speeches*, pp. 92, 107.

20. Soards, *The Speeches*, pp. 34, 68.

21. Richard, *Acts 6:1-8:4*, p. 103.

22. Colmenero-Atienza, 'Hechos', p. 42.

23. Barrett, *The Acts of the Apostles*, pp. 363-65.

24. See Carter, 'Introduction', pp. 1-17, esp. pp. 4-6, for a well-argued call to a linguistically-based literary criticism.

2. *Major Participants in the Stephen Episode*

Of the various theories that have been put forward regarding the structure of the speech (more on this below), the biographical criterion as presented by Colmenero-Atienza[25] seems to best fit the data. In the following pages, I hope to show that the entire Stephen episode (Acts 6–7) is designed by the author to underline one single feature that unites the careers of Stephen, Joseph, and Moses. Far from a slightly revised 'neutral' account of Israelite history,[26] the narrative and speech form a cohesive and masterfully crafted chronicle that successfully advances the writer's overall theses in Acts.

In his essay entitled 'Participant Reference in Koine Greek Narrative',[27] Stephen Levinsohn explores the various means available to koine Greek writers for the introduction of and further reference to the characters in a narrative. More specifically, Levinsohn suggests the classification of 'default' and 'marked' encoding of participants, a notion based on the observation that the more significant a character is in a narrative, the more coding material is normally assigned to it to mark that significance. Thus, Levinsohn notes that in the Gospels, any explicit reference to Jesus as subject of a clause when he has already been introduced is marked encoding, while the absence of an explicit subject is generally the norm and is considered the 'default' encoding.[28] While I am generally in agreement with Levinsohn's theory, I would add that, at least until an exhaustive study of participant reference in the New Testament is carried out, statements of 'norm' or 'default', of which 'marked' encoding is held to be a departure, should only be made relative to specific texts. I will later discuss a particular means of

25. Colmenero-Atienza ('Hechos', pp. 41-43) rejects both a chronologically-based and a geographically-based structure, arguing instead for a biographical arrangement as follows: A. vv. 2-8, Abraham; B. vv. 9-16, Joseph; C. vv. 17-43, Moses; D. vv. 44-50, the house of God; E. vv. 51-53, the final invective. Though I am in agreement with the choice of a biographical structure, I do not concur with Colmenero's inclusion of Abraham as a figure of equal importance to Joseph and Moses in the structure of the speech. See below on this point.

26. See Haenchen, *The Acts of the Apostles*, p. 288.

27. In D.A. Black *et al.* (eds.), *Linguistics and New Testament Interpretation: Essays in Discourse Analysis* (Nashville: Broadman Press, 1992), pp. 31-44.

28. Levinsohn, 'Participant Reference', p. 35; see also Porter, 'Word Order', p. 194.

participant reference that seems unique to the author of Acts, and can be properly understood only in light of his agenda in the Acts of the Apostles. First, however, I wish to suggest the following cline as a means of summarizing the ways in which the various participants are referred to in the Stephen episode:

1. Full explicit subject (proper noun used)
   e.g. Στέφανος δὲ...ἐποίει τέρατα καὶ σημεῖα
2. Abbreviated explicit subject (pronoun or article used)
   πρὶν ἢ κατοικῆσαι αὐτὸν ἐν Χαρράν
3. Non-explicit subject (indicated by personal verb suffixes)
   ἦν ἀστεῖος τῷ θεῷ
4. Non-subject participant[29] (e.g. direct or indirect object)
   Ὁ θεὸς τῆς δόξης ὤφθη τῷ πατρὶ ἡμῶν Ἀβραάμ

In reading a narrative such as the Stephen episode, even the literarily untrained reader will acquire impressions concerning what participants strike him or her as 'more important'. The above scale is a means of grounding such impressions in the language system and the author's use of it. Thus, in a narrative such as the Stephen episode, the importance or centrality of a character may be gauged by the frequency of his or her appearing as full or abbreviated explicit subject (categories 1 and 2). Conversely, the centrality of the characters in the story will decrease proportionately to their appearance as non-explicit subjects or non-subject participants. Though this method of participant referent analysis is somewhat more complex than Levinsohn's described above, it takes full account of the fact that a participant may appear often as other than the subject of a clause or sentence, a fact that may yield important hermeneutical insights, as we shall see below. Further, the above scale is, unlike Levinsohn's 'default' and 'marked' notion, capable of accounting for the transitivity choices[30] that are often made by writers to

---

29. In Hallidayan functional grammar, the semantic framework for the representation of processes consists of three essential elements: the process itself (realized in texts by a verbal form), the participants (realized by actors or subjects and goals or direct objects) and circumstances (realized by adjuncts or circumstantial complements). Therefore, a particular character such as Abraham may appear several times as a participant in the narrative, though not as an actor or subject. See Halliday, *Introduction to Functional Grammar*, pp. 101-44.

30. The term transitivity is here used in the rather wide functional grammatical sense of 'the different types of processes that are recognized in the language, and the structures by which they are expressed'. The key types of processes (and corre-

differentiate a participant or participants from the rest.

In the Stephen episode, animate (i.e. human participants and God) participants are many and varied, including: 'the disciples' (6.1-2), Jewish and Greek Christians (6.1), the 'seven' (6.3), Stephen (6.5–7.2; 7.54-60), priests (6.7), certain synagogue members (6.9-10), 'men' (6.11); false witnesses (6.13), Jesus (6.14), Moses (6.11, 14), the high priest (7.1), God (7.2), Abraham (7.2-8), the patriarchs (7.8), Joseph (7.9-18), 'another king' (7.18-19), Moses (7.20-44), the Pharaoh's daughter (7.21), the sons of Israel (7.23, 37), an Egyptian (7.24, 28), a prophet (7.37), our fathers (7.39), Aaron (7.40), David (7.46), the prophet (7.48), your fathers (7.52), the witnesses (7.58). Of these participants, four stand out from the rest because of the sheer bulk of material dedicated to them, namely Stephen himself, Abraham, Joseph and Moses. Using the above scale, I shall examine each in turn.

(a) *Stephen*

In the 16 verses that recount his appointment and early career, arrest, defense, and stoning, Stephen appears 19 times as participant. The distribution of these references is as follows:

Participant reference to Stephen: Acts 6.5–7.1; 7.55-60

1. Full explicit subject $1\times^{31}$
2. Abbreviated explicit subject $2\times^{32}$
3. Non-explicit subject $10\times^{33}$
4. Non-subject participant $6\times^{34}$

sponding clause-types) that Halliday recognizes are material processes (processes of doing), mental processes (processes of sensing), and relational processes (processes of being). See Halliday, *An Introduction to Functional Grammar*, pp. 101-105. See also Hopper and Thompson, 'Transitivity in Grammar', pp. 251-99; and, for a critique of the latter, García-Miguel, *Transitividad y Complementación*.

31. Once in an independent clause: Στέφανος δὲ πλήρης χάριτος καὶ δυνάμεως ἐποίει τέρατα καὶ σημεῖα μεγάλα, 6.8.

32. Twice in independent clauses: ὁ ἄνθρωπος οὗτος οὐ παύεται λαλῶν, 6.13; and ὁ δὲ ἔφη, 7.2 (in the second case we have the article functioning as pronoun, a usage not at all infrequent in Luke–Acts. BDF, p. 131 [#251].

33. ἐλάλει, 6.10; ὑπάρχων...ἀτενίσας εἰς τὸν οὐρανὸν εἶδεν...7.55; εἶπεν, Ἰδοὺ θεωρῶ...7.56; θεὶς δὲ τὰ γόνατα ἔκραξεν...καὶ τοῦτο εἰπὼν ἐκοιμήθη, 7.60.

34. ἐξελέξαντο Στέφανον, 6.5; συζητοῦντες τῷ Στεφάνῳ, 6.9; Ἀκηκόαμεν

The analysis of these references yields some unexpected observations. Though in these 16 verses Stephen's presence 'on stage' is strong from the outset (of the seven 'deacons', it is he alone who is set aside for specific description in 6.5, and is referred to four times by name), the types of clauses in which these references appear encode processes that lack an external agent in all but two cases, that is, they make no reference to causation: they are non-ergative clauses. In other words, though the spotlight is clearly on Stephen, he is not described as a dynamic protagonist who is directly involved in bringing about events and doing things. Of the 13 clauses where he is the subject participant, only two encode material processes, processes of 'doing' where Stephen is an agent acting upon a medium in an ergative clause.[35] The other eleven clauses encode relational processes (processes of being), or mental and verbal processes, where Stephen is speaking in his defense, crying out, looking to the heavens, seeing the glory of God, being full of the Holy Spirit, and so on. The six references under my fourth category above (non-subject participant) appear in clauses where Stephen is on the receiving end of largely hostile actions (5 out of 6). It is interesting to note that the first and last times that Stephen is mentioned by name fall under my 'non-subject participant' category: 'they chose Stephen' (6.6) and 'they stoned Stephen' (7.59).

The cumulative effect of these choices made by the writer in the transitivity system of Greek amounts to what we might call the incapacitation of Stephen through linguistic means. In the 16 verses discussed above, Stephen is consistently found in situations where he appears to be carried along by events, rather than effecting them in any way; he is a patient victim, who in the face of opposition, arrest and deadly force responds only with words. Lastly, Stephen's role as a 'persecuted one', described in terms reminiscent of Christ's passion,[36] is further underlined by his relationship to the Holy Spirit in this story. As

αὐτοῦ, 6.11; συνήρπασαν αὐτὸν, 6.12; ἀκηκόαμεν γὰρ αὐτοῦ, 6.14; ἐλιθοβόλουν τὸν Στέφανον, 7.59.

35. These two clauses are: Στέφανος δὲ...ἐποίει τέρατα καὶ σημεῖα ('Stephen...used to do signs and wonders', 6.8), and θεὶς δὲ τὰ γόνατα ('he fell on his knees', 7.60), which Stephen does as he is being stoned!

36. For the parallels between Stephen and Christ in this story, see Charles Talbert, 'Martyrdom in Luke–Acts and the Lucan Social Ethic', in Richard Cassidy and Philip Scharper (eds.), *Political Issues in Luke–Acts* (Maryknoll, NY: Orbis Books, 1983), pp. 99-110; Robert F. O'Toole, *The Unity of Luke's Theology* (Wilmington, DE: Michael Glazier, 1984), pp. 63-67.

Sylva has noted,[37] the strong invective of 7.51-53 includes the only instance in which the Spirit is mentioned in reference to someone other than Stephen: Σκληροτράχηλοι καὶ ἀπερίτμητοι καρδίαις καὶ τοῖς ὡσίν, ὑμεῖς ἀεὶ τῷ πνεύματι τῷ ἁγίῳ ἀντιπίπτετε ὡς οἱ πατέρες ὑμῶν καὶ ὑμεῖς ('oh stiff-necked and uncircumcised of hearts and ears! you always resist the Holy Spirit: as your fathers did so you do...', 7.51). The other four references to the Holy Spirit, both before and after the invective, consistently describe Stephen as being full of the Holy Spirit (6.5; 6.3; 7.55) or speaking in or by the Spirit (6.10). The message is clear: those who have consistently opposed the Holy Spirit in Moses and the prophets will naturally continue opposing that same Spirit in Stephen, for as he is true heir of the saints of old, Stephen's accusers are true children of their murderous ancestors.[38]

(b) *Abraham*
Given that Stephen begins his speech with Abraham, and roughly seven verses are taken up with his career, the exegete is immediately tempted to consider the patriarch a central character in the structure of the speech, on a par with Joseph and Moses.[39] Upon closer examination of participant reference and clause structure, however, a different picture emerges:

Participant reference to Abraham: Acts 7.2-8

1.	Full explicit subject	0×
2.	Abbreviated explicit subject	0×
3.	Non-explicit subject	5×[40]
4.	Non-subject participant	7×[41]

---

37. Sylva, 'Acts 7:46-50', pp. 273-74.

38. Sylva seems wholly justified in seeing vv. 51-53 as a direct reply to the charges leveled against Stephen: '...the function of Acts 7:51-53 is to claim that the false accusations leveled against Stephen are but another example of the Jewish resistance to God's message because the Holy Spirit is linked to Stephen in Acts 6:1–8:1, and because Stephen's claim that the Jews, like their fathers, always resist the Holy Spirit immediately follows Stephen's response to the false accusations leveled against him' (Sylva, 'Acts 7:46-50', p. 274).

39. See for example Colmenero-Atienza, 'Hechos', p. 43; Soards, *The Speeches*, p. 59; Kilgallen, *The Stephen Speech*, p. 35, though Kilgallen notes that 'God is the one who brings about all that happens to Abraham...' (p. 43).

40. Twice in dependent clauses: πρὶν ἢ κατοικῆσαι αὐτὸν ἐν Χαρράν (7.2), and ἐξελθὼν ἐκ γῆς Χαλδαίων (7.4); three times in independent clauses:

Two features of the above scale are particularly striking. First, Abraham is never referred to by means of an explicit subject, a frequent means of highlighting a character in Greek.[42] Secondly, in the syntax of these verses, Abraham occupies primarily the slot of complement (direct or indirect object) in clauses where the subject is God, who appears three times as full explicit subject,[43] seven times as non-explicit subject,[44] and once as a non-subject participant.[45] It seems clear, then, that in this brief overture to Stephen's particular history of Israel it is the 'God of glory',[46] rather than Abraham, who occupies center stage. The writer thus emphasizes the role of Abraham's God as the great initiator of Israel's life as a nation, a fact he conveys with great force by means of two ergative clauses in 7.4 and 7.8.[47] Once this fundamental point is made, the author is ready to focus on the individual careers of Joseph and Moses: 'And [God] gave him the covenant, and it was thus that [Abraham] begat Isaac...and Isaac Jacob, and Jacob the twelve patriarchs'.

κατῴκησεν ἐν Χαρράν (7.4), ἐγέννησεν τὸν Ἰσαὰκ καὶ περιέτεμεν αὐτὸν (7.8).

41. Ὁ θεὸς τῆς δόξης ὤφθη τῷ πατρὶ ἡμῶν Ἀβραάμ (7.2); εἶπεν πρὸς αὐτόν (7.3); σοι δείξω (7.3); μετῴκισεν αὐτὸν εἰς τὴν γῆν ταύτην (7.4); οὐκ ἔδωκεν αὐτῷ κληρονομίαν (7.5); ἐπηγγείλατο δοῦναι αὐτῷ (7.5); ἔδωκεν αὐτῷ διαθήκην (7.8).

42. See Porter, 'Word Order', p. 200. However, as I argued in Chapter 2 above, claims concerning the 'highlighted' nature of explicit subjects or any other lexico-grammatical choices must be justified in light of the author's larger 'highlighting', or foregrounding strategy in the work.

43. Ὁ θεὸς τῆς δόξης ὤφθη τῷ πατρὶ ἡμῶν (7.2); ἐλάλησεν δὲ οὕτως ὁ θεὸς (7.6); and ὁ θεὸς εἶπεν (7.7).

44. εἶπεν πρὸς αὐτόν (7.3a); εἰς τὴν γῆν ἣν ἄν σοι δείξω (7.3b); μετῴκισεν αὐτὸν (7.4); οὐκ ἔδωκεν αὐτῷ κληρονομίαν (7.5a); ἐπηγγείλατο δοῦναι αὐτῷ (7.5b); κρινῶ ἐγώ (7.7); ἔδωκεν αὐτῷ διαθήκην περιτομῆς (7.8).

45. λατρεύσουσίν μοι (7.7).

46. This expression occurs one other time only in the Old Testament: Ps. 28.3 in the LXX or Ps. 29.3 in the MT (אֵל־הַכָּבוֹד).

47. μετῴκισεν αὐτὸν εἰς τὴν γῆν ταύτην εἰς ἣν ὑμεῖς νῦν κατοικεῖτε (7.4); ἔδωκεν αὐτῷ διαθήκην περιτομῆς (7.8). See also Nils A. Dahl, 'The Story of Abraham in Luke–Acts', in Leander E. Keck and J. Louis Martyn (eds.), *Studies in Luke–Acts* (London: SPCK, 1976), pp. 139-44 (143-44), where Dahl argues that the remainder of the speech is fundamentally an account of the fulfillment of God's word to Abraham.

(c) *Joseph*

Participant reference to Joseph: Acts 7.9-14, 18

1. Full explicit subject $2\times^{48}$
2. Abbreviated explicit subject $0\times$
3. Non-explicit subject $1\times^{49}$
4. Non-subject participant $5\times^{50}$

Although in the above clauses Joseph appears for the most part in the complement slot (i.e. as a non-subject participant), he is referred to four times by name, two of which are explicit subjects. The writer begins his account of Joseph by detaching him from the rest of the patriarchs in the following manner: '...and Isaac [begat] Jacob, and Jacob the twelve patriarchs' (7.8). '*And the patriachs were jealous of Joseph and sold him into Egypt. But God was with him*' (7.9). The verses that follow are primarily an elaboration of this theme—a point argued in a slightly different manner by Richard[51]—and may be summarized aptly as follows:

(1) *Adversity* (7.9a). Joseph's brothers sell him into slavery.
(2) *Blessing* (7.9b-10). God delivers him, gives him wisdom, and he is subsequently made prime minister of Egypt.
(3) *Adversity* (7.11). Famine comes, accompanied by 'great tribulation', with the result that 'our fathers could not find food'.
(4) *Blessing* (7.12-16). Joseph brings his family to Egypt and they are spared.

The betrayal of Joseph by his brothers, expressed in the strongest terms, is followed by an equally strong affirmation of God's presence and blessing in his life, a blessing that results in salvation for Joseph's

48. ἀνεγνωρίσθη Ἰωσὴφ τοῖς ἀδελφοῖς αὐτοῦ (7.13); Ἰωσὴφ μετεκαλέσατο Ἰακὼβ τὸν πατέρα αὐτοῦ (7.14).

49. In a dependent clause: ἀποστείλας (7.14).

50. οἱ πατριάρχαι ζηλώσαντες τὸν Ἰωσὴφ (7.9); ἐξείλατο αὐτὸν ἐκ πασῶν τῶν θλίψεων αὐτοῦ (7.10); ἔδωκεν αὐτῷ χάριν καὶ σοφίαν (7.10); κατέστησεν αὐτὸν ἡγούμενον (7.10); ἀνέστη βασιλεὺς ἕτερος [ἐπ' Αἴγυπτον] ὃς οὐκ ᾔδει τὸν Ἰωσήφ (7.18).

51. See Richard, 'The Polemical Character', pp. 258-62. Richard's essay has shown beyond reasonable doubt the intentionality of the writer's choice of words in 7.9: both ζηλώσαντες and ἀπέδοντο, predicated of Joseph's brothers and without further comment on the events that preceeded this development in the Genesis account, serve to emphasize the victimization of Joseph at the hands of his brothers.

family at the time of their greatest need. The christological allusions of this passage cannot be missed.[52]

(d) *Moses*

Participant reference to Moses: Acts 6.14; 7.20-40, 44

1. Full explicit subject   7×[53]
2. Abbreviated explicit subject   8×[54]
3. Non-explicit subject   16×[55]
4. Non-subject participant   15×[56]

The size of the Moses section of the speech (it takes up roughly 35% of the total, versus 11.6% for the Joseph section), together with its careful chronological structure (three 'forty year' periods) and the 'more than human dignity'[57] with which its protagonist is invested, reveal something of the centrality of the figure of Moses in Stephen's oration. Far from being a 'neutral' account of the great Old Testament hero's

52. See Kilgallen, *The Stephen Speech*, p. 52.
53. ἃ παρέδωκεν ἡμῖν Μωϋσῆς (6.14); ἐγεννήθη Μωϋσῆς (7.20); ἐπαιδεύθη Μωϋσῆς (7.22); ἔφυγεν δὲ Μωϋσῆς (7.29); ὁ δὲ Μωϋσῆς ἰδὼν ἐθαύμαζεν (7.31); ἔντρομος δὲ γενόμενος Μωϋσῆς (7.32); ὁ γὰρ Μωϋσῆς οὗτος...οὐκ οἴδαμεν τί ἐγένετο αὐτῷ (7.40).
54. ὃς ἀνετράφη μῆνας τρεῖς (7.20); ἐκτεθέντος δὲ αὐτοῦ (7.21); μὴ ἀνελεῖν με σὺ θέλεις (7.28); προσερχομένου δὲ αὐτοῦ κατανοῆσαι (7.31); οὗτος ἐξήγα-γεν αὐτοὺς (7.6); οὗτός ἐστιν ὁ Μωϋσῆς (7.37); οὗτός ἐστιν ὁ γενόμενος (7.38); ὃς ἐξήγαγεν ἡμᾶς ἐκ γῆς Αἰγύπτου (7.40).
55. ἦν ἀστεῖος τῷ θεῷ (7.20); ἦν δὲ δυνατὸς (7.22); ἰδών τινα ἀδικούμενον (7.24); ἠμύνατο (7.24); ἐποίησεν ἐκδίκησιν (7.24); πατάξας τὸν Αἰγύπτιον (7.24); ἐνόμιζεν δὲ συνιέναι τοὺς ἀδελφοὺς (7.25); ὤφθη αὐτοῖς μαχομένοις (7.26); συνήλλασσεν αὐτοὺς εἰς εἰρήνην (7.26); εἰπών (7.26); ἀνεῖλες ἐχθὲς τὸν Αἰγύπτιον (7.28); ἐγένετο πάροικος (7.29); ἐγέννησεν υἱοὺς δύο (7.29); ἰδὼν (7.31); οὐκ ἐτόλμα κατανοῆσαι (7.32); ποιήσας τέρατα καὶ σημεῖα (7.36).
56. ἀνείλατο αὐτὸν (7.21); ἀνεθρέψατο αὐτὸν (7.21); Ὡς δὲ ἐπληροῦτο αὐτῷ (7.23); ἀπώσατο αὐτὸν (7.27); Τίς σε κατέστησεν (7.27); ὤφθη αὐτῷ (7.30); εἶπεν δὲ αὐτῷ ὁ κύριος (7.33); ἀποστείλω σε (7.34); Τοῦτον τὸν Μωϋσῆν...ὁ θεὸς [καὶ] ἄρχοντα καὶ λυτρωτὴν ἀπέσταλκεν (7.35); ὃν ἠρνήσαντο (7.35); τοῦτον ὁ θεὸς... (7.35); ἀγγέλου τοῦ ὀφθέντος αὐτῷ (7.35); τοῦ ἀγγέλου τοῦ λαλοῦντος αὐτῷ (7.38); ᾧ οὐκ ἠθέλησαν ὑπήκοοι γενέσθαι (7.39); τί ἐγένετο αὐτῷ (7.40); ὁ λαλῶν τῷ Μωϋσῇ (7.44).
57. Barrett, *Acts*, p. 338. Similarly, Munck has written that in Stephen's speech one finds 'the highest appreciation of Moses that we meet in the New Testament' (Munck, *Acts*, p. 221 n. 1).

career, however, this is the climactic point of the writer's unique history of Israel, carefully crafted to cohere with and consummate all that has preceeded it. Like Joseph in the preceeding section, Moses is described in terms reminiscent of Christ.[58] As was the case with both Stephen and Joseph above, however, the reader is left with the impression that Moses is hardly in control of the events of his life, but rather seems often overwhelmed by them. This impression is created by the syntax of this section: of the 31 clauses in which Moses appears as a subject (explicit or non), only five are ergative, that is, only five have him as an agent external to the process in question.[59] Conversely, all of these clauses but five are non-ergative, that is, the processes in which Moses is involved are represented as self-engendered, as in ἔφυγεν δὲ Μωϋσῆς ('Moses fled') (process + medium, 7.29), rather than engendered by himself, as in πατάξας τὸν Αἰγύπτιον ('Having filled the Egyptian') (agent + process + medium, 7.24).[60] Lastly, as he did with Joseph in the previous paragraphs, the writer focuses on one specific aspect of Moses' life, with very little attention to everything else: Moses, rejected by men, but blessed and chosen by God: 'This very Moses, whom they denied...even this man God has sent as both ruler and deliverer...' (7.35).

The question asked of Stephen by the high priest in 7.1 is simply this: 'Are these things so?', that is, are you blaspheming against Moses and God? (6.11), are you indeed announcing that Jesus will alter the traditions we have received from Moses, and what concerns the temple in particular? (6.13-14).[61] Stephen's speech, culminating so poignantly with the Moses account represents a strong and well argued reply to

---

58. Compare for example 7.20-22 with Luke's account of the birth and childhood of Jesus in Lk. 2.

59. Of these five clauses where Moses is an agent, three refer to the same event, namely, his killing of the Egyptian: μὴ ἀνελεῖν με σὺ θέλεις (7.28); ἐποίησεν ἐκδίκησιν (7.24); πατάξας τὸν Αἰγύπτιον (7.24). The other two are: ἃ παρέδωκεν ἡμῖν Μωϋσῆς (6.14), and οὗτος ἐξήγαγεν αὐτοὺς (7.36).

60. See Halliday, *An Introduction to Functional Grammar*, p. 147.

61. Sylva is correct when he argues that Acts 6.13-14 is an elaboration and specification of the one fundamental charge, namely, to have spoken blasphemies against Moses and God. See Sylva, 'Acts 7:46-50', p. 268. Similarly, Barrett sees the charges of 6.13-14 as a second, more formal stage of the accusation, rather than a separate indictment. Furthermore, Barrett argues that 'to speak against Moses and to speak against the law are...synonymous' (Barrett, *Acts*, p. 327).

these charges.[62] There are only two kinds of Israelite, argues the martyr, God's faithful envoys together with those who submit to their message, and those who, throughout the history of the nation, have opposed, persecuted and murdered them. The high praise that Stephen directs at Moses and the law that was given through his mediation (7.38, 44) makes clear where he stands with respect to this great divide: it is not he who has rejected Moses and the law, but 'your fathers' (7.39), of whom Stephen's audience, in their prejudiced and malevolent opposition to him, are showing themselves to be true heirs.

The Moses theme leads to the disquisition on the temple in vv. 44-50. In this regard, Barrett is incorrect when he affirms that in the speech, 'the temple is treated with no respect at all'.[63] Quite the contrary, Stephen begins his brief commentary on Israel's place of worship by connecting it, in its original form, to Moses himself (7.44), to whom the command to build (ποιῆσαι) such a structure was originally given. Secondly, David's desire to find (εὑρεῖν) a temple (σκήνωμα[64]) is described approvingly by the writer, and it is only Solomon's construction (οἰκοδόμησεν) of a house (οἶκον) that receives the harsh condemnation of the writer. A sounder reading of this section of the speech is

62. Supporting this view see also Kilgallen, *The Stephen Speech*, esp. pp. 107-19; Sylva, 'Acts 7:46-50', p. 263; F.F. Bruce, *The Acts of the Apostles* (London: Tyndale Press, 4th edn, 1956), pp. 160-64. Against this view, see Colmenero-Atienza, 'Hechos', pp. 38-39; Haenchen, *The Acts of the Apostles*, p. 288; F.J. Foakes Jackson, *The Acts of the Apostles* (London: Hodder & Stoughton, 1945), p. 61. Barrett's may be considered an intermediate position regarding this fundamental issue in the study of the speech, since he argues that the speech is most likely 'a qualified kind of answer' to the charges. Barrett, *Acts*, p. 335.

63. Barrett, *Acts*, p. 338. See also Haenchen, *The Acts of the Apostles*, p. 290; Philip F. Esler, *Community and Gospel in Luke–Acts* (Cambridge: Cambridge University Press, 1987), pp. 135-63. Similarly, the now standard work by J.T. Sanders, *The Jews in Luke–Acts* (London: SCM Press, 1987), pp. 33-34, where Sanders writes: '...a peculiar part of Luke's attitude towards the Temple is that it is inherently perverse because it was χειροποίητος...' This is a serious misunderstanding of the Stephen speech. One basic problem with this view is that while matters related to the law did concern early Christian communities in cities such as Jerusalem and Antioch, there is no historical evidence to suggest that the temple was a point of similar controversy. See Hill, 'Division or Diversity?', p. 143. See also Ben Witherington III, *The Acts of the Apostles: A Socio-Rhetorical Commentary* (Grand Rapids: Eerdmans, 1998), pp. 261-62.

64. The term is used in the Septuagint of both the tabernacle and the temple. See Sylva, 'Acts 7:46-50', p. 264.

offered by Kilgallen and by Sylva,[65] who argue that it is a particular view of the temple, rather than the temple per se, that is under attack in this section of the speech. The 'Most High', affirms the martyr, using a divine name that highlights God's transcendence, is not contained by structures made with hands (χειροποιήτοις, v. 48), for he himself is the maker of all things. The writer's account of Israel's worship progresses as follows:

- *False worship* by the fathers involving a σκηνὴ (7.43)
- *True worship* by Moses and David involving σκηνὴ and σκήνωμα (44-46)
- *False worship* by Solomon involving οἶκος (47-50)
- *The invective:* you are just like your fathers! they killed the prophets and did not keep the law (51-53)

Thus, the thematic links of this brief section to both the previous material and the invective are clear: failure to understand the true purpose and meaning of the temple is presented as one last defining characteristic of those who persecuted the prophets and did not keep the law.[66]

In order to complete my analysis of participant reference in the Stephen episode, I must now return to Luke's account of the activity of the divine actor in this episode, a subject I referred to only briefly in connection to the account of Abraham's career. It is important to note that God is not introduced directly until the start of Stephen's narrative of Israel's history in 7.2, and 'leaves the stage' just before Stephen's invective marks the end of his speech (7.50). God's participation in the narrative of the Stephen episode is, therefore, limited to Stephen's historical summary of 7.2-50. As the data below show, however, God's activity in this historical summary is relentless and overpowering, and reveals that for Luke, the history of Israel is nothing if not the history of God's activity on her behalf. The references to God as participant in his episode are distributed as follows:

---

65. Kilgallen, *The Stephen Speech*, pp. 87-92; Sylva, 'Acts 7:46-50', pp. 266-67. See also Dahl, 'The Story of Abraham', pp. 145-46.

66. This is to be expected, since one of the most recurrent themes in the prophetic writings is precisely to warn Israel against placing her trust in the physical structure of the temple, while at the same time neglecting the commandments. See especially Jer. 7.4-15.

1. Full explicit subject   13[67]
2. Abbreviated explicit subject 1[68]
3. Non-explicit subject   13[69]
4. Non-subject participant 5[70]

In the middle of his account of the martyrdom of Stephen, Luke chooses to insert a carefully crafted (more on this in my excursus below) digest of several Old Testament accounts of God's sovereign agency in the history of his people. God's activity in history is thus made to cast a shadow of hope over and put in perspective what appears to be the defeat of God's present purposes in the murder of his servant Stephen. Further, Luke's transitivity choices in his depiction of Abraham, Joseph, and Moses, serve to identify these Old Testament heroes, both in their suffering and in their final vindication by God, with Stephen's own experience.

When presenting arguments for the literary unity of the Stephen episode, or for its unity in relation to the rest of Acts, it has been customary since Harnack's time to focus primarily on lexis. Yet, Harnack notwithstanding, lexical features alone may not be considered 'proof' of unity of style and cohesiveness in Luke–Acts, as the famous debate between Harnack and Cadbury showed.[71] Without denying the relative value of lexis in determining cohesion in this text or in Luke–Acts as a whole, I have turned my attention to other linguistic features of the

67. ὁ θεὸς τῆς δόξης ὤφθη (7.2); ἐλάλησεν δὲ οὕτως ὁ θεὸς (6); ὁ θεὸς εἶπεν (7b); ἦν ὁ θεὸς μετ᾽ αὐτοῦ (9); ὡμολόγησεν ὁ θεὸς (17); ὁ θεὸς διὰ χειρὸς αὐτοῦ δίδωσιν (25); εἶπεν δὲ αὐτῷ ὁ κύριος (33); ὁ θεὸς [καὶ] ἄρχοντα καὶ λυτρωτὴν ἀπέσταλκεν (35); ἀναστήσει ὁ θεὸς (37); ἔστρεψεν δὲ ὁ θεὸς (42); ἔξωσεν ὁ θεὸς (45); οὐχ ὁ ὕψιστος ἐν χειροποιήτοις κατοικεῖ: (48); λέγει κύριος (49).

68. κρινῶ ἐγώ (7).

69. εἶπεν (3a); δείξω (3b); μετῴκισεν (4); οὐκ ἔδωκεν (5a); ἐπηγγείλατο δοῦναι (5b); ἔδωκεν (8); ἐξείλατο (10a); ἔδωκεν (10b); ἰδὼν εἶδον (34a); ἀποστείλω (34b); παρέδωκεν (42); μετοικιῶ (43); ἐποίησεν (50).

70. λατρεύσουσίν μοι (7); ἦν ἀστεῖος τῷ θεῷ (20); προσηνέγκατέ μοι (42); ὁ οὐρανός μοι θρόνος (49a); οἰκοδομήσετέ μοι (49b).

71. Harnack concluded his lexical analysis with the words 'the proof is now complete' (*Luke the Physician*, p. 81). But see Cadbury's reply in, among others, Cadbury, *The Making*, passim. For the problems inherent in 'counting words' in order to prove cohesiveness, authorship or unity of style, see the classic by G.U. Yule, *The Statistical Study of Literary Vocabulary* (Cambridge: Cambridge University Press, 1944), esp. chapter 6 'Word Distributions from Different Works of the Same Author: Macaulay and Bunyan', esp. p. 133.

Stephen story that seem to be both consistent, and purposefully placed, and may therefore be considered contributive to its texture.[72] Specifically, the transitivity choices made by the writer in the description of Stephen, Joseph, and Moses, the consistency of clause structure (I shall have more to say on this in the next section), and the repeated theme of 'human opposition–divine blessing' make the literary unity of the Stephen episode very difficult to dispute. A method of participant reference and clause structure analysis such as the one offered here allows us to record these observations in a manner that is concrete, linguistically principled, and replicable by other scholars using the same method.

3. Foregrounded Syntax in Acts 7.35: Its Relation to the Speech, the Episode, and the Book of Acts

In the previous section I have attempted to show that the literary structure of the Stephen episode centres around the biographical sketches of Stephen, Joseph, and Moses. More specifically, I pointed out that the writer is focusing on the status of these three men as relatively passive victims of unrighteous opposition, who nonetheless bear the seal of God's approval and are blessed and chosen by him. I now turn my attention to a particular passage in this story, namely, Acts 7.35, that is used by the writer to culminate and bring this theme to the fore with unparalleled impetus and clarity.

> Τοῦτον τὸν Μωϋσῆν, ὃν ἠρνήσαντο
> εἰπόντες, τίς σε κατέστησεν ἄρχοντα καὶ δικαστήν...
> τοῦτον ὁ θεὸς [καὶ] ἄρχοντα καὶ λυτρωτὴν ἀπέσταλκεν
> σὺν χειρὶ ἀγγέλου τοῦ ὀφθέντος αὐτῷ ἐν τῇ βάτῳ.

> This very Moses whom they denied saying, who appoined you ruler and judge?
> Even this man God sent as both ruler and deliverer by the hand of the angel who appeared to him at the bush.

Two features of this passage, missed almost entirely by the major commentaries, as I will show, call for some detailed discussion.

---

72. In Hallidayan functional grammar, texture, or the cluster of properties that separate a text from non-text, involves three essential elements: cohesion (both grammatical and lexical), theme and information systems (pertaining to the internal structure of the clause), and the macrostructure of the text or its genre, such as narrative or conversation. See M.A.K. Halliday and R. Hasan, *Cohesion in English* (London: Longman, 6th edn, 1984), esp. pp. 324-33.

(a) *The Adjectival–Demonstrative Use of* οὗτος *in Acts*

Haenchen, Bruce, and Barrett[73] have all argued that οὗτος is 'emphatic' in 7.35-38. Unfortunately, however, such an affirmation does not carry conviction for two fundamental reasons: no linguistic arguments are offered to back such an assertion (see my comments under section I above), and no proper differentiation is made between the adjectival use of the pronoun in v. 35, and its nominal use in vv. 36-38.[74] Yet, this distinction is significant enough to merit separate treatment. In its nominal usage, the demonstrative pronoun οὗτος functions most often as an anaphoric and, less often, cataphoric referential tie. That is, it points, without mentioning it explicitly, to a referent present either before or after in the text, as in Acts 2.15: οὐ γὰρ ὡς ὑμεῖς ὑπολαμβάνετε **οὗτοι** μεθύουσιν ('for *these men* [in this case, the tongue-speaking apostles] are not drunk, as you suppose'), or Acts 7.36: **οὗτος** ἐξήγαγεν αὐτοὺς ('*This man* [Moses] led them out'). The adjectival function of οὗτος, however, is the qualification, description or highlighting of the noun to which it is attached. The use of the adjectival demonstrative pronoun οὗτος (henceforth ADP οὗτος) in Acts calls for specific comment.

The 28 instances of the ADP οὗτος when used of human participants in Acts are distributed as follows:

1.	Qualifying Paul	10^{75}
2.	Qualifying the apostles	6^{76}
3.	Qualifying Jesus	5^{77}
4.	Qualifying Moses	2^{78}
5.	Qualifying Paul's nephew	2^{79}
6.	Qualifying other Christians	2^{80}
7.	Qualifying Stephen	1^{81}

---

73. See Haenchen, *The Acts of the Apostles*, p. 282; Bruce, *Acts*, p. 171; Barrett, *Acts*, p. 364. For Barrett, the 'emphatic' use of the pronoun apparently begins in v. 36.

74. For a discussion of the various uses of οὗτος, see BDF, p. 289. BDF does not, however, use the terms adjectival and nominal when describing the various uses of οὗτος.

75. ἀπεκρίθη δὲ Ἀνανίας· κύριε, ἤκουσα ἀπὸ πολλῶν περὶ τοῦ ἀνδρὸς **τούτου** ὅσα κακὰ τοῖς ἁγίοις σου ἐποίησεν ἐν Ἰερουσαλήμ· (9.13); τινὲς δὲ καὶ τῶν Ἐπικουρείων καὶ Στοϊκῶν φιλοσόφων συνέβαλλον αὐτῷ, καί τινες ἔλεγον· τί ἂν θέλοι ὁ σπερμολόγος **οὗτος** λέγειν; (17.18); καὶ θεωρεῖτε καὶ ἀκούετε ὅτι οὐ μόνον Ἐφέσου ἀλλὰ σχεδὸν πάσης τῆς Ἀσίας ὁ Παῦλος **οὗτος** πείσας

In 26 out of the above 28 instances (93%), the ADP οὗτος is used to qualify a central New Testament figure or Moses, and it is used exclusively of Christian figures or Moses. Further, the participants that are singled out for reference by means of ADP οὗτος are already 'on stage' or in the spotlight, due most often (in 23 out of 28 cases) to their being under investigation or accusation by a hostile audience or tribunal. It is perhaps on the basis of some of these examples that Blass and

μετέστησεν ἱκανὸν ὄχλον (19.26); ἀκούσας δὲ ὁ ἑκατοντάρχης προσελθὼν τῷ χιλιάρχῳ ἀπήγγειλεν λέγων· τί μέλλεις ποιεῖν; ὁ γὰρ ἄνθρωπος **οὗτος** Ῥωμαῖός ἐστιν (22.26); ἀναστάντες τινὲς τῶν γραμματέων τοῦ μέρους τῶν Φαρισαίων διεμάχοντο λέγοντες· οὐδὲν κακὸν εὑρίσκομεν ἐν τῷ ἀνθρώπῳ **τούτῳ** (23.9); Τὸν ἄνδρα **τοῦτον** συλλημφθέντα ὑπὸ τῶν Ἰουδαίων καὶ μέλλοντα ἀναιρεῖσθαι ὑπ' αὐτῶν (23.27) εὑρόντες γὰρ τὸν ἄνδρα **τοῦτον** λοιμὸν καὶ κινοῦντα στάσεις πᾶσιν τοῖς Ἰουδαίοις (24.5); καὶ ἀναχωρήσαντες ἐλάλουν πρὸς ἀλλήλους λέγοντες ὅτι οὐδὲν θανάτου ἢ δεσμῶν ἄξιον [τι] πράσσει ὁ ἄνθρωπος **οὗτος**. (26.31) Ἀγρίππας δὲ τῷ Φήστῳ ἔφη· ἀπολελύσθαι ἐδύνατο ὁ ἄνθρωπος **οὗτος** εἰ μὴ ἐπεκέκλητο Καίσαρα. (26.32); πρὸς ἀλλήλους ἔλεγον· πάντως φονεύς ἐστιν ὁ ἄνθρωπος **οὗτος** (28.4).

76. τί ποιήσωμεν τοῖς ἀνθρώποις **τούτοις**; (4.16); εἶπέν τε πρὸς αὐτούς· ἄνδρες Ἰσραηλῖται, προσέχετε ἑαυτοῖς ἐπὶ τοῖς ἀνθρώποις **τούτοις** τί μέλλετε πράσσειν. (5.35); καὶ τὰ νῦν λέγω ὑμῖν, ἀπόστητε ἀπὸ τῶν ἀνθρώπων **τούτων** καὶ ἄφετε αὐτούς· (5.38); αὕτη κατακολουθοῦσα τῷ Παύλῳ καὶ ἡμῖν ἔκραζεν λέουσα· **οὗτοι** οἱ ἄνθρωποι δοῦλοι τοῦ θεοῦ τοῦ ὑψίστου εἰσίν (16.17); **οὗτοι** οἱ ἄνθρωποι ἐκταράσσουσιν ἡμῶν τὴν πόλιν, Ἰουδαῖοι ὑπάρχοντες (16.20); ἠγάγετε γὰρ τοὺς ἄνδρας **τούτους** οὔτε ἱεροσύλους οὔτε βλασφημοῦντας τὴν θεὸν ἡμῶν (19.37).

77. **οὗτος** ὁ Ἰησοῦς ὁ ἀναλημφθεὶς ἀφ' ὑμῶν εἰς τὸν οὐρανὸν οὕτως ἐλεύσεται ὃν τρόπον ἐθεάσασθε (1.11); **τοῦτον** τὸν Ἰησοῦν ἀνέστησεν ὁ θεός, οὗ πάντες ἡμεῖς ἐσμεν μάρτυρες· (2.32); καὶ κύριον αὐτὸν καὶ χριστὸν ἐποίησεν ὁ θεός, **τοῦτον** τὸν Ἰησοῦν ὃν ὑμεῖς ἐσταυρώσατε. (2.36); βούλεσθε ἐπαγαγεῖν ἐφ' ἡμᾶς τὸ αἷμα τοῦ ἀνθρώπου **τούτου**. (5.28); ἀκηκόαμεν γὰρ αὐτοῦ λέγοντος ὅτι Ἰησοῦς ὁ Ναζωραῖος **οὗτος** καταλύσει τὸν τόπον (6.14).

78. **Τοῦτον** τὸν Μωϋσῆν ὃν ἠρνήσαντο εἰπόντες· τίς σε κατέστησεν ἄρχοντα καὶ δικαστήν; τοῦτον ὁ θεὸς [καὶ] ἄρχοντα καὶ λυτρωτὴν ἀπέσταλκεν (7.35); ὁ γὰρ Μωϋσῆς **οὗτος**, ὃς ἐξήγαγεν ἡμᾶς ἐκ γῆς Αἰγύπτου, οὐκ οἴδαμεν τί ἐγένετο αὐτῷ (7.40).

79. τὸν νεανίαν **τοῦτον** ἀπάγαγε πρὸς τὸν χιλίαρχον (23.17); ἠρώτησεν **τοῦτον** τὸν νεανίσκον ἀγαγεῖν πρὸς σε (23.18).

80. σὺ κύριε καρδιογνῶστα πάντων, ἀνάδειξον ὃν ἐξελέξω ἐκ **τούτων** τῶν δύο ἕνα (1.24); ἦλθον δὲ σὺν ἐμοὶ καὶ οἱ ἓξ ἀδελφοὶ **οὗτοι** καὶ εἰσήλθομεν εἰς τὸν οἶκον τοῦ ἀνδρός (11.12).

81. ἔστησάν τε μάρτυρας ψευδεῖς λέγοντας· ὁ ἄνθρωπος **οὗτος** οὐ παύεται λαλῶν ῥήματα κατὰ τοῦ τόπου τοῦ ἁγίου (6.13).

Debrunner write that 'οὗτος appears to be used in a contemptuous sense (like *iste*) of a person present: Lk 15:30'.[82] Barrett's comment on οὗτος in Acts 6.13 and 14 is taken directly from Blass and Debrunner, a grammar he is heavily dependent on.[83] But the above list shows that the meaning of the ADP οὗτος in Acts is more complex than Blass and Debrunner and Barrett have supposed. It appears that, in Acts, this particular form of participant reference is used consistently by the writer to mark either key Christian figures or Moses, who are typically found under unjust persecution. These references occur in the words either of an accuser or opponent, or of a Christian speaker or the narrator for specific comment: *this very one(s)* whom...you murdered, you bring before me, the fathers rejected...we now preach, you must leave alone, is not worthy of death, and so on.[84]

The use of the ADP οὗτος in Acts 7.35 is consistent with the above explanation, and is particularly significant, in light of the fact that it is also used of both Stephen and Jesus in 6.13 and 14 respectively. The ADP οὗτος, therefore, appears to be a linguistic means used by the writer to further highlight the characteristic that his key protagonists have in common in the Stephen episode: 'this very one whom men reject God has both chosen and blessed'.

82. BDF, p. 151 [§290(6)]. Similarly, Turner writes, somewhat more helpfully, 'οὗτος is very frequent in papyri and New Testament and as in earlier Greek refers to someone actually present (often contemptuously: Lk 15:30, ὁ υἱός σου οὗτος; 18.11...), not necessarily referring to the noun which is nearest, but to the noun which is most vividly in the writer's mind (deictic)' (*Grammar of New Testament Greek*, pp. 44-45). It is important to note that neither BDF nor Turner make a distinction between the nominal and adjectival uses of οὗτος. Concerning the usage of οὗτος in Homeric Greek, Monro writes, '[it] is chiefly used (Like iste in Latin) of what belongs to or concerns the person spoken to, or else in a hostile or contemptuous tone...used of one of the enemy...' (D.B. Monro, *Homeric Grammar* [Oxford: Clarendon Press, 1891], pp. 217-18).

83. See Barrett, *Acts*, pp. 327-28, where he writes that ὁ ἄνθρωπος οὗτος in 6.13 'gives a derogatory tone to the reference', and that Ἰησοῦς ὁ Ναζωραῖος οὗτος in 6.14 'is contemptuous as in 13'. For Barrett's dependence on BDF, see also Barrett, *Acts*, pp. 346, 348, 349, 350, 353, 355, 359, 361, 362, 364, etc. That a commentary published in 1994 could be so dependent on a century-old grammar, largely unaffected by the findings of modern linguistics, seems at best difficult to accept. See Porter and Reed, 'Greek Grammar since BDF', pp. 143-64.

84. Thus for example 7.35 (cited above) of Moses, 9.13 of Paul, and 2.36 of Jesus.

(b) Complement–Subject–Predicate: *A Strikingly Rare Clause Type in Acts 7.35*[85]

In commenting upon Acts 7.35, Barrett writes that 'the object of ἀπέσταλκεν is brought to the beginning of the sentence for emphasis',[86] providing no reasons for such an assertion. All that we can gather from a thorough analysis of clause structure in the Stephen episode and elsewhere in Acts, is that the structure Complement–Subject–Predicate (τοῦτον τὸν Μωϋσῆν, ὃν ἠρνήσαντο...τοῦτον ὁ θεὸς [καὶ] ἄρχοντα καὶ λυτρωτὴν ἀπέσταλκεν; 'This very Moses whom they denied... even this man God sent as both ruler and redeemer') is very rare; indeed it is the most unusual clause type there is in Acts. In independent clauses, the complement is not likely to come first in either clauses with an explicit subject (0 instances in the narrative section of 6.1–7.1, and 5 [4.8%] in the speech) or those without it (1 in the narrative section of 6.1–7.1 [3.5%] and 6 [5.8%] in the speech).[87] In isolation from other linguistic or literary data about the Stephen episode, however, this observation is of limited value. If one wishes to argue, as Barrett does, that a particular clause type is purposely being used by the writer as an indicator of prominence in this story, one must be able to show how that prominence relates to the 'big picture' of the text, that is, to the writer's theme(s) or agenda(s) in the Stephen episode, and in the Acts of the Apostles. In his classic essay on linguistic foregrounding, Michael Halliday states:

> Foregrounding, as I understand it, is prominence that is motivated. It is not difficult to find patterns of prominence in a poem or prose text...that stand out in some way, or may be brought out by careful reading; and one may often be led in this way towards a new insight, through finding that such prominence contributes to the writer's total meaning. *But unless it does, it will seem to lack motivation; a feature that is brought into prominence will be 'foregrounded' only if it relates to the meaning of the text as a whole.*[88]

---

85. As throughout this book, I am using the method of clause structure analysis proposed by Porter in his 'Word Order' article, especially on pp. 189-92.

86. Barrett, *Acts*, p. 363.

87. The most frequent clause structure in both speech and narrative is Pred.–Comp. The data here presented are roughly equivalent to that gathered by myself from the sample texts of Acts 1 and 27.

88. Halliday, 'Linguistic Function and Literary Style', p. 112. Emphasis mine.

The real significance of Acts 7.35 is not the rarity of its Greek syntax or grammar. Rather, it is that these unusual features of language are used by the writer to highlight and drive home, that is, to foreground, the theme he has been focusing on from the beginning of the Stephen episode. The key protagonist of Stephen's speech appears once more in the complement slot of the clause: 'this very Moses whom they denied...even this man God has sent as both ruler and deliverer'. The presence of the ADP οὗτος, together with the writer's choice of clause structure, has the effect of capturing the reader's attention and bringing the central theme of the Stephen episode to a climax.

The relevance of this theme to the speech, the episode, and the book of Acts seems clear. It is relevant to the speech because by means of the theme of 'rejected by men/chosen by God' as embodied in the lexico-grammar and explicitly stated at key points of the text, the careers of Abraham, Joseph, Moses and Stephen are related and their shared significance explained. It is relevant to the episode as a whole, because in relating Stephen to Abraham, Joseph and Moses, and his persecutors to theirs, the speech is shown to be a reply to the charges brought against him, and the narrative and speech portions are seen to possess both coherence and cohesiveness. Lastly, the theme that we see foregrounded in Acts 7.35 is relevant to the 'big picture' of the Acts of the Apostles, because it clearly reflects what appears to be one of the author's primary concerns, namely, to narrate the sovereign unfolding of the 'plan of God' (βουλὴ τοῦ θεοῦ) in the face of human and demonic opposition.[89] My findings in Acts 6–7 and 27 thus confirm Hopper and Thompson's transitivity hypothesis, namely, that narrative characters who do not initiate events and appear in clauses with a low transitivity coefficient are likely to receive a backgrounded interpretation.[90] In Hallidayan terms, participants who are represented consistently as mediums in non-ergative clauses appear to readers as incapacitated or sidelined vis-à-vis any participants represented as agents in ergative clauses.

Having said this, the two episodes of the Acts narrative I have exam-

---

89. See Squires, *The Plan*.

90. '...the likelihood that a clause will receive a foregrounded interpretation is proportional to the height of that clause on the scale of transitivity. From the performer's viewpoint, the decision to foreground a clause will be reflected in the decision to encode more (rather than fewer) transitivity features in the clause' (Hopper and Thompson, 'Transitivity in Grammar', p. 284).

ined thus far have further interest for two reasons. First, it is the main characters, the veritable heroes of the story, who are being back-grounded through the linguistic means I have described. In the ship-wreck narrative, the highly dynamic 'they' subject (most often the soldiers and sailors on the ship) appears foregrounded in contrast with the more passive 'we' subject and Paul, yet only in order to underline the absolute futility of their actions, as all their efforts to oppose 'what is necessary', that is, what God deems necessary, fail. The message is clear: though seemingly engaged in the bringing about of events, the soldiers and sailors are in fact as overwhelmed by them as the rest of the ship's passengers. In the Stephen episode, the account of the mar-tyr's interrupted career is placed alongside those of Abraham, Joseph and Moses, in order to highlight the feature held in common by the four: an apparent passivity and helplessness in the face of human oppo-sition that is in each case accompanied by God's approval and blessing. Luke's summary of Israelite history, the essence, as I have shown, of Stephen's speech, leaves no doubt concerning God's sovereign will in the Old Testament. The purpose of this historical digest is none other than to remind his readership that the past is intimately connected with the present, and, insofar as the βουλή τοῦ θεοῦ is concerned, though appearances may indicate otherwise, 'the history of Israel has never come to an end, but continues in linear progression into the church'.[91]

4. *Conclusion*

In discussing the major trends in twentieth-century Acts scholarship, and research into the speeches in particular, C.K. Barrett exposes the reductionism to which the well known 'sources' versus 'free composi-tion' debate has often led. Instead of the somewhat doctrinaire and necessarily restricted approaches of Bultmann (whom Barrett proposes as the champion of sources) and Haenchen (whom Barrett considers the champion of free composition), Barrett has issued a timely call for a greater openness to *all relevant methods* in the study of Acts.[92]

Although significant ground has been gained in various types of his-torical study of Acts, the potential insights that modern linguistics offers remain largely unexplored. Functional grammar reminds us that,

91. Jacob Jervell, *The Theology of the Acts of the Apostles* (New Testament Theology; Cambridge: Cambridge University Press, 1996), p. 24.
92. Barrett, *Acts*, p. 16

in interpreting a text, we are primarily involved in a response to language, and this must encompass lexis, as well as syntax and style in the widest sense. Foregrounding theory, especially when understood within the framework of functional grammar, serves as a link between the lexico-grammatical features of a text, and the effects that those features have upon the reader. As such, foregrounding is capable of yielding important clues into the author's agenda in composing the Stephen episode, and thus begins to offer linguistically grounded solutions to such age-old problems as the literary unity of Acts 6–7, or the connection of Stephen's speech to the charges leveled against him.

Chapter 4

LUKE'S SECOND SURVEY OF ISRAEL'S HISTORY (ACTS 13.16B-25): REDACTION AND REGISTER VARIATION

The following pages represent a natural excursus to my discussion of the historical summary in Stephen's speech of Acts 7.2-49. In the process of studying Stephen's speech, I became aware of the fact that the literary function(s) of Luke's summaries of biblical history in Acts 7 and 13, together with the similarities and differences between the two accounts, are a largely unexplored area of study. Correspondence with Joachim Jeska of the University of Münster, Germany confirmed this assessment. Jeska's doctoral thesis,[1] though still at an early stage, may well be the first complete literary study of the two major historical synopses in Acts within the context of early Jewish historical narrative. Continuing with my own functional-grammatical study of Acts, I now turn my attention to the historical survey of Acts 13.16b-25 in order to explore its relationship to that of Acts 7.2-49, the Septuagint passages on which it is based, and its function within Paul's speech at Pisidian Antioch. Further, I will assess the value of the formal category of the 'mission speech', a category to which Paul's Pisidian Antioch oration is often said to belong, and suggest this is in fact a rather blunt tool, in need of linguistically-based refinement along the lines of register analysis. This is a slight aside from the primary subject of this volume, yet one which seems amply justified in light of the inadequate attention this subject has thus far received.

1. Joachim Jeska, 'Lukanische Summarien der Geschichte Israels (Act 7 und 13) im Kontext fruhjüdischer Geschichtssummarien' (PhD dissertation in progress, University of Münster, Germany, 1998).

1. *Acts 7.2-53 and 13.16-25: Two Different Perspectives on Israel's History*

Addressing the question of the purpose of Acts, Jervell argues that the two major surveys of Jewish history in Acts 7 and 13 are Luke's way of reaffirming the fact that the Church *is* Israel.[2] His thesis is well known: the church in the last quarter of the first century was going through a deep identity crisis as Gentiles began to join its ranks in increasing numbers. The poignant question being raised (mainly by Jewish opponents of the church) was 'how can Gentiles be considered the people of God?' This question—argues Jervell—is answered by Luke by showing how in the Church the promises made by God to Israel are fulfilled and salvation is given through Israel's Messiah. Though Jervell's hypothesis is largely overstated in his recent monograph,[3] his non-speculative attempt to ground his proposal concerning the context of Acts in the text of Acts as we have it is commendable. Far from 'sacred history told for its own sake and with no other theme',[4] Jervell argues convincingly that the two surveys of Acts 7 and 13 are carefully crafted reports, designed by Luke to influence his readers' self-understanding at a time of profound identity crisis. Be that as it may, a detailed analysis of the two summaries reveals both similarities and significant differences apparently missed by Jervell.

When one turns to the transitivity choices made by Luke in both synopses, it becomes apparent that, at least at this level, the two surveys are composed from the same perspective, namely, God's.[5] As was the case in Acts 7, Luke's editorial hand altered the LXX text in Acts 13 so as to make God the primary initiator of the processes narrated in Paul's

---

2. Jervell, *The Theology*, p. 24. Concerning the historical survey in Acts 13.16b-25 see also Jervell, 'The Future of the Past', in Witherington III (ed.), *History*, pp. 104-26; Arnold, 'Luke's Characterizing Use', p. 319; David P. Moessner, 'The "Script" of the Scriptures in Acts', in Witherington (ed.), *History*, pp. 233-41; Squires, *The Plan*, p. 70; Soards, *The Speeches*, pp. 80-84; Bruce, *Acts*, pp. 262-70; Barrett, *Acts*, p. 623; Witherington, *Acts*, pp. 406-17.

3. See my review of Jacob Jervell, *The Theology of the Acts of the Apostles* forthcoming (JSNTSup, 69; Sheffield: Sheffield Academic Press, 1998), p. 113.

4. Haenchen, *The Acts of the Apostles*, p. 288.

5. Contra Witherington, who writes that Paul's speech in Acts 13 is a 'more theocentric speech', while Acts 7 is 'more ecclesiocentric' (Witherington, *Acts*, p. 409).

account of Israel's history. Luke's strategy is particularly clear in vv. 19 and 22 and merits some detailed discussion. In Acts 13.19, the words κατεκληρονόμησεν τὴν γῆν αὐτῶν are taken from Josh. 14.1, which states that Eleazar caused them (the sons of Israel) to inherit the land. Following exactly its Hebrew *Vorlage*, the LXX first refers to the sons of Israel and their status as inheritors: 'These are the sons of Israel who inherited (qal stem of נחל in Hebrew) in the land of Canaan...', and then reveals the cause of their inheritance: 'which Eleazar caused them to inherit' (piel stem of נחל with a causative sense in Hebrew). For Luke, the final cause of all that happens to τοῦ λαοῦ τούτου Ἰσραὴλ is none other than God himself, and Josh. 14.1b thus provides him with the ideal wording to express his high view of divine sovereignty. Secondly, v. 22 is likewise the product of Luke's purposeful reworking of two or more LXX passages, shaped so as to cohere with the larger transitivity pattern evident in this second historical survey. As I will show below, the survey of Israelite history in Acts 13.16-25 pays particular attention to David's reign, a period of perceived spiritual and political splendor in the life of the nation. It is this focus which, among other features, gives this passage, in contrast to its counterpart in Acts 7, its positive, hopeful flavor. In painting his unique picture of David, Luke forces the reader to see the king from God's perspective alone, for it is God who, having deposed Saul, raised David up for them; it is God who affirms of David that 'he is a man after *my* heart (LXX of 1 Sam. 13.14 has *his* heart)', and who ποιήσει πάντα τὰ θελήματά μου ('shall carry out all my wishes'). For the latter clause Luke has turned not to 1 Samuel but to Isa. 44.28, and not to an account of David but of Cyrus the Persian. The context of the Isaiah quotation (esp. 44.4-13) is the complete authority and power of יהוה over the gods of the nations and their rulers. The conclusion of God's election and call of Cyrus is that אני יהוה עשׂה כל־אלה, 'I the Lord do all these things' (45.7). Thus, though the clause in Acts 13.22b has David as the agent of an ergative clause, its Old Testament context, together with the complement 'all my wishes' serves to underline not David's power and initiative, but rather God's. As Steyn has noted, the chronological jump from David to Jesus in this account of biblical history is indicative of Jesus' complete submission to God, a submission that mirrors David's own as depicted by Luke.[6]

6.   Gert J. Steyn, *Septuagint Quotations in the Context of the Petrine and Pauline Speeches of the Acta Apostolorum* (Contributions to Biblical Exegesis and

The structure of the clauses in this passage is according to expectation. As is the case in the other episodes of Acts I examine (i.e. chs. 1, 2, 6–7, 21–22, and 27), Pred.–Comp. and Pred. clauses clearly predominate, and Comp. initial clauses are the most rare. In Acts 13.16-25, the single instance of a complement initial independent clause is found in 13.17b τὸν λαὸν ὕψωσεν, 'the people he exalted'. As is the case in the other Acts episodes I discuss, complements in the initial position of the clause draw attention to the patient status of individuals acted upon in various ways by God. This attention-drawing effect is achieved *both* by the unusualness of the complement-initial clause and by its relation to the other transitivity choices (particularly those of agent) made throughout the episode.

Yet, all the above notwithstanding, the two summaries of Acts 7 and 13 are also different in fundamental ways.[7] Consistent with the notion that Luke was both a historian and a skilled narrator is the view that what we find in Acts 13 is not merely an abbreviated form of the historical survey of Acts 7,[8] but rather a separate synopsis which complements the previous one and fits within its own literary context. While Acts 7 covers in some detail the careers of Abraham, Joseph and, particularly, Moses, mentioning David and Solomon only in connection with the planning and building of the temple, Acts 13 does the opposite, that is, it surveys briefly the desert experience without mentioning proper names, and concentrates instead on the monarchy, mentioning Samuel as the last of the judges, Saul, and, finally, David (vv. 22-23), who serves as bridge to the concluding christological section. Further, as Squires has noted,[9] the element of human opposition, so strong in the survey of ch. 7, is absent from the historical section of Paul's speech in ch. 13, and mentioned only at the end, in connection with the death of Jesus. These compositional differences between the two accounts are understandable in light of the very different settings in which the two

Theology, 12; Kampen: Kok), p. 165.

7. Though using arguments different from my own, Klijn affirms emphatically that 'the way in which Stephen interprets Jewish history is wholly different from what is to be found in the rest of Acts' ('Stephen's Speech', p. 27).

8. On this point, see Squires, *The Plan*, p. 70, who refutes Schubert and Vielhauer's thesis that the survey of Acts 13 is essentially a summary of its Acts 7 counterpart.

9. Squires, *The Plan*, p. 70.

speeches are given.[10] In the first instance, the aim of Stephen's speech is largely 'defense by attack', and, therefore, its focal point is the account of Israel's rejection of Moses in the desert, one of the lowest points in Israel's history in terms of its adherence to the covenant. In Paul's speech, however, the aim is evangelistic and, consequently, in his version of biblical history, the emphasis is on a far more virtuous epoch of the nation's life, the reign of David, from whom Jesus is seen to descend.

2. *Acts 13.16b-41: A 'Mission Speech'?*

In his recent work *The Paul of Acts*, Porter issues a much needed call for a more context-sensitive analysis of the speeches in Acts than has heretofore been attempted.[11] This call is the result of Porter's awareness that the discussion of the purpose(s) of these speeches is often too generic to be truly useful (i.e. is their purpose within the Acts narrative stylistic, historiographical or theological?). The form-critical category of 'mission speech', under which Paul's speeches in Acts 13, 14 and 17 are often placed,[12] however, suffers from similar limitations. The discussion of 'mission speeches' in Acts by Edward Schweizer is illustrative of this problem.[13] Schweizer begins his study by referring to the long-standing scholarly opinion that the speeches in Acts are Lukan compositions. Being in agreement with this thesis, Schweizer's aim is to provide further support for it by means of an 'analysis of the speeches which contain the missionary proclamation of the apostles to Jews and Gentiles'.[14] Yet, among all these speeches, Schweizer finds Paul's speech at Pisidian Antioch 'far more complicated' than the rest, as it contains 'a sort of parallel' to Stephen's speech and a unique

10. Contra Haenchen, for whom, the differences between the two surveys are the result of Luke's desire to avoid repetition. Haenchen, *The Acts of the Apostles*, p. 415.

11. Porter, *The Paul of Acts*, ch.6.

12. Porter, *The Paul of Acts*, ch. 6. See also Edward Schweizer, 'Concerning the Speeches in Acts', in L. Keck and J. Martyn (eds.), *Studies in Luke–Acts* (London: SPCK, 1978), pp. 208-16; Robert F. O'Toole, 'Acts 2:30 and the Davidic Covenant of Pentecost', *JBL* 102.2 (1983), pp. 245-58 (253); Sanders, *The Jews in Luke–Acts*, p. 54; Powell, *What are they Saying*, p. 30; Steyn, *Septuagint Quotations*, pp. 162-63.

13. Schweizer, 'Concerning the Speeches', esp. pp. 210-14.

14. Schweizer, 'Concerning the Speeches', p. 208.

indictment of the Jerusalemite Jews. Further, Schweizer places Paul's addresses to Gentile audiences in Acts 14 and 17 under a separate heading, but retains for them the category of 'mission speech', affirming of these two and all the rest that they share the same basic structure. It seems clear in light of this and similar analyses that the category in question is in need of refinement. First, although, by its very name, the category of 'mission speech' makes reference to the purpose of the oration, that is, these are speeches aimed at winning an audience over to the Christian gospel, the inability of this category to discriminate between speeches addressed to audiences as diverse as a Jewish and God-fearer synagogue audience (Acts 13) and a Gentile Athenian crowd (Acts 17) makes the category of 'mission speech' a very blunt tool indeed. In his psycholinguistic analysis of the Stephen episode, Jacques Steyn addresses the important issue of audience design in a narrative which contains speeches:

> There are actually two kinds of Audience Design in the passage. Firstly, the author designed his text for some specific readers. Secondly, the author reconstructed a design from Stephen's point of view. Because Stephen has a specific audience his speech has a different Audience Design from the rest of the book of Acts.[15]

The same is true of every speech in Acts. Secondly, and directly related to the above, the argumentation of a speech will almost always vary from one audience to another. To wit, while at Pisidian Antioch Paul uses biblical history as the basis of his speech to Jews and God-fearers (Acts 13), when facing purely Gentile audiences in Lystra and Athens (Acts 14 and 17) he bases his arguments on a natural theology easily understandable by his listeners. This important difference, along with other more subtle features I will discuss below, is swept aside by

15. Steyn, 'Some Psycholinguistic Factors', p. 62. In contrast to those who use the 'mission speech' category, Bruce took full account of audience design in the speeches of Acts (though he does not come to the discussion from Steyn's psycholinguistic angle). See F.F. Bruce, 'The Significance of the Speeches for Interpreting Acts', *Southwestern Journal of Theology* 33 (1990), pp. 20-28, where he groups the speeches on the basis of both speaker and audience: Paul's Preaching to Jews and God-fearers ('it conforms to well-attested patterns for synagogue sermons'), Paul's Preaching to Pagans ('more praeparatio evangelica than direct gospel'), etc. Schweizer likewise places speeches to Gentile audiences under a separate heading, but refers to them as 'missionary speeches' nonetheless. See Schweizer, 'Concerning the Speeches', p. 214.

those intent on seeing 'a far reaching identity of structure' in all the so-
called mission speeches of Acts.[16]

In chapter 1, I discussed at some length the Hallidayan notion of
register, defined within the framework of functional grammar as a language variety according to use. As Porter and Reed have done in their
respective recent works,[17] I will argue that the Hallidayan notion of
register[18] possesses the necessary linguistic basis, functional orientation
and flexibility to shed light on the subject of my present inquiry: the
nature and functional significance of those features of language that
make Luke's second historical survey a unique narrative. Through the
remainder of this excursus, I will explore the different ways in which
biblical history is brought to bear upon Stephen's and Paul's audiences
in Acts 7 and 13 respectively. Further, I will show that the interpersonal
function is central to this Lukan rhetorical/literary strategy and essential
to understanding register variation from the first historical summary to
the second.

3. *The Rhetoric of Historical Surveys: Interpersonal Links between Past and Present*

In 'The Future of the Past', Jervell puts forth yet another discussion of
Luke's purpose in Acts and concludes that Luke is above all else a
'pragmatic historian' in the tradition of Thucydides and Polybius.[19]
Biblical/salvation history, the only history there is for Luke, argues
Jervell, is his subject matter, and when he narrates the events of the
birth and early development of the Church, Luke does so consciously as
one who is writing but a new chapter in the history of God's unfolding
plan. Although historical summaries are common in both the Old

16. Schweizer, 'Concerning the Speeches', p. 210.

17. Porter, 'Dialect and Register', and 'Register'; Jeffrey T. Reed, *A Discourse Analysis of Philippians: Method and Rhetoric in the Debate over Literary Integrity* (JSNTSup, 136; Sheffield: Sheffield Academic Press, 1997).

18. The concept is at least as old as Rousseau's 'Essay on the Origin of Lan-guages', published post-humously in 1781. As I mentioned in Chapter 1, the term was coined by T.B.W. Reid in 1956, and has been widely used within sociolinguis-tics since then. However, Porter, Reed, and I have focused primarily on Halliday's utilization of register theory within the framework of his functional grammar, an approach to the subject that seems particularly well-suited to the study of New Testament Greek.

19. Jervell, 'The Future', p. 113.

Testament and early Jewish literature, Luke's two summaries are different, insofar as their design is ultimately paraenetic, writes Jervell. Luke's concern is to show his audience how Israel's history relates to their experience, and how it has contemporary relevance and meaning.[20] To this end,

> The criteria employed were of an aesthetic character, namely, what affected the mind of the reader pleasantly... The criterion is once more the reader: he or she, through the reading, should become a spectator and be engaged in the occurrences told.[21]

Although I am in fundamental agreement with Jervell on this point, it appears to me that the linguistic means which Luke has used to connect his different audience(s)[22] to the individuals and events of biblical history have been overlooked by Jervell and others. In their respective speeches, Stephen and Paul make it clear to their audiences that the events of biblical history they have narrated, though in rather different ways in each case, have very much to do with them. There is, however, an important key to understanding Luke's means of achieving this effect that goes beyond the interpretation of the paraenetic sections at the end of each speech. I am referring to the use of first and second person plural pronouns throughout both Stephen's and Paul's orations. A careful study of the use of these personal and possessive pronouns in Acts 7 and 13 reveals the very different roles that Stephen and Paul adopt vis-à-vis their audiences throughout their respective speeches. Luke demonstrates that the use of pronouns is an effective means of establishing a vinculum or nexus between an audience and the historical events and people being recounted. In Acts 7, Stephen weaves in and out of Old Testament history to include himself and his audience by means of first and second person plural pronouns (see below). This connection is then masterfully exploited in vv. 51-53 as Stephen's audience suddenly finds itself associated with individuals and events of a most malevolent nature. Stephen concludes his oration by underlining

20. Jervell, 'The Future', p. 116.
21. Jervell, 'The Future', p. 122.
22. I am referring, as above, to the issue of audience design. Two audiences are involved here: Stephen's and Paul's audiences in Acts 7 and 13 respectively, and the audience/readership of Acts. It is the former that I will be primarily concerned with, as any theory about Luke's own literary/rhetorical strategy can only be based upon Luke's composition of Stephen's and Paul's speeches and the events that surrounded them.

this connection in no uncertain terms, thus moving from the apparent role of an instructor or teacher to that of an accuser, with devastating rhetorical effect. In Acts 13, however, Paul's strategy is different at several points. Like Stephen, Paul begins his speech with an historical summary and reference to its protagonists as 'our fathers'. Unlike Stephen, Paul completes his historical summary (vv. 17-25) exclusively in the third person, thus leaving intact the sensation of distance inherent in the narration of events of the far-off past. Direct engagement with the audience is picked up again at v. 26 by means of the second person plural pronoun ἡμῖν, and throughout the remainder of the speech Paul drives home the message that it is his listeners who are in fact the intended beneficiaries of the promises God made to the historical Israel. The prominence of the choices of first and second (in vv. 27-30 'they' refers to the Jerusalemite Jewish leaders, and is contrasted with 'you' and 'us') person plural in vv. 26-38 is an important indicator of the overall thrust of the speech, and of the irenic teacher–evangelist role adopted by Paul. A detailed look at the use of these pronouns in both speeches will further bear up this interpretation.

Acts 7.2-53: Stephen addresses Jewish leaders in Jerusalem

- ἄνδρες ἀδελφοὶ καὶ πατέρες, ἀκούσατε· (v. 2)
- πατρὶ ἡμῶν Ἀβραὰμ (v. 2)
- τὴν γῆν ταύτην εἰς ἣν ὑμεῖς νῦν κατοικεῖτε (v. 4)
- οὐχ ηὕρισκον χορτάσματα οἱ πατέρες ἡμῶν (v. 11)
- ἐξαπέστειλεν τοὺς πατέρας ἡμῶν (v. 12)
- ἐτελεύτησεν αὐτὸς καὶ οἱ πατέρες ἡμῶν (v. 15)
- οὗτος κατασοφισάμενος τὸ γένος ἡμῶν (v. 19)
- μετὰ τοῦ ἀγγέλου…καὶ τῶν πατέρων ἡμῶν (v. 38)
- ὃς ἐδέξατο λόγια ζῶντα δοῦναι ἡμῖν (v. 38b)
- ᾧ οὐκ ἠθέλησαν ὑπήκοοι γενέσθαι οἱ πατέρες ἡμῶν (v. 39)
- Ἡ σκηνὴ τοῦ μαρτυρίου ἦν τοῖς πατράσιν ἡμῶν (v. 44)
- ἣν καὶ εἰσήγαγον διαδεξάμενοι οἱ πατέρες ἡμῶν (v. 45)
- ὧν ἔξωσεν ὁ θεὸς ἀπὸ προσώπου τῶν πατέρων ἡμῶν (v. 45b)

The Invective
- ὑμεῖς ἀεὶ τῷ πνεύματι τῷ ἁγίῳ ἀντιπίπτετε, ὡς οἱ πατέρες ὑμῶν καὶ ὑμεῖς (v. 51)
- τίνα τῶν προφητῶν οὐκ ἐδίωξαν οἱ πατέρες ὑμῶν… (v. 52)

- [...τοῦ δικαίου οὗ νῦν <u>ὑμεῖς</u> προδόται καὶ φονεῖς ἐγένε<u>σθε</u> (v. 52b)
- οἵτινες ἐλά<u>βετε</u> τὸν νόμον εἰς διαταγὰς ἀγγέλων, καὶ οὐκ ἐφυλά<u>ξατε</u> (v. 53)

Acts 13.16b-41—Paul Addresses Jews and God-fearers in Pisidian Antioch

- ἄνδρες Ἰσραηλῖται καὶ οἱ φοβούμενοι τὸν θεόν, ἀκού<u>σατε</u> (v. 16b)
- ἐξελέξατο τοὺς πατέρας <u>ἡμῶν</u> (v. 17)

17b-25: Third Person Historical Narrative
- ἄνδρες ἀδελφοί, υἱοὶ γένους Ἀβραὰμ καὶ οἱ ἐν <u>ὑμῖν</u> φοβούμενοι τὸν θεόν (v. 26)
- <u>ἡμῖν</u> ὁ λόγος τῆς σωτηρίας ταύτης ἐξαπεστάλη (v. 26b)
- καὶ <u>ἡμεῖς ὑμᾶς</u> εὐαγγελιζόμεθα τὴν πρὸς τοὺς πατέρας ἐπαγγελίαν (v. 32)
- ὅτι ταύτην ὁ θεὸς ἐκπεπλήρωκεν τοῖς τέκνοις [αὐτῶν] <u>ἡμῖν</u> (v. 33)
- γνωστὸν οὖν ἔστω <u>ὑμῖν</u>, ἄνδρες ἀδελφοί, ὅτι διὰ τούτου <u>ὑμῖν</u> ἄφεσις ἁμαρτιῶν καταγγέλλεται (v. 38)

The use of historical summaries for didactic purposes is a fairly common feature of Jewish literature (see, e.g., Deut. 29; Ps. 105 and so on). What is particularly striking about Stephen's speech is the rather abrupt shift from first-person to second-person plural (i.e. from 'our fathers' to 'your fathers') at v. 51, and the accusatory invective with which the oration concludes. This sudden shift is found puzzling by Klijn, who argues that the only possible solution to this issue is to posit two separate groups of fathers.[23] Such a 'solution', however, is unnecessary if we understand the shift in person to be a rhetorical device aimed at suddenly creating distance between speaker and audience at a strategic juncture of the speech, as Stephen takes on the role of accuser. Thus, while the group of Israelites who both 'denied' and refused to obey Moses and the law is referred to as '*our fathers*' in v. 39, in the invective of vv. 51-53 rebellion and disobedience are ascribed exclu-

---

23. 'Stephen's Speech', p. 27. Facing the same apparent dilemma, Grundmann opted for a two source hypothesis. Cited in Klijn, 'Stephen's Speech', p. 27.

sively to 'your fathers' and 'you', with the added emphasis of the explicit subject: even you yourselves always resist the Holy Spirit! As your fathers did, so you do!

By contrast, as we have seen, Paul in Acts 13 chooses the third person narrative style for the historical summary, and then spends the remainder of his speech stressing to his audience that those past events have very much to do with them. The prominence of pronouns in this final section is striking and merits more detailed discussion.[24] After repeating his now slightly altered formula of address (brethren, sons of Abraham, and those among you who fear God, v. 26) Paul asserts that ἡμῖν ὁ λόγος τῆς σωτηρίας ταύτης ἐξαπεστάλη, '*to us* has been sent this word of salvation' (v. 26b). This complement-initial clause draws attention to the beneficiaries of the promise, who will be the focus throughout Paul's concluding words. By contrast, Paul continues, those who live in Jerusalem and their rulers, having disregarded this [man] (τοῦτον),[25] together with the words of the prophets...*they* asked Pilate to have him executed, thus fulfilling all that was written about him. But God raised him from the dead.[26] Being witnesses of this fact, Paul proceeds, καὶ ἡμεῖς ὑμᾶς εὐαγγελιζόμεθα τὴν πρὸς τοὺς πατέρας ἐπαγγελίαν γενομένην, 'even *we ourselves* announce to *you* the promise which was given to the fathers' (v. 32), 'for God has fulfilled this promise to their sons, even *us*...' (v. 33). Thus, γνωστὸν οὖν ἔστω ὑμῖν, ἄνδρες ἀδελφοί, ὅτι διὰ τούτου ὑμῖν ἄφεσις ἁμαρτιῶν καταγγέλλεται, 'let it be known to *you*, brethren, that on this account to *you* [note again the complement initial position of the pronoun] forgiveness of sins is proclaimed' (v. 38). These verses make it clear that, as far as the promises of God 'to the fathers' is concerned, 'we' and 'you' are one and the same group of people. By contrast, the Jerusalemite Jewish leadership ('they') has, by its own rejection of Jesus, placed itself

24. See Witherington, *Acts*, p. 407.

25. The referent of the demonstrative τοῦτον here is not completely clear, and another possible option is: having ignored this (namely, that the promise is for us), together with the oracles of the prophets which are read every Sabbath, they fulfilled them in condemning [him], and having found no reason for capital punishment, they asked Pilate for him to be executed (vv. 27-28). See Sanders, *The Jews in Luke–Acts*, p. 354 n. 93, who agrees with this reading.

26. Compare this to Peter's formula to his Jerusalem audiences in Acts 2.23-24: 'This man...you killed, whom God raised'; 2.36: 'God made him both Lord and Christ, this Jesus whom you crucified'; 3.10 'Jesus Christ the Nazarene, whom you crucified, whom God raised...'.

outside of the household of those who inherit the promise.

Very little has been written concerning the use of person deixis and the rhetorical implications of the presence or absence of pronouns in Acts.[27] One writer who has dealt with the subject, albeit briefly and without much linguistic or literary support, is Jack T. Sanders,[28] and his passing comments on person reference in Acts 7 and 13, among other passages, merit a response. Sanders's thesis concerning the alleged antisemitism of Luke–Acts is well known, and I will not attempt to add to the rebuttals carried out (I think successfully) by others.[29] That overarching thesis is an essential framework, however, for understanding Sanders's comments regarding Luke's use of personal reference in Acts 7 and 13. For Sanders, Luke is above all else interested in showing the irredeemable guilt of the Jews, who systematically reject the gospel and persecute its messengers. One of the primary ways in which Luke achieves this desired effect, argues Sanders,[30] is the insertion or deletion of a subject. Occasionally, Luke inserts a subject, but most often he omits a subject or other personal reference, by which 'he wants to imply that "the Jews" are guilty of something but does not quite want to say it'.[31] Concerning the insertion of subjects or other personal references, Sanders is, at least partly, on the right track. That is, where a pronoun such as 'you' is either formally unnecessary (e.g. it is a 'redundant' or explicit subject) or unexpected (e.g. it was missing in a

27. See Porter's comments in regard to person in Mark's Gospel: 'Register', p. 22. See also Halliday's discussion of person in *Introduction to Functional Grammar*, p. 98. The latter is one of Halliday's frequent analyses of text produced by his son, Nigel. Person switching from third to first is seen to reorient the discourse, and 'the ongoing selection of subjects by a speaker…does give a characteristic flavour' to that discourse. Hasan, in 'Linguistics', esp. pp. 11-121, provides a provocative analysis of pronominals in Angus Wilson's *Necessity's Child*, concluding that the juxtaposition of first and third person pronominals establishes a 'definite patern of exclusion', and serves to underline the 'undesirability' or 'otherness' of the child protagonist, Rodney.

28. Sanders, *The Jews in Luke–Acts*, pp. 49, 51, 79.

29. See, for a recent example, Witherington's response to Sanders in Witherington, *Acts*, pp. 839-40. For a view exactly opposite to Sanders', that is, that Judaism is almost always portrayed in a positive light by Luke, see Jervell, *The Theology*, passim. Both Sanders and Jervell have significantly overstated their respective theses, it would appear.

30. Sanders, *The Jews in Luke–Acts*, p. 51, referring to Acts 4.11: 'the stone that was considered of no account by YOU the builders'.

31. Sanders, *The Jews in Luke–Acts*, p. 79.

LXX passage being cited), then a stylistic or rhetorical explanation may be put forth (though this explanation may not necessarily coincide with Sanders'). In the second case, however, Sanders is essentially arguing from silence, and works on the basis of the assumption that, when Luke uses third person plural subjects or seems to omit an explicit personal reference, he is intending to refer to *all Jews everywhere*.[32] Sanders argues in this manner even in passages where the intended referents of pronouns are made clear in other ways. His brief discussion of Paul's speech in Acts 13 is a case in point. Addressing specifically the manner in which Paul concludes his speech, Sanders writes as though Paul's audience is, for all practical purposes, exclusively Jewish, and assumes again that the 'they' of v. 42 refers to 'the Jews':

> One might expect that the Lucan Paul would move from [the 13:27-29] accusation to an appeal: 'Please, Antiochene Jews, do not follow the footsteps of your Palestinian relatives and join in the condemnation of Jesus...' Instead...the choice before the Lucan Jews in Antioch of Pisidia...is whether to behave like Jews or to show good sense and be converted.[33]

According to Sanders's exegesis of the entire speech, the Lukan Paul phrases his 'appeal' to his audience in such a way that the conversion of the Jews will actually be prevented.[34] Thus, Sanders's assumptions prevent him from recognizing the inclusive sense of 'we' in v. 26, and the rhetorical significance of the interplay in personal reference throughout the speech, and especially in vv. 26-41. Lastly, Sanders fails to recognize the importance of the God-fearing contingent in Paul's audience, a group the historicity of which he questions elsewhere.[35] God-fearers,

---

32. See Sanders, *The Jews in Luke–Acts*, p. 73, concerning Stephen's audience in Acts 7. Sanders admits that Stephen is being tried by the Sanhedrin, yet goes on to argue: 'you who received the Law in angelic ordinances and did not keep it', spoken with all the Jewish people in mind [!], is followed immediately by all those subjectless third-person verbs that describe his martyrdom...what is the reader to think?' See, along the same lines, pp. 79, 51.

33. Sanders, *The Jews in Luke–Acts*, p. 261.

34. Sanders, *The Jews in Luke–Acts*, p. 262.

35. Sanders, *The Jews in Luke–Act*, p. 137. But see Irina Levinskaya, *Diaspora Setting* (A1CS, 5; Grand Rapids: Eerdmans; Carlisle: Paternoster Press, 1996), pp. 51-126. Levinskaya concludes: 'it is no surprise that God-fearers were such an important issue for Luke, the historian. They could be (and actually were) either the backbone of the Gentile Christian communities or the greatest impediment to the spread of the Christian mission. Which way they chose to adopt depended upon the

however, surely carried significant weight at the time of audience design in the composition of this speech. As Levinskaya has shown, this was a group fought over by both Jews and Christians, as they often represented a crucial hinge between the synagogue and Graeco-Roman society.[36] The fact that many God-fearers were often merely sympathetic to Judaism, and had little if any knowledge of the Scriptures of Israel,[37] represents a possible explanation of Paul's omission of first and second person pronouns throughout all but the first sentence of his historical summary. The strong presence of God-fearers in the audience may also explain Paul's emphatic affirmation that the promises made to Israel by 'the fathers' are in fact meant for 'you', an emphasis hardly necessary when addressing a purely Jewish audience.

I wish to argue, therefore, that the positioning, omission or insertion of personal deictic markers (especially personal pronouns) within the clause is central to the very different rhetorical strategies inherent in Stephen's and Paul's utilization of historical summaries within their respective speeches. These specific choices made by Luke from the network of person, are a fundamental element of the interpersonal function of language,[38] which is in turn, according to Halliday's functional grammar, determined by the situational element of tenor, or 'who is taking part' (see my chart of the situational elements and metafunctions in Chapter 1). The tenor of discourse together with the other situational elements of field ('what is going on') and mode (the role of language in the situation), are determinants of register, that is, a situation-specific language variety.

---

reaction of Jewish communities to Christian propaganda' (p. 126).

36. See Levinskaya, *Diaspora Setting*, pp. 51-136. Jewish attempts to secure the allegiance of high status God-fearers was not, however, part of a larger Jewish missionary endeavor. See Levinskaya, *Diaspora Setting,* pp. 19-49, where the author examines both Jewish and Christian evidence and concludes (contra Sandmel and others) that first-century Judaism was not a missionary religion.

37. See esp. Levinskaya's discussion of the Aphrodisias inscription, *Disapora Setting*, pp. 78-79. Dated c. 212 CE, this two-faced marble block was probably the door frame of a synagogue, and contains on its b-face 52 names preceded by the heading: *kai hosoi theosebis*, 'and as many as [are] God-fearers', of which several were also Aphrodisian city councillors. This and other inscriptional evidence, argues Leviskaya, confirms Luke's presentation of the God-fearers as an extremely significant group of Gentiles on the fringe of the Jewish faith.

38. See Halliday, *Introduction to Functional Grammar*, pp. 68-100.

In his recent essay on register,[39] Porter addresses the issue of where, within Halliday's functional grammar, rhetorical analysis might fit. Although Halliday seems to place rhetoric within the textual function of language, Porter suggests that, insofar as it concerns participant relations, rhetoric is perhaps better subsumed under the interpersonal function. The problem arises from the fact that Halliday is simply not sufficiently explicit about this issue, often arguing simply that his functional grammar as a whole has a fundamental rhetorical orientation,[40] in contrast to the logical emphasis of the transformational approach. Porter's point, however, is well argued, and my discussion of person deixis in the present chapter lends support to his view. My comparative analysis of Luke's two historical summaries shows that the shift in person in both speeches is directly related to both the exploitation of distance between speaker and audience and the change in speaker roles vis-à-vis each audience. This fact notwithstanding, my discussion of other Acts episodes throughout this thesis shows that rhetorical analysis must also extend to the textual function of language.[41] A further issue raised by Porter also bears upon my present discussion. In conclusion to his treatment of tenor in Mark's gospel, Porter expresses confidence in the benefits of sociolinguistic analysis of the sort practiced by Halliday, for 'at least the rudiments exist of a framework of criteria to evaluate the reconstruction of the context of situation'.[42] As I expressed in Chapter 1, this is one of the features of functional grammar which holds great potential for the linguistic study of the New Testament. The real potential for recovering something of the 'rhetorical exigence' (see Chapter 1 on this) of the various New Testament texts varies from, for

39. Porter, 'Dialect and Register'.

40. Halliday, *Introduction to Functional Grammar*, p. xxviii.

41. As my main title indicates, the subject of this book is Luke's transitivity-based foregrounding scheme in several key Acts episodes. In Chapter 1 (see n. 86) I argued that the phenomenon of foregrounding, regardless of the linguistic items through which it is manifested, is a consistent feature throughout a text, contributes to its overall 'texture', and thus belongs to the textual function of language.

42. Porter, 'Dialect and Register'. Porter phrases this somewhat more conservatively than Halliday, Hasan and others have done (see my discussion in Chapter 1 where I make reference to the alleged potentially 'predictive element' of the functional grammatical analysis of texts). In light of the limitations faced by all analysts of 2000+ year old texts, Porter's is a realistic assessment of the potential of functional grammar as *a useful aid* in recovering something of the context on the basis of the text.

example, the Gospels (possibly the least potential, though see Porter's analysis[43]) to the Pauline epistles and some of the speeches in Acts, where valuable information about the context of situation is often made explicit by the author. In all instances, however, a careful, systematic deployment of functional grammar will yield essential information regarding the specific functional orientation of the text, that is, regarding its register(s). Such linguistic information is, therefore, a necessary basis for any theory purporting to explain the context of situation of a New Testament text.

Analyses such as my present study, or Porter's discussion of register in Mark's Gospel, are significant both for New Testament and general linguistic research. Concerning the latter, Butler, Berry and others have expressed concern that Halliday's register theory, and, in particular, the matter of the determining relationship between situational elements and metafunctions, is a rather complex construct based on insufficient data.[44] Since that criticism was issued in Butler's volume, successful applications of Halliday's model to many types of texts and languages have been many and varied, as was evidenced in the 1996 compendium *Functional Descriptions: Theory in Practice.*[45] The cumulative result of all these studies cannot be ignored.

---

43. Porter, 'Register', esp. pp. 18-25.

44. See the chapter entitled 'Systemic Functional Grammar: A Critical Appraisal', in Butler, *Systemic Linguistics*.

45. R. Hasan, C. Cloran and D. Butt (eds.), *Functional Descriptions: Theory in Practice* (Amsterdam: John Benjamins, 1996).

Chapter 5

FOREGROUNDING SCHEME AND RHETORICAL STRATEGY IN THE
EPISODE OF PAUL'S ARREST AND DEFENSE (ACTS 21–22)

In his incisive essay entitled 'The Value of Acts as a Source for the Study of Paul',[1] A.J. Mattill has discerned four major ways in which twentieth-century Luke–Acts scholars have assessed Luke's portrayal of St Paul. From the conservative approaches of Bruce and Gasque ('School of Historical Research') to the rather speculative analyses of Zeller and Haenchen ('School of Creative Edification'), one's assessment of the 'we' sections of Acts is shown by Mattill to be determinative of one's conclusions regarding the plausibility and historicity of the Lukan Paul.[2] The author shows that the bulk of the scholarly work he has examined represents the various attempts made to answer questions of a primarily historical and source-critical nature.

As is the case with other areas of Luke–Acts study, more recent analyses of the Lukan Paul have begun to steer away from a mainly historical emphasis to a literary one. John C. Lentz's 1993 monograph *Luke's Portrait of Paul* is an example of this trend.[3] Though Lentz sets out to show that Luke's Paul (especially his double Pharisaic *and* Roman identity) is an unhistorical literary creation of the author of Acts, he

1. Mattill, 'The Value of Acts', pp. 77-98.

2. See Mattill, 'The Value of Acts', p. 97. See also Vielhauer, 'On the Paulinism of Acts', pp. 33-48; Edwin R. Goodenough, 'The Perspective of Acts', pp. 50-55; C.F.D. Moule 'The Christology of Acts', p. 173, all in Keck and Martyn (eds.), *Studies in Luke–Acts*. Vielhauer and Goodenough argue against the historicity of the Lukan Paul and his theology, while Moule writes: '…it needs to be remembered that it is a priori likely that there should be differences between a speaker's initial presentation of the gospel to a non-Christian audience [i.e. Paul's speeches in Acts], and the same speaker's address to those who have already become Christians [i.e. the Pauline epistles]' (p. 173).

3. John C. Lentz, *Luke's Portrait of Paul* (SNTMS, 77; Cambridge: Cambridge University Press, 1993).

places significant emphasis on 'the more subtle literary techniques that Luke used to highlight Paul's authority and control'.[4] For Lentz, these techniques boil down to the consistent highlighting of Paul's *persona* as an authoritative and virtuous Roman citizen, a device characteristic of judicial Graeco-Roman rhetoric. Following Neyrey, Lentz sees the entire speech of Acts 22 as a forensic defense speech, the structure of which is laid out by Quintilian in his *Institutio Oratoria*.[5]

Continuing with the methodological approach I have defined in previous chapters, the present chapter is a linguistically-based analysis

---

4.   Lentz, *Luke's Portrait*, p. 3.

5.   See Jerome H. Neyrey, 'The Forensic Defense Speech and Paul's Trial Speeches in Acts 22–26: Form and Function', in Charles Talbert (ed.), *Luke–Acts: New Perspectives from the SBL Seminar* (New York: Crossroad, 1984), pp. 210-24. In this essay, Neyrey affirms that 'knowledge of [Graeco-Roman] forensic speeches is indispensable for understanding Acts' (p. 220). Twelve years later, Neyrey's dogmatic affirmation is repeated in Bruce J. Malina and Jerome H. Neyrey, *Portraits of Paul* (Louisville: John Knox Press, 1996), p. 91. The most influential presentation of this view in recent years was offered by George Kennedy in *Rhetorical Criticism*, pp. 134-38. See also, following Kennedy, Soards, *The Speeches*, p. 111. In another work, 'Luke's Social Location of Paul: Cultural Anthropology and the Status of Paul in Acts', in Witherington (ed.), *History*, pp. 251-79, Neyrey moves away from a strict dependence on the rhetorical manuals of antiquity, and turns his attention to a method of analysis gleaned from sociology and anthropology. Neyrey's use of the terms 'rhetoric' and 'rhetorical' seems to have widened in this work. See 'Luke's Social Location'. Robert L. Brawley has provided a well-balanced analysis of these speeches in his essay 'Paul in Acts: Lucan Apology and Conciliation', in Talbert (ed.), *New Perspectives*, pp. 129-47, where he compares literary techniques of legitimation in Acts and various ancient writings (both Hellenistic and non-Hellenistic), concluding that these devices were widespread in ancient literature both Jewish and Graeco-Roman, and one cannot, therefore, demonstrate direct literary borrowing; indeed, 'no one category is sufficient to encompass Luke's efforts to authenticate Paul. Luke uses whatever means he considers appropriate' (p. 135). Similarly, Jacob Jervell has seen 'a pattern' in two of the speeches, namely Acts 22 and 26, but stops short of recognizing a unified composition or structure. See Jervell's chapter 'Paul: The Teacher of Israel, The Apologetic Speeches of Paul in Acts', in Jervell, *Luke and the People of God* (Minneapolis: Augsburg, 1972), pp. 153-83, and for a slight revision of the same thesis, *idem*, *The Theology*, pp. 82-95. Similarly, see Fred Veltman, 'The Defense Speeches of Paul in Acts', in Talbert (ed.), *New Perspectives*, pp. 243-59. See also the essays in the section entitled 'Rhetoric and Questions of Method' in Porter and Olbricht (eds.), *Rhetoric and the New Testament*, where various noted experts in the field of rhetorical criticism argue for methodological expansion in this discipline.

of Luke's portrayal of Paul in the arrest and defense episode of Acts 21.27–22.29, with a view to examining how that portrayal reveals Luke's own interests as a writer, and, ultimately, his overall literary/ rhetorical strategy. I shall first evaluate Neyrey's and Lentz's thesis that the speech is modeled after Roman forensic oratory, and focuses, there-fore, on the *persona* of Paul. Secondly, I will proceed to investigate clause structure, together with Luke's choices in the transitivity network of Greek, as indicators of linguistic foregrounding in this important episode of Acts. I will attempt to further support my claim that Halliday's functional grammar is a method of textual analysis capable of accounting for foregrounding strategies in literary texts, thus yielding significant insights into Luke's literary/rhetorical agenda.

1. *Acts 22.1-21: A Forensic Defense Speech?*

Jerome Neyrey's hypothesis is, in his own words, 'that the trial speeches of Paul in Acts 22–26 are formally structured according to the profile of forensic defense speeches as these are described in the rhetor-ical handbooks'.[6] Having introduced the fivefold structure of a forensic speech as given by Quintilian, Neyrey attempts to show that Paul's speeches in Acts 22–26 match the the pattern of Exordium–Narratio– Probatio. Consequently, Neyrey argues that these speeches ought to be understood and interpreted on the basis of the rhetorical manuals; indeed, he asserts confidently, 'knowledge of forensic speeches...is in-dispensable for understanding Acts'.[7] However, Neyrey's method of analysing both the Acts material and the rhetorical manuals is hardly convincing.

Regarding Neyrey's analysis of the Acts speeches, at least two objections must be raised. First, instead of providing a complete anal-ysis of each of the three speeches in chs. 22, 24 and 26, and then show-ing how each one conforms to the structure of a forensic speech, Ney-rey follows what might be called a 'cut and paste' approach, by which he picks and chooses from each one of these speeches in Acts to fill the gaps in his structure as seems best to him. For example when Neyrey discusses the exordium, he proceeds to complete his 'forensic defense puzzle' by pasting together references from both the Acts 22 and 26 speeches, and from the narrative of Acts 21.38-39 (!). Or, under

6.   Neyrey, 'Forensic Defense Speech', p. 210.
7.   Neyrey, 'Forensic Defense Speech', pp. 220-21.

narratio, Neyrey pastes together material from the speeches in Acts 23, 24 and 26, while at the same time admitting the distinct settings of each speech.[8] Secondly, Neyrey fails to address a fundamental question, namely, how many of the sections of a forensic defense speech as laid out in the manuals must be present in order to class an ancient (or modern!) speech as such? According to Quintilian, the peroratio is the most important section of a forensic speech,[9] yet, Neyrey has neither referred to it in his analysis, nor justified his exclusion of it. The author begins his essay by confidently asserting, on the basis of *Inst. Orat.* 3.9.1, that forensic speeches consist of five parts. Yet, he goes on to argue for the identification of Paul's trial speeches in Acts as forensic oratory on the basis of only three of these headings. Neyrey's failure to address this question detracts significantly from the credibility of his thesis.

Concerning Neyrey's understanding of Quintilian and Cicero, it appears that he has gravely misread their manuals at several points. First, Neyrey cites Cicero's *De Inventione* on the persona of the defendant in order to support Neyrey's section on the exordium.[10] However, the passage cited is part of Cicero's discussion of confirmation or proof (confirmatio), and not of the exordium.[11] According to Quintilian, discussion of the defendant's birth, education and achievements may be included under either exordium (though only very briefly), probatio (an in depth presentation is more fitting here), or peroratio (again, only a brief summary).[12] Secondly, Neyrey fails to come to terms with what is perhaps the most repeated theme in Quintilian's description of forensic speeches, namely, the fundamental requirement that they adhere strictly to the charges, and be as credible and rational as possible. Thus Quintilian asserts that the rhetor must avoid irrelevance,[13] limit himself to *quantum opus est et quantum satis est* ('as much as is necessary and as much as is sufficient')[14] and be based on certainty.[15] Even when using fiction, argues Quintilian, one must ensure that the argument is kept within the bounds of possibility, must not be beyond belief, and must

8. Neyrey, 'Forensic Defense Speech', pp. 212, 215.
9. Quintilian, *Inst. Orat.* 6.2.1.
10. Neyrey, 'Forensic Defense Speech', p. 212.
11. Cicero, *De Inventione* 1.24.34
12. Quintilian, *Inst. Orat.* 4.1.13-14; 5.10.23-28; 6.1.21.
13. Quintilian, *Inst. Orat.* 4.2.40.
14. Quintilian, *Inst. Orat.* 4.2. 45.
15. Quintilian, *Inst. Orat.* 5.12.2.

always be tied to something that is demonstrably true.[16] Consequently, he reminds his readers, arguments based on superstition and dreams have lost their value.[17] Yet, though in terms of its content the forensic speech had to be tightly connected to the facts of the case, stylistically it was expected to be polished, pleasant and entertaining, for 'it is natural that the judges should give readier credence to those to whom they find it a pleasure to listen'.[18] Indeed, such literary sensitivity and polished style was often demanded by the judges, who took such skills as evidence of conscientious preparation on the part of the advocate.[19] Such 'literaturization' of the courts in the early empire was due to a combination of factors, not least of which were the phenomenal increase in litigation in the first century CE and the attendant demand for more lively and endurable judicial oratory, together with the fact that neither judges nor lawyers were legal experts, but rather men of letters who, though capable of weighing the facts of the case, were better disposed if these facts were appropriately dressed in pleasant garb.[20] It seems clear, then, that Paul's speech to the Jewish audience in Acts 22 would not be recognized by Quintilian as a forensic defense speech for a number of reasons: (1) it is not primarily a refutation of the charges brought against him;[21] (2) it dwells instead on a set of super-

16. Quintilian, *Inst. Orat.* 4.2.89. See also Cicero, *De Inventione* 1.20.28; 1.21.29, where he argues that the three essential qualities of narratio are that it be brief, clear, and plausible, by which he means 'characteristics which are accustomed to appear in real life'.

17. Quintilian, *Inst. Orat.* 4.2.94. Cicero relegates references to oracles and portents to the peroratio. See *De Inventione* 1.53.101. See also Brawley, who points out that the two major traditions of authentication in antiquity, namely, 'the wise man' and 'the miracle worker', tended to exclude one another, and that authors in the 'wise man' tradition frequently rejected the miraculous. This makes the trial speeches particularly unique ('Paul in Acts', pp. 134-35).

18. Quintilian, *Inst. Orat.* 4.1.12.

19. Quintilian, *Inst. Orat.* 4.1.57.

20. The standard court procedure in the first century was for the litigant parties to appear before a *praetor* who, properly trained in legal maters, would draw up the formula for the case. He would then set the time for the second phase of the trial and hand over the formula to the *judex*, who would listen to the arguments from both advocates and reach a decision on the case. See Parks, *The Roman Rhetorical Schools*, pp. 43-44. See also Kennedy, *The Art of Rhetoric in the Roman World* (Princeton, NJ: Princeton University Press, 1972), p. 491.

21. Quintilian argues that when the forensic orator is taking up the case of the defendant, his duty consists only in refutation. See *Inst. Orat.* 5.13.1.

natural phenomena including a vision and a healing; (3) and it lacks most of the typical stylistic marks of forensic oratory, including enthymemes[22] as well as a peroratio. I will later argue that, although the speech makes reference to Paul's birth, education and character, this is by no means the focus of the oration. Lastly, If Luke was indeed intending to pattern this speech according to the forensic model and thus emphasize the persona of Paul, it would seem almost certain that he would have included within it a reference to Paul's Roman citizenship (a fact revealed after the speech, in the dialogue of Acts 22.25-29). In 4.2.113, Quintilian tells of the case of a certain Philodamus, a Roman citizen unjustly beaten, an event which, Quintilian points out, Cicero included in the narratio section of his defense of that citizen.

In 'The Forensic Defense Speech', Neyrey argues his case with great conviction, and the potential implications of his thesis for the interpretation of Acts are enormous. He has, however, failed to show that Acts 22 is patterned after the Roman model of a forensic speech. One cannot, therefore, simply accept his conclusion that Acts cannot be properly understood without reference to the rhetorical manuals. Further, to 'demonstrate' that any speech, be it ancient or modern, is patterned after Quintilian's model may be nearly impossible; for, in the final analysis, all Quintilian maintains is that rhetoric—of any genus—is fundamentally *bene dicendi scientia* ('the science of speaking well'),[23] that all of the sections in a forensic speech except for probatio may be rearranged and/or dispensed with,[24] and that those who do not see that rhetorical genera are at the service of the case in question, rather than the other way around, are but ivory-tower school boys, out of touch with the real demands of professional oratory.[25]

In the next section, I shall turn my attention to the grammar of the clause in its ideational function in Acts 21.27–22.29 (see my discussion of the clause in Chapter 1), the episode of Paul's arrest and defense before the Jews in Jerusalem. My analysis will be twofold. On the one hand, I will examine the presence or absence of the 'agent' element in the clauses of narrative and speech, and compare my findings with those obtained from other episodes of Acts. On the other hand, I will

22. On the importance of enthymemes in forensic speeches see Aristotle, *Rhetoric* 1.1, 1.9; Quintilian, *Inst. Orat.* 5.14.1.
23. Quintilian, *Inst. Orat.* 5.10.54.
24. Quintilian, *Inst. Orat.* 4.1.25; 4.2.4; 4.2.24; 5. Preface.
25. Quintilian, *Inst. Orat.* 5.13.59; 4.2.85.

provide a complete analysis of clause structure in this episode following the method suggested by Porter.[26] The data resulting from this analysis add to that obtained in previous studies of Acts, and will provide more accurate knowledge of what may be considered standard clause structure in both narrative and speech sections of Acts, and, conversely, what may count as a departure from that standard structure. My study of the clause in Acts 21.27–22.29 is carried out with a view to revealing its role as an indicator of transitivity-based foregrounding in this episode, and its bearing on Luke's portrait of Paul.

2. Luke's Portrayal of Paul: Acts 21.27–22.29

One of the most repeated statements in John Lentz's monograph on Luke's Paul is that, in Acts, Paul is depicted as being in authority and in control. This is so, argues Lentz, 'always'[27] and '[in] all situations',[28] but particularly so in the trial scenes of Acts 21–28.[29] Given the fact that such a notion is nowhere stated explicitly by Luke, Lentz sets out to explore the 'more subtle literary techniques' by which the author of Acts allegedly highlights this feature of his protagonist's persona. Unfortunately, Lentz never offers a strictly literary and, therefore, language-based defense of his thesis, and opts instead for a sociological/historical analysis of the legitimating techniques he discerns in Acts. I wish to argue, however, that a linguistic-literary examination of the data is well worth pursuing.

In order to test Lentz's claim linguistically, let me begin with a question: What linguistic resources are available to a writer who wishes to portray a particular character as being 'in control'? What is involved here is language in its ideational function. More specifically, we are talking about the representation of a process in which participant 'A' exerts authority and/or control over participant 'B'. This is one of the primary functions of the transitivity system. According to Hopper and Thompson's influential study,[30] transitivity is a matter of degree, and its presence in a clause may be weighed as high or low, depending on the number of transitivity features that are discernible in it. Thus, if a clause

---

26. Porter, 'Word Order', pp. 177-206.
27. Lentz, *Luke's Portrayal*, p. 2.
28. Lentz, *Luke's Portrayal*, p. 107.
29. Lentz, *Luke's Portrayal*, pp. 107, 118.
30. Hopper and Thompson, 'Transitivity in Grammar', pp. 251-99.

exhibits the features of volitionality (the agent is acting purposefully, e.g., 'I wrote your name' as opposed to 'I forgot your name'), agency (high potency of the agent), and affectedness of the object (the degree to which the agent's action is transferred to the object), the clause in question will score high on the transitivity scale. As I have mentioned above in Chapter 2, this interpretation of 'high' or 'cardinal' transitivity coincides with Halliday's notion of ergativity, a term descriptive of any clause which includes the elements of agent, process and medium, as in ὃς ταύτην τὴν ὁδὸν ἐδίωξα ('who persecuted this way') (see above). Characters who appear consistently in the position of 'agent' in ergative clauses are thus the 'movers and shakers' of a story, those who are perceived as the initiators and advancers of the story line, in control of events as opposed to controlled by them.

In the episode of Paul's arrest and defense,[31] Paul appears some 81 times as participant in various types of processes.[32] Of these, however, he is the agent of ergative clauses in eight instances:

1. Ἕλληνας εἰσήγαγεν ('he brought in Greek') (medium + agent + process, 21.28)
2. καὶ κεκοίνωκεν τὸν ἅγιον τόπον τοῦτον ('and corrupted this holy place') (agent + process + medium, 21.28b)
3. ὃν... εἰσήγαγεν ὁ Παῦλος[33] ('whom Paul brought in') (medium? + process + agent, 21.29)
4. ὃς ταύτην τὴν ὁδὸν ἐδίωξα ('who persecuted this way') (agent + medium + process, 22.4)
5. δεσμεύων καὶ παραδιδοὺς εἰς φυλακὰς ἄνδρας τε καὶ γυναῖκας ('binding and delivering to sail both men and women') (agent + process + medium, 22.4b)
6. ἄξων καὶ τοὺς ἐκεῖσε ὄντας δεδεμένους ('intending to bring those who live there bound') (agent + process + medium, 22.5)

---

31. I agree with Veltman that narrative and speech are inseparable parts of the episode of Paul's arrest and defense before the Jerusalem crowd. See Veltman, 'The Defense Speeches', p. 244.

32. Of these, Paul is fully explicit subject in 6 instances, abbreviated subject in 19, non-explicit subject in 32, and non-subject participant (that is, occupies the complement position) in 24.

33. This case is somewhat questionable, since the medium is stated only in the previous clause (ὃν ἐνόμιζον).

7.   ἐγὼ ἤμην φυλακίζων καὶ δέρων...τοὺς πιστεύοντας ἐπὶ σέ
     ('I myself was imprisoning and beating those who believe in
     you?') (agent + process + medium, 22.19)
8.   αὐτὸς ἤμηνφυλάσσων τὰ ἱμάτια ('I myself was keeping the
     garments') (agent + process + medium, 22.20)

Several observations may be made on the basis of these clauses. First,
though they are few in number when compared to the total (9.8%),
these eight clauses do represent Paul as an active, purposeful and dynamic agent, who is in a relationship of causation to the medium in each
case. Secondly, the eight clauses above are either part of the accusation
made against Paul by the Jews in the temple (nos. 1-3), or autobiographical statements by Paul about his life as persecutor of 'the way'
(nos. 4-8). Of the latter, the first three occur at the beginning of the
speech, and the last two near the end, as part of the dialogue which Paul
has with the risen Christ. While in the three clauses at the beginning of
the speech Paul describes his past life as persecutor of Christians, in the
final two he makes Christ the final object of his past persecution of 'the
way', for the Christians were merely τοὺς πιστεύοντας ἐπὶ σέ ('those
who believe in you'), and Stephen was τοῦ μάρτυρός σου ('your witness') (22.19-20). Further, these two clauses stand out from the rest
because of their grammaticalized, 'superfluous' subjects (agents): ἐγὼ
ἤμην φυλακίζων... ('I myself used to imprison...', 22.19), and καὶ
αὐτὸς ἤμην ἐφεστὼς καὶ συνευδοκῶν καὶ φυλάσσων τὰ ἱμάτια...
('even I myself was present, and approving, and keeping the gar-
ments...', 22.20). Though these two clauses are essentially a restate-
ment of Paul's previous autobiographical remarks, the grammatical
features I have referred to give them the unique flavor of a confession.
Thirdly, the zeal and determination of Saul in eradicating Christianity is
described most poignantly in Acts 22.5, where Paul recalls the
commission he received from the high priest, by which his authority
was extended as far as Damascus. To Damascus Saul went, ἄξων καὶ
τοὺς ἐκεῖσε ὄντας, δεδεμένους εἰς Ἰερουσαλὴμ ἵνα τιμωρηθῶσιν,
'intending to bring even those [Christians] who lived there bound to
Jerusalem, that they may be punished'. The future participle form used
here is extremely rare in the New Testament[34] and denotes the strong

---

34.   12 instances in the New Testament, of which 5 are in Acts (8.27; 20.22;
22.5; 24.11; 24.17), 2 in Hebrews (3.5; 13.17), and 1 each in Luke's Gospel
(22.49), John (6.64), 1 Corinthians (15.37), and 1 Peter (3.13).

intention or purpose of its subject.[35] Lastly, the key transitivity features of kinesis, volition, agency and affectedness of object are clearly present in all but the last two clauses.[36] In summary, these eight ergative clauses have in each case a highly dynamic agent, namely, Paul, who is purposefully and directly involved in engendering the processes in question. In the first half of the episode, these processes take the form of aorist or perfect tense forms (first three) or participle periphrastic constructions (last two), and refer to events that are past from the perspective of the speaker. Before deciding on the significance of these clauses, however, more needs to be said about the structure of the speech.

Concerning the structure of the speech, several theories have been put forth from the ranks of form criticism.[37] Among these is Hubbard's, who divides the core of Paul's oration into three separate 'commission accounts', each having the same formal elements and patterned after the same model:[38]

---

35. See the above references, and BDF §351.

36. Kinesis refers to the clause being 'action' or 'non-action', actions being transferable from one participant to another (I tackled John), while states cannot (I love John). Volition has to do with the intentionality or lack thereof on the part of the agent. Agency distinguishes animate (thus high in agency) from inanimate (low or lacking in agency) subjects. Affectedness of object refers to the degree to which the action is transferred from agent to medium. On the last two clauses, see below. See Hopper and Thompson, 'Transitivity in Grammar', p. 252.

37. See, for example, J. Munck, 'La vocation de l'Apôtre Paul', *ST* 1 (1947), pp. 130-45; Terence Y. Mullins, 'New Testament Commission Forms, Especially in Luke–Acts', *JBL* 96 (1976), pp. 603-14; Benjamin J. Hubbard, 'The Role of Commissioning Accounts in Acts', in Talbert (ed.), *Perspectives*, p. 197; Charles W. Hedrick, 'Paul's Conversion/Call: A Comparative Analysis of the Three Reports in Acts', *JBL* 100.3 (1981), pp. 415-32; Gerhard Lohfink, *Paulus vor Damaskus* (Stuttgarter Bibelstudien, 4; Stuttgart: Verlag Katholisches Bibelwerk, 1967), pp. 53-60, where Lohfink sees 22.7-10 as having the structure of an *Erscheinungsgespräch*, or 'apparition dialogue', a literary form common to the Old Testament and other Jewish literature.

38. Hubbard argues that the literary form of commission has the following seven elements: introduction, confrontation, reaction, commission, protest, reassurance, and conclusion. He admits, however, that only four of these elements appear in all the 'commissions' he has discerned in Luke–Acts. Hubbard, 'Commissioning Accounts', pp. 187-89. See also Soards, *The Speeches*, pp. 111-12.

22.6-11   Paul's apostolic commission
22.12-16   Commission by Ananias
22.17-21   Temple christophany and commission

Yet, due attention to the language of the speech, and to transitivity and clause structure in particular, will show the implausibility of this form-critical hypothesis. Paul's account of his anti-Christian activity, expressed by means of three ergative clauses in vv. 4 and 5, comes to an abrupt turning point in v. 6, where Paul moves from the subject-agent position of the clause to the object-medium position, not to appear again as agent until v. 19. This turning point is brought about in the syntax of the speech by means of an unusual ἐγένετο + infinitive clause (its structure repeated with slight variations in v. 17), which continues to puzzle commentators and grammarians. These two clauses are akin to two pegs on which the entire speech hangs, and hold the key to the structure and the meaning of the episode.

Acts 22.6	Acts 22.17
Ἐγένετο δέ μοι	**Ἐγένετο δέ μοι**
πορευομένῳ καὶ ἐγγίζοντι	ὑποστρέψαντι εἰς
τῇ Δαμασκῷ περὶ	Ἰερουσαλὴμ καὶ
μεσημβρίαν ἐξαίφνης ἐκ	προσευχομένου
τοῦ οὐρανοῦ	μου ἐν τῷ ἱερῷ
περιαστράψαι φῶς ἱκανὸν περὶ ἐμέ	γενέσθαι με ἐν ἐκστάσει

While referring to both clauses, Bruce reserves his comments for the latter and designates this 'an awkward sentence in more ways than one'.[39] Conzelmann goes further and considers this clause 'an impossible construction',[40] with no further comment on the matter. Of the old-school grammarians, Blass and Debrunner seem equally puzzled, and view this as 'a very clumsy sentence',[41] pointing out that ἐγένετο is

39. Namely, 'in the double sense of γινομαι, avoided in 21.35; in the lack of concord in the pronouns μοι...μου...με (cf 15.22); in the gen. abs. προσευχομένου μου referring to a noun or pronoun already in the sentence, with no attempt to assimilate the cases' (Bruce, *The Acts of the Apostles*, p. 404).

40. *Hans Conzelmann, *Acts of the Apostles* (trans. J. Limburg, A.T. Kraabel and D.H. Juel; Hermeneia; Philadelphia: Fortress Press, 1987), p. 188.

41. BDF, §409.4. This statement from BDF is due, presumably, to the 'failure' of this clause to conform to 'good classical form'. See their introductory 'The New Testament and Hellenistic Greek', p. 2. See also Haenchen, who, referring to Acts 22.17, calls it a 'quite unclassical construction', and adds that it has a 'counterpart'

often used with accusative and infinitive, and that even when a dative is used, as in Acts 22.6, 'the acc. with infinitive is possible or even necessary'.[42] Turner, however, argues that in ἐγένετο clauses, the accusative with infinitive is as possible as is the dative with infinitive, and gives Acts 22.6 and Acts 22.17 as examples of the latter.[43] Thus, it seems that the very matter that is a bone of contention among New Testament Greek grammarians and is ignored by most commentators, namely, the relationship of μοι to the rest of the clause in each verse, is in fact the crucial piece in this syntactical puzzle.

Both Blass and Debrunner and Turner have noted the similarities of these two clauses, and refer to both in their discussion, as summarized above. Yet, the generic vocabulary used in describing them ('goes with', 'possible', etc.) tends to cloud, rather than shed light on, the issue. It is helpful to begin any discussion of these clauses by noting that similarly to Hebrew (cf. the recurrent וַיְהִי construction), the καὶ ἐγένετο/ἐγένετο δε +___ formula ('and it happened that…') should be considered one of the chief building blocks used by writers in the composition of koine Greek narrative texts.[44] Within this large group of clauses, we find the ἐγένετο + infinitive construction, where the infinitive is the subject of ἐγένετο, of which Acts 22.6 and 22.17 are two examples. This construction occurs exclusively in narrative, and in 22 out of 23 instances[45] in Luke–Acts.[46] As for the infinitival clause in

in Lk. 3.21. This is not exactly so, as I will show below (Haenchen, *The Acts of the Apostles*, p. 627).

42. BDF §409.4.

43. Turner, *Grammar of New Testament Greek*, p. 149.

44. This was also the case in earlier Greek, although συμβαίνω was far more frequent than γίγνομαι. Only one instance of συνέβη + infinitive is attested in the New Testament (Acts 21.35), and the tendency is for the simplification of these constructions via direct speech or ὅτι periphrases. See Turner, *Grammar of New Testament Greek*, p. 148; Turner, 'The Quality of the Greek of Luke–Acts', pp. 393-94. See also Paul Burguière, *Histoire de l'infinitif en grec* (Etudes et Commentaires, 33; Paris: Librairie C. Klincksieck, 1960), esp. the chapter entitled 'Anomalies Symptomatiques en Grec Postclassique', pp. 177-98, for a discussion of this construction in Hellenistic Greek.

45. The data that follow are gathered with the aid of GRAMCORD software. For a discussion of this program, its benefits and drawbacks vis-à-vis similar programs, see Harry Hahne, 'Interpretive Implications of Using Bible-Search Software for New Testament Grammatical Analysis'. Paper presented at the annual meeting of the Evangelical Theological Society, 24 November 1994.

46. See Mk 2.23; Lk. 1.59; 6.1; 6.6; 6.12; 14.1; 16.22; Acts 4.5; 9.3; 9.32; 9.37;

ἐγένετο + infinitive constructions, our two samples conform to the standard pattern in the Greek of the New Testament. In the two clauses of Acts 22.6, 17, although the dative pronoun μοι does, to use Blass and Debrunner's expression, 'go with' the infinitive in each case, it does not go with it in the sense of being its subject, for, as is standard in the New Testament, the subject of the two infinives is in each case an explicit accusative noun/pronoun.[47] These observations clarify the central issue in our discussion. Since the infinitival clauses in vv. 6 and 17 have accusative subjects in conformity with expectation, the question remains: What exactly is the function and relationship of μοι to the rest of the clause in each case? Before I suggest an answer to this question, however, we must further examine the 21 other clauses that together with our two samples fit the structure ἐγένετο + infinitive (where the infinitive is the subject of ἐγένετο) in the Greek New Testament (see n. 46 above). All but three of these clauses have an adjunct[48] (i.e. a circumstantial clause) which in 13 of 20 instances appears immediately after ἐγένετο or ἐγένετο δε. When the order ἐγένετο/ἐγένετο δε + adjunct is altered, this is due to (1) the adjunct preceding ἐγένετο;[49] (2) the subject of the infinitive, in either the accusative case[50] or in the

9.43; 11.26; 14.1; 16.16; 19.1; 21.1; 21.5; 22.6; 22.17; 27.44; 28.8; 28.17.

47. Namely, φῶς (22.6) and με (22.17). There is one single instance of ἐγένετο plus an infinitive with its subject in the dative in the entire Greek New Testament, namely ἐγένετο δὲ αὐτοῖς καὶ ἐνιαυτὸν ὅλον συναχθῆναι ἐν τῇ ἐκκλησίᾳ καὶ διδάξαι ὄχλον ἱκανόν (Acts 11.26). On this issue see K.L. McKay, *A New Syntax of the Verb in New Testament Greek* (Studies in Biblical Greek, 5; New York: Peter Lang, 1994), p. 57. Such a construction was more frequent in the non-literary papyri as well as in previous Greek. For this construction in the non-literary papyri, see Basil G. Mandilaras, *The Verb in the Greek Non-Literary Papyri* (Athens: Hellenic Ministry of Culture and Sciences, 1973), pp. 326-28. For this construction in classical Greek see W.W. Goodwin, *Syntax of the Moods and Tenses of the Greek Verb* (London: Macmillan, 1929), p. 299; W.W. Goodwin and C.B. Gulick, *Greek Grammar* (Boston: Ginn, 1930), pp. 197, 320.

48. As I have mentioned before, there are three components to a process: the process itself, realized in texts in the element of 'process' (a verb form); participants, realized in the elements of 'agent(s)' and 'medium(s)'; and circumstances attending the process, realized in the element of 'adjunct', that is, in circumstancial clauses generally answering questions such as 'how', 'when', or 'why'.

49. ἐν δὲ τῷ πορεύεσθαι ἐγένετο αὐτὸν ἐγγίζειν τῇ Δαμασκῷ, (Acts 9.3); καὶ οὕτως ἐγένετο πάντας διασωθῆναι ἐπὶ τὴν γῆν (Acts 27.44).

50. καὶ ἐγένετο αὐτὸν ἐν τοῖς σάββασιν παραπορεύεσθαι (Mk 2.23); ἐγένετο

dative,[51] being interposed between ἐγένετο and the adjunct; or (3) the dative pronoun μοι, though it is not the grammatical subject of the infinitive, being interposed between ἐγένετο and the adjunct in Acts 22.6 and 17. The peculiarity of the last case is underlined by comparing the two clauses of Acts 22.6 and 7 with another clause that is structurally equivalent to them, but without the dative pronoun μοι:

Acts 16.16
(a) ἐγένετο δε
(b) (Adj. subject 1) **πορευομένων ἡμῶν** εἰς τὴν προσευχὴν
(c) (Inf. clause, subject 2) **παιδίσκην τινα**; ἔχουσαν πνεῦμα Πύθωνα ὑπαντῆσαι ἡμῖν

'And it happened that, as we were going to the place of prayer, a certain slave girl who had a spirit of divination met us.'

Acts 22.6
(a) ἐγένετο δέ μοι
(b) (Adj. subject 1) πορευομένῳ καὶ ἐγγίζοντι τῇ Δαμασκῷ περὶ μεσημβρίαν ἐξαίφνης ἐκ τοῦ οὐρανοῦ
(c) (Inf. clause, subject 2) περιαστράψαι **φῶς ἱκανὸν** περὶ ἐμέ

'And it happened to me that, while travelling and getting close to Damascus at about midday, suddenly from heaven, a great light shone about me.'

Acts 22.17
(a) ἐγένετο δέ μοι
(b) (Adj. subject 1) ὑποστρέψαντι εἰς Ἰερουσαλὴμ καὶ προσευχομένου **μου** ἐν τῷ ἱερῷ
(c̓) (Inf. clause, subject 2) γενέσθαι **με** ἐν ἐκστάσει

'And it happened to me that, having returned to Jerusalem and praying in the temple, I fell into a trance.'

As is the case in Acts 22.6 and 17, the clause in Acts 16.16 fits the pattern of ἐγένετο + adjunct + infinitive clause, the infinitive being the subject of ἐγένετο. Further, as is true of Acts 22.6, 17, the adjunct in Acts 16.16 has its own grammatical subject apart from that of the infini-

---

δὲ τὸν πατέρα τοῦ Ποπλίου πυρετοῖς καὶ δυσεντερίῳ συνεχόμενον κατακεῖσθαι (Acts 28.8).
    51. ἐγένετο δὲ αὐτοῖς καὶ ἐνιαυτὸν ὅλον συναχθῆναι ἐν τῇ ἐκκλησίᾳ καὶ διδάξαι ὄχλον ἱκανόν (Acts 11.26).

tival clause.[52] Unlike the clauses in Acts 22, however, the subject of the adjunct in Acts 16.16, being different from that of the infinitive, is placed within the bounds of the adjunct, rather than outside. This confirms my primary observation drawn from all the clauses that fit this pattern in the Greek New Testament: ἐγένετο being the principal verb and the infinitive clause its subject, any participant other than the grammatical subject of the infinite clause is enclosed within the bounds of an adjunct, as it is considered tangential to, rather than part and parcel of, the 'main event'.

It could be argued that, given the case concord of the dative pronoun μοι and the participle that follows it in the two clauses of 22.6 and 17, pronoun and participle belong together grammatically (e.g. as a 'dative absolute') and may not be considered as belonging to two distinct elements within the clause. Having examined the 350 dative participles in the Greek New Testament, that possibility seems highly unlikely, since there are two single cases of what might be called a 'dative absolute' in the entire New Testament, both in Matthew.[53] Secondly, the strong likelihood that μοι is in fact a complement (indirect object) of ἐγένετο in Acts 22.6, 17 (thus, 'it happened to me...'. rather than 'it happened...'[54]) is seen in the distribution of the pronouns με and μοι as complements throughout the speech: once before v. 6, but 13 times after v. 6. Lastly, I wish to emphasize that, although morphological considerations are by no means unimportant, the linguistic method I am

52. Though the referent of μου (grammatical subject in the adjunct) and με (grammatical subject in the infinitival clause) are the same in Acts 22.17, I am treating them as separate since they are grammaticalized explicitly within the bounds of each clause. According to Goodwin and Gulick, a basic grammatical principle applicable in Greek infinitive clauses of all periods is that 'the subject of the infinitive is generally omitted when it is the same as the subject or the object of the leading verb... [or] *when it is the same with any important adjunct of the leading verb*' (Goodwin and Gulick, *Grammar*, p. 196).

53. Mt. 8.23 καὶ ἐμβάντι αὐτῷ εἰς τὸ πλοῖον ἠκολούθησαν αὐτῷ οἱ μαθηταὶ αὐτοῦ; and Mt. 14.6 γενεσίοις δὲ γενομένοις τοῦ Ἡρῴδου ὠρχήσατο ἡ θυγάτηρ τῆς Ἡρῳδιάδος ἐν τῷ μέσῳ καὶ ἤρεσεν τῷ Ἡρῴδῃ. Moule mentions only the latter, though he is uncertain concerning its identification as a 'dative absolute'. See Moule, *An Idiom Book*, pp. 44-45. For a possible example of a dative absolute in post-New Testament Christian literature see *Mart. Pol.* 9.1: τῷ δὲ Πολυκάρπῳ εἰσιόντι εἰς τὸ στάδιον φωνή ἐξ οὐρανοῦ ἐγένετο...

54. Thus Haenchen, *The Acts of the Apostles*, p. 623, where he renders Acts 22.6 'It happened to me, however...', and 22.17 'Now, it happened to me...'

deploying in the present argument focuses on the function rather than the form of linguistic elements, such as complements and adjuncts. There are at least five clauses in the New Testament that contain a structure analogous (two of them directly so[55]) to the one present in both Acts 22.6 and 17, namely, a main verb followed by a dative pronoun or noun and a dative participle. Two of these clauses will illustrate the last point:

Lk. 1.3: **ἔδοξε κἀμοὶ παρηκολουθηκότι** ἄνωθεν πᾶσιν ἀκρι-βῶς καθεξῆς σοι γράψαι, κράτιστε Θεόφιλε

Acts 7.2: Ὁ θεὸς τῆς δόξης **ὤφθη τῷ πατρὶ ἡμῶν Ἀβραὰμ ὄντι** ἐν τῇ Μεσοποταμίᾳ πρὶν ἢ κατοικῆσαι αὐτὸν ἐν Χαρράν.[56]

Though the participles following the dative pronoun and noun agree with these in case, the functional role of the participial phrases is, in each case, that of modifying the pronoun and noun adverbially, that is, they fulfill the role of adjuncts, answering the question 'how?' or perhaps 'why', and 'when?' In the same clauses the dative pronoun μοι and the dative noun πατρὶ answer the question 'whom or what', that is, they fulfill the role of complement. The same analysis applies in the two clauses of Acts 22.6 and 17.

Thus, it can be claimed with a considerable degree of certainty that the dative pronoun μοι is 'out of place' in Acts 22.6 and 17, and, consequently, that its appearance immediately following ἐγένετο calls for an explanation.

As I mentioned above, in vv. 4-5 of the speech, Paul appears as the highly dynamic agent of three ergative clauses: 'I...—Paul declares—persecuted this way unto death, binding and delivering to prison both men and women...I went [to Damascus] intending to bring those [Christians] who were there bound to Jerusalem...'. At this juncture, both the story and its syntax reach a fundamental turning point: '...But

55. Namely, Lk. 1.3 and Acts 15.25, both having an impersonal main verb and an infinitive clause as its subject. See below.

56. The other three are Acts 15.25 ἔδοξεν ἡμῖν γενομένοις ὁμοθυμαδὸν ἐκλεξαμένοις ἄνδρας πέμψαι πρὸς ὑμᾶς σὺν τοῖς ἀγαπητοῖς ἡμῶν Βαρναβᾷ καὶ Παύλῳ; Lk. 9.59b ἐπίτρεψόν μοι ἀπελθόντι πρῶτον θάψαι τὸν πατέρα μου; Heb. 7.1 Οὗτος γὰρ ὁ Μελχισέδεκ, βασιλεὺς Σαλήμ, ἱερεὺς τοῦ θεοῦ τοῦ ὑψίστου, ὁ συναντήσας Ἀβραὰμ ὑποστρέφοντι ἀπὸ τῆς κοπῆς τῶν βασιλέων καὶ εὐλογήσας αὐτόν.

it happened *to me* that, as I was travelling and getting close to Damascus, a great light shone about me'. Luke's shifting of Paul from the agent to the complement position in v. 6 signals the end of his pre-eminent role in the speech, for, after this point, all of Paul's actions are merely responses to the two encounters with Jesus, introduced in identical form, as we have seen. Once the speech proper begins, Paul does not appear in the complement position of the clause until v. 6 but does so 10 times after that, as he appears on the receiving end of actions/processes attributed to a great light (22.6), a voice (22.7, 9), 'unspecified' (i.e. 'it will be said to you', 'it is appointed for you...', 22.10), Ananias (22.12), God of our fathers (22.14), a trance (22.17), 'him', that is, Jesus (22.18, 21). As I noted above, of the eight ergative clauses with Paul as agent in the episode, the last two are in the penultimate verse of the speech, and have the form and flavor of a confession, effectively drawing Paul's testimony to a close.

The shift in focus away from Paul is not only revealed by the syntax of the episode, however. The autobiographical remarks that have often been interpreted as a legitimating technique by Luke, namely the references to Paul's birth in Tarsus, education and 'achievements', are strictly limited to Acts 21.37–22.5 in the episode, and clearly fade into the background as the determined and zealous Jew is intercepted by Christ and his purpose frustrated in vv. 22.6. This negation of Paul's own design is further repeated when, having returned to Jerusalem and while praying in the temple, he is met by Jesus once more and his own plans are again redirected, this time toward the Gentile mission. It seems fair to say that by the end of Paul's autobiographical account, very little indeed remains of the Saul we had met in vv. 22.3-5, for now his *persona* is only significant in relation to the risen Christ. Consequently, while in the brief account of his life prior to the Damascus road, the high priest is cited as a witness to Paul (22.5), after v. 6 it is Paul who becomes a witness to Christ before all men (22.15, 18). In his introduction to his recent commentary on Acts, Witherington inserts a very interesting footnote concerning the likely acceptability of much of the content of Acts to a Roman reader such as Tacitus.[57] He concludes that Acts would most likely not have suited Tacitus due to its rather strong Greek and Eastern flavor. Tacitus would also have been rather skeptical, argues Witherington, of

---

57. Witherington, *Socio-Rhetorical Commentary*, p. 39 n. 137.

all the stories in Luke–Acts about people going through character transformation by conversion, for 'Tacitus, like most Roman writers, usually
regarded moral character as fixed at birth and the human personality as
essentially static'.

It is surprising that Witherington does not bring this matter to bear upon
his reading of Paul's apologetic speech in Acts 22, a reading carried out
along the rather rigid lines of Graeco-Roman rhetorical analysis,[58]
including the emphasis on Paul's *persona* and character.

The narrative that follows the speech (Acts 22–29) presents no major
changes in terms of the transitivity patterns. Thus, of the 16 clauses that
have Paul as participant, he occupies the complement slot in seven,
where he is on the receiving end of processes initiated by either the
Jewish crowd or the Roman tribune. Of the rest, Paul is the subject of
clauses encoding verbal processes (processes of saying, three instances), relational processes (processes of being, four instances), and
on two occasions, the passive subject of actions carried out by the
Roman soldiers (v. 24). Concerning the apparent abruptness of the
speech's ending at v. 21, I concur with Conzelmann that this is not an
indication of an incomplete source, but rather a literary technique used
by Luke to highlight the offensiveness to Jews of the Gentile mission.[59]

By fronting the dative pronoun μοι in verses 22.6 and 17 of the
speech, Luke highlights the fundamental shift in focus that takes place
as Paul ceases to be the driving force of the narrative, that is, he ceases
to be 'in control', and finds himself overwhelmed by a power far superior to his own. These two foregrounded clauses give a clear structure

---

58. Witherington, *Social-Rhetorical Commentary*, pp. 659-75. For Witherington, this is a forensic defense speech for which he suggests the structure of (i) exordium (vv. 1-2); (ii) narratio (vv. 3-21) and some hints of proofs included in the
narratio. Witherington believes this basic structure reflects the model set forth in
Quintilian, *Inst. Orat.* 4.1.1-79, 4.2.1-132, and in Cicero, *De Inventione* 1.19.27.
Luke's alleged dependency on the manuals when composing the speech is for
Witherington apparently not at odds with its essentially Jewish theme (see p. 659),
and the fact that what is happening in ch. 22 is not a trial. The problematic nature of
this method of analysis becomes further apparent when, on p. 667, Witherington
refers to the readings of this speech carried out by others with the same dependency
upon the manuals that Witherington has, and yet, resulting in different conclusions,
while citing the same classical authors in support on those conflicting readings!

59. Conzelmann, *Acts*, p. 189. But see Foakes Jackson for the opposite view in
The Acts of the Apostles, p. 202.

to the speech and represent the climactic points of the entire episode.[60] From the perspective of the reader/hearer, the clauses of Acts 22.6, 17 appear foregrounded due to the quality of 'departure from the norm' that I have noted both in their structure and in the transitivity shift that v. 6 introduces. Yet, mere deviation from 'norms', be these internal or external to the text, is not in itself sufficient to interpret a stretch of text as foregrounded, if it is not also shown to have 'value in the game', that is, to be significant in light of the overall theme(s) of that text.

The interpretation I have just offered of Acts 21–22 coheres with the conclusions I reached in the above studies of the shipwreck story of Acts 27, and of the episode of Stephen's martyrdom in Acts 6–7. These episodes are selected because they are in each case complete sub-units within the larger work of Acts, sufficiently long to allow the kind of linguistic study I have carried out, and contain in each case both narrative and speech(es). As is the case in narrative texts of many of the world's languages, the transitivity system of Greek is shown to be a fundamental tool used by the author of Acts to differentiate from the rest those participants he wishes to portray as 'efficacious'. In each case, however, Luke utilizes a syntax-based foregrounding scheme to highlight the inability of human actions, grammaticalized by means of ergative clauses, to resist the unfolding and irresistible will of God (see my discussion of τὸ δεῖν in Chapter 2). In discussing Paul's speech in Acts 22, Haenchen notes that Jesus is in most instances not mentioned by name.[61] This fact is not as unusual as Haenchen may think, however. As I noted in my previous studies of Acts 27 and 6–7, the systematic 'incapacitation' of his key characters (Stephen, Paul, Moses) achieved by Luke through the syntax of these episodes leads the reader/hearer to ask: 'Who then, is behind these events?' Yet, Luke seems often to avoid giving an explicit answer to this question, allowing the reader instead to experience an element of suspense in the narrative. Thus, as we have seen, the 10 clauses in which Paul occupies the object/complement slot

---

60. Paul Schubert sees the Damascus road experience as the 'center' of the speech. Schubert, '*The Final Cycle*', p. 5. Marguerat argues that it is the ecstasy in the temple that constitutes the climax of the speech. Daniel Marguerat, 'Saul's Conversion (Acts 9, 22, 26) and the Multiplication of Narrative in Acts', in C.M. Tuckett (ed.), *Luke's Literary Achievement* (JSNTSup, 116; Sheffield: Sheffield Academic Press, 1995), pp. 127-55 (149). Hedrick, however, sees the 'commission' by Ananias as the climax. Hedrick, 'Paul's Conversion', p. 424.

61. Haenchen, *The Acts of the Apostles*, pp. 627, 630.

after the encounter with 'a great light' in v. 22.6 encode processes that are attributed to a light (22.6), a voice (22.7, 9), 'unspecified' (i.e. 'it will be said to you', 'it is appointed for you...', 22.10), a trance (22.17), 'him', that is, Jesus (22.18, 21), Ananias (22.12), and 'God of our fathers' (22.14). In Luke's overall purpose, this device reminds readers that the divine plan (βουλή τοῦ θεοῦ), though often invisible to the human eye, is nonetheless constantly moving forward, even in the face of human efforts to thwart it. Thus I conclude with Lohfink that this speech has a clear religious/theological purpose in Luke's literary scheme, rather than primarily a political/rhetorical one,[62] and that, as Walaskay has noted, even the references to Paul's rights as a Roman are seen by Luke as part and parcel of the divine necessity by which Paul is brought to his appointed destination, Rome.[63]

4. *Conclusion*

In this chapter, I have sought to offer both an interpretation of Acts 21–22 and to explain *how that text means* what it does. It is the latter that is missing in John Lentz's proposal concerning Paul in the trial episodes of Acts. Lentz's and Neyrey's interest in rhetoric could be far more fruitful if, with Halliday, they understood rhetoric as inseparable from grammatical analysis, thus substantiating their claims regarding the effect of language upon readers/hearers by relating these claims to the functionally-oriented choices made by the writer from the language system. This necessarily involves breaking free from an exaggerated dependence on the Graeco-Roman manuals, a dependency Quintilian himself warned against, as I have pointed out:

62. Referring to the speeches of Acts in general, Lohfink affirms that these speeches are essentially 'Predigt und Anrede', rather than the rhetorical and stylistic exercises of a Hellenistic author. See Lohfink, *Paulus vor Damaskus*, pp. 51-52. See also Jervell's chapter 'Paul: The Teacher of Israel', in his *Luke and the People of God*, esp. pp. 156-61, where he presents arguments against the political orientation of Paul's apologetic speeches in Acts 22–26.

63. Paul W. Walaskay, *And so we Came to Rome: The Political Perspective of St Luke* (SNTSMS, 49; Cambridge: Cambridge University Press, 1983), p. 58. Similarly, Jervell writes: 'the girder of Luke's theological thinking is the notion of God being in complete control of history...it is impossible for men to resist his will, at least in the long run...' (Jervell, *The Theology*, p. 129). See also Hubbard, 'Commissioning Accounts', p. 198.

> Eloquence therefore must not restrict itself to narrow tracks, but range at large over the open fields. Its streams must not be conveyed through narrow pipes like the water of fountains, but flow as mighty rivers flow, filling whole valleys; *and if it cannot find a channel it must make one for itself.* For what can be more distressing than to be fettered by petty rules, like children who trace the letters of the alphabet which others have first written for them, or, as the Greeks say, insist on keeping the coat their mother gave themMust not the orator breathe life into the argument and develop it? Must he not vary and diversify it by a thousand figures, and do all this in such a way that it seems to come into being as the very child of nature...?[64]

The undue fixation upon the manuals that is apparent in some of the work of Neyrey, Lentz and others is lacking among rhetoricians who study texts other than the New Testament. Instead, scholars of communication theory, language teachers and public speaking consultants regularly draw upon the insights of Burkean rhetoric, speech act theory, pragmatics, and various forms of functional linguistics. Of these, I have suggested the last is ideally suited for the task of relating the linguistic features of New Testament texts such as Paul's apologetic speeches in Acts, to the effects they have upon their readers/hearers. This was, in the final analysis, Quintilian's own agenda.

---

64. Quintilian, *Inst. Orat.* 5.24.31-32.

Chapter 6

FOREGROUNDED TRANSITIVITY PATTERNS
IN THE PENTECOST EPISODE (ACTS 2)

1. *Introduction: The Pentecost Episode in Recent Discussion*

In his 1971 monograph entitled *Peter's Pentecost Discourse*,[1] Richard
Zehnle affirmed that Peter's speech in the second chapter of Acts is 'the
finest mission discourse composed by Luke',[2] and serves as a 'keynote
address',[3] a programmatic statement of sorts, setting forth the Lucan
theology to be unfolded throughout the rest of Luke's 'second treatise'.
The widespread recognition of the significance of Peter's speech for our
understanding of Acts has motivated an important number of recent
studies,[4] ranging from source-critical analyses to linguistic and socio-

---

1.   Richard F. Zehnle, *Peter's Pentecost Discourse* (SBLMS, 15; Nashville:
Abingdon Press, 1971). The title is somewhat misleading, since the book is actually
a comparative study of the speeches of Acts 2 and 3. Zehnle concludes that the
speech of Acts 3 contains the earliest Christology in the New Testament.

2.   Zehnle, *Pentecost Discourse*, p. 60.

3.   Zehnle, *Pentecost Discourse*, p. 130.

4.   Of all the scholarly work published on the Pentecost episode of Acts 2,
Dionisio Mínguez's 1976 monograph *Pentecostés* is unequaled in thoroughness and
linguistic erudition. See also Craig A. Evans, 'The Prophetic Setting of the Pentecost Sermon', *ZNW* 74 (1983), pp. 148-50; O'Toole, 'Acts 2.30', pp. 245-58;
Sanders, *The Jews in Luke–Acts*, pp. 232-35, where Sanders sets forth his well
known theory of Luke's thorough antisemitism; José Rius-Camps, 'Pentecostés
versus Babel: Estudio crítico de Hechos 2', *FN* 1 (1988), pp. 35-61; Tannehill, *The
Narrative Unity of Luke–Acts*, esp. pp. 26-36; Robert B. Sloan, 'Signs and Wonders: A Rhetorical Clue to the Pentecost Discourse', *EvQ* 63 (1991), pp. 225-40;
Soards, *The Speeches*, pp. 31-37; A.J.M. Wedderburn, 'Tradition and Redaction in
Acts 2:1-13', *JSNT* 55 (1994), pp. 27-54; Robert L. Brawley 'Hermeneutical Voices
of Scripture in Acts 2', in *idem*, *Text to Text Pours Forth Speech* (Bloomington, IN:
Indiana University Press, 1995), pp. 75-90; Gerhard Mussies, 'Variation in the
Book of Acts' [Part 2], *FN* 8 (1995), pp. 23-61; Mark L. Strauss, *The Davidic*

logical ones. Regardless of the methodological angle chosen, however, discussion of this episode has centred primarily on the issue of its unity and coherence, or lack thereof: Are the two apparently different types of speech (namely the 'ecstatic' speech resembling the glossolalia of 1 Cor. 14 [v. 4] and the language miracle [vv. 6-13]) indicators of two different sources behind this episode?[5] Is the apparently undeveloped Christology of the speech evidence of an early tradition which Luke has, hesitantly but faithfully, preserved?[6] Lastly, is the entire speech sufficiently connected to the Pentecost event that precedes it?[7] Like the previous chapters, the present chapter is part of my investigation of clause structure and, more specifically, the transitivity choices made by the author of Acts. My aim is to shed light on such issues as cohesiveness, coherence, and, above all, foregrounding strategy, that is, the systematic, purposeful utilization of various linguistic means to highlight those elements of the narrative of Acts 2 that are most significant to the writer's overall literary purpose(s). My starting point is the text

Messiah in Luke–Acts (JSNTSup, 110; Sheffield: Sheffield Academic Press, 1995), pp. 131-47. Of the commentaries, the best treatments are found in Bruce, *The Acts of the Apostles*, pp. 80-99; Haenchen, *The Acts of the Apostles*, pp. 166-89; Conzelmann, *Acts*, pp. 13-21; Barrett, *Acts*, pp. 106-157 and Witherington, *Socio-Rhetorical Commentary*, pp. 128-63. For a well-informed discussion of the issue of 'tongues' in Acts 2, see Bob Zerhusen, 'An Overlooked Judean Diglossia in Acts 2?', *BTB* 25 (1995), pp. 118-30.

5.   Thus Wedderburn, 'Tradition and Redaction', p. 53. For a brief discussion of other options see Conzelmann, *Acts*, pp. 15-16; Haenchen, *The Acts of the Apostles*, pp. 172-73. But see Rius-Camps' proposal in 'Pentecostés', esp. pp. 40-42.

6.   Thus Barrett, *Acts*, p. 151. On this issue, Barrett seems to contradict himself. On the same page, Barrett first writes that '...we have here that primitive kind of adoptionism that Paul was obliged to correct...' and later 'We are dealing here with an unreflecting Christology' (it is better to say unreflecting than primitive, or early) (p. 152). For a different view on this, see Conzelmann, *Acts*, p. 21.

7.   See Barrett, *Acts*, pp. 132-33. Barrett argues that the speech is made up of two parts, one connected to the Pentecost event (vv. 14-21) and the rest, which 'contains nothing to connect it with the occasion'. The two verses that seem to connect the latter half of the speech to the previous narrative (i.e. vv. 33 and 39) must be, argues Barrett, Luke's own interpolations. Barrett adds that the latter half of the speech shows no interest in the manifestations of the Spirit or in universality (though these themes appear in vv. 33 and 39!). I shall deal with Barrett's hypothesis below.

of the Pentecost episode as we have it;[8] consequently, the debate over sources and the exact nature of the speech miracle(s) will be entered into only insofar as it touches upon linguistic or literary matters.

In previous chapters I have noted in explicit terms the significance of participant reference and transitivity patterns for understanding Luke's compositional design. Though both these issues are largely ignored in the scholarly discussion of the shipwreck episode (Acts 27), the story of Stephen's arrest, defense and martyrdom (Acts 6–7) and the episode of Paul's arrest and defense (Acts 22), the greater perspicuity of these features of language in Acts 2 has provoked remarks of varying depth and usefulness from commentators and other researchers.[9] Insightful as several of these discussions appear to be, a fuller, more systematic and explicit treatment of the data is needed, in particular, one carried out within the framework of a modern linguistic method. Thus, my findings concerning transitivity choices such as 'agent' and 'medium' in the present episode need to be understood and interpreted in relation to Luke's choices from the same network elsewhere in Acts, as well as the choices Luke *did not* make, though these were equally open to him, given the Greek language system.

2. *The Pentecost Episode: Its Structure*

Speaking of Acts 2, Soards writes that '[it] is a neatly structured unit of material that is practically self-contained'.[10] Though I do not entirely agree with the arguments Soards uses to suport this statement,[11] I fully

8.   On the Western textual variants in Acts 2, see José Rius-Camps, 'Las variantes de la recensión occidental de los hechos de los apóstoles (V): Hch 2.14-40', *FN* 15 (1995), pp. 63-78. See also Eldon J. Epp *The Theological Tendency of Codex Bezae Cantabrigiensis in Acts* (SNTSMS, 3; Cambridge: Cambridge University Press, 1966), p. 69. Epp's thoroughgoing treatise shows the tendentious anti-Judaism of the Codex Bezae in Acts.

9.   The most explicit treatment of transitivity in Acts 2 is found in Mínguez, *Semiótica Narrativa*, esp. pp. 46-48. See also Tannehill, *Narrative Unity of Luke–Acts*, p. 36; Sloan, 'Signs and Wonders', pp. 229-30; Squires, *The Plan*, pp. 64-65; Brawley, 'Hermeneutical Voices', p. 86.

10. Soards, *The Speeches*, p. 31.

11. As I have mentioned in previous chapters, Soards is intent throughout his work on proving the dependence of Luke upon the specific structures of the three classical rhetorical genera. Concerning Acts 2, he argues that, although the entire speech is unified, the 'first continuous portion…is judicial rhetoric', while 'the final

concur with his assessment that the Pentecost episode is in fact a literary unity. The narrative describing the sudden incursion of the Spirit into the 'house' where the eleven were assembled, the 'other tongues' the disciples began to speak, and the resulting mixed reaction of the crowd assembled outside, is connected to the speech that follows in ways that are not always recognized in discussions of the episode. First and foremost, it is a brief account of the event that was initially a cause of great puzzlement to part of the audience (τί θέλει τοῦτο εἶναι, 'what might this mean?' 2.12), but was later explained by Peter (τοῦτό ἐστιν τὸ εἰρημένον διὰ τοῦ προφήτου, 'this is that which was spoken through the prophet' 2.16; ἐξέχεεν τοῦτο ὃ ὑμεῖς [καὶ] βλέπετε καὶ ἀκούετε, 'He poured out this which you both see and hear' 2.33). The clear anaphoric function of the demonstrative pronoun both at the beginning and end sections of the speech is not given sufficient attention by those who argue against the cohesiveness of the entire episode.[12] In Halliday's functional grammar, a single instance of cohesion such as the one I have just referred to is known as a 'tie', and a text may be described in terms of the number and kind of cohesive ties it possesses, thus displaying relatively high or low cohesiveness.[13] Other cohesive ties discernible in the Pentecost episode as a whole will be discussed below. Closely related to this is the masterful way in which the writer utilizes suspense to hold the reader's attention until the end. Thus, explicit mention of the identity of and cause behind the 'violent rushing wind' is avoided in vv. 1-3, partially disclosed in vv. 4-5, and fully revealed only at the end of Peter's speech (2.33). The enigmatic referent of ἐκάθισεν in v. 3 significantly heightens this suspenseful element.[14] Further, the twofold reaction of the crowd narrated briefly in vv. 12-13 seems to evoke a specific response to each group in Peter's speech. Thus the 'others' of v. 13 are addressed first in vv. 15-21 (οὐ γὰρ ὡς ὑμεῖς ὑπολαμβάνετε οὗτοι μεθύουσιν, 'these are not drunk as you suppose...' v. 13), while the rest (the πάντες of v. 12) are addressed throughout.[15] The abrupt and unexplained move in the narrative from

two brief remarks' are deliberative rhetoric (*The Speeches*, p. 31).

    12. See especially Barrett, *Acts*, pp. 132-33.

    13. Halliday and Hasan, *Cohesion in English*, pp. 1-4.

    14. Acts 2.3: ὤφθησαν αὐτοῖς διαμεριζόμεναι γλῶσσαι ὡσεὶ πυρός, καὶ ἐκάθισεν ἐφ' ἕνα ἕκαστον αὐτῶν... Due most likely to the grammatical difficulty, Codex Bezae emends to ἐκ́θισαν.

    15. Making reference to two groups of individuals reacting to the same event in

indoors to outdoors in v. 5, lexical choices such as ἄφνω ('suddenly') and πνοῆς βιαίας ('violent wind'), and the polysyndeton of vv. 1-4 together invest this narrative overture to the Pentecost episode with a powerful sense of swiftness, of containing a rapid succession of events that calls for the kind of detailed interpretation provided by Peter's oration.

When one considers the structure of Peter's speech in Acts 2.16-36, the word 'architecture'[16] seems ideally suited for its description. Its three major sections, demarcated by the thrice-repeated form used for direct address ἄνδρη... at vv. 14, 22 and 29, become apparent upon the first reading of these lines. Rather than indicators of two different groups within Peter's audience, the three formulae of address ἄνδρες Ἰουδαῖοι (v. 14), ἄνδρες Ἰσραηλῖται (v. 22), and ἄνδρες ἀδελφοί (v. 29) are the product of Luke's rhetorical concern to avoid repetition, a feature characteristic of the entire work.[17] More detailed analysis of the speech reveals a clear progression from first to third section that may be summarized as follows:

1. First section: Briefest address by Peter (vv. 14b-16) and lengthiest LXX quotation (vv. 17-21)
2. Second section: Lengthier address by Peter (vv. 22-25a) and briefer LXX quotation (vv. 25b-28)
3. Third section: Lengthiest address by Peter (vv. 29-34a) and briefest LXX quotation (vv. 34b-35)
4. Peroratio-colophon (v. 36).

The speech proper concludes at v. 36 with a peroratio-like statement that sums up and drives home the core of Peter's message, preceded by a new and powerful formula of address: ἀσφαλῶς οὖν γινωσκέτω πᾶς

---

mutually opposed ways is a common feature of the Acts narrative. See also 5.33-34; 14.4; 17.18; 23.6-9; 28.24. On this, see Rius-Camps, 'Pentecostés', pp. 39-40. Rius-Camps pushes this alleged differentiation in the speech too far, however, basing it largely on (1) variant readings in the Western Text, (2) his (hardly warranted) omission of Ἰουδαῖοι in v. 5, and (3) his interpretation of ἄνδρες Ἰουδαῖοι (v. 14) and ἄνδρες Ἰσραηλῖται (v. 22) as two different groups. In his conclusion, Rius-Camps argues that the early insertion of Ἰουδαῖοι in v. 5 'ha contaminado ambas recensiones'. One could also argue, however, that the omission of Ἰουδαῖοι in v. 5 has contaminated both Codex Sinaiticus *and* Rius-Camps's essay.

16. The term is Talbert's. See Talbert, *Literary Patterns*, p. 5.

17. Rius-Camp's thesis as explained above becomes very difficult to accept at this point. See Mussies, 'Variation', p. 45.

οἶκος Ἰσραήλ... 'therefore, let the whole house of Israel know with certainty...' To this, the response of the crowd follows, addressing Peter and the apostles in a manner that echoes Peter's own at the outset of the third section: τί ποιήσωμεν, ἄνδρες ἀδελφοί 'what shall we do, men brothers?' It is interesting to note that the skeptical 'others' of v. 13 have at this point either disappeared from the scene or joined the ranks of the persuaded.

Upon closer examination of Peter's oration, one discovers a less obvious yet far more fundamental structure, built upon what is perhaps Luke's favourite theme in Acts. In the first section (vv. 12b-21), Peter addresses the question 'what?'—that is, stating what the phenomenon in question *is not*, he identifies it as 'that which was prophesied'. Throughout the remainder of the speech, the so-called christological kerygma, the focus is on 'who', and Peter now explains how the Spirit's outpouring is related to three major participants, namely, God, the Jews and Jesus, together with the processes engendered by them.[18] More specifically, vv. 22-36 spells out 'who does what to whom' in Luke's account of Pentecost. The bare backbone of this theme in sections 2-4, at once simple and powerful, may be summarized as follows:

> JESUS [complement] YOU killed><GOD raised (vv. 22-24, section 2)
> JESUS [complement] GOD raised><HE (Jesus) poured (vv. 32-33, section 3)
> LORD AND CHRIST [complement] GOD made><YOU killed (v. 36, peroratio)

In three separate clauses at key points of sections 2, 3 and in the peroratio, Jesus appears in the complement–initial position of the clause, on the receiving end of processes initiated by the Jews ('you') and God. The one exception, interestingly enough, is v. 33: ἐξέχεεν τοῦτο ὃ ὑμεῖς [καὶ] βλέπετε καὶ ἀκούετε,[19] 'He [that is, Jesus] poured *this* out, which you both hear and see'. This is the only clause in the Pentecost episode in which Jesus appears as agent in an ergative (i.e. a highly transitive) clause, and it is by means of this clause that Luke brings

---

18.   Though, as we shall see, the actions of each participant carry very different weight in Luke's narrative plot.

19.   An interesting textual variant of v. 33 is ἐξέχεεν ὑμῖν τοῦτο..., attested only by Dd, a fifth- to sixth-century Latin portion of Codex Bezae. In this regard, Epp writes: 'in this case...there is strong Western support against D, so that there is no need to regard D here as representing the Western text' (*Theological Tendency*, p. 69).

closure to the preceding explanation of the Pentecost event.[20] The chiasm[21] evident in the first and last of the dyads mentioned

> Jesus you killed><God raised (relative clause)
> Lord and Christ God made><You killed (relative clause)

ensures the memorability of Peter's message and underlines the fundamental importance of the transitivity network in Luke's narrative strategy.

As I mentioned at the outset of this chapter, the striking set of linguistic choices made by Luke in this episode has not been overlooked in several of the monographs and essays. Thus, Sloan speaks of a 'theocentric syntax' discernible throughout Peter's speech,[22] and Mínguez concludes that the activity of God with Jesus as the object appears 'invasoramente irresistible' ('invasively irresistible').[23] In the pages that follow I shall attempt to provide a more complete and principled analysis of these features of language than any offered in previous discussions of the Pentecost episode. Having done this, I shall turn my attention to an issue of a theological/historical nature, namely, the alleged primitive and/or adoptionistic Christology of Peter's speech, and suggest a purely linguistic and literary solution to the problem.

3. *Functional Elements of the Clause and Clause Structure in Acts 2*

Following the pattern of previous chapters, this analysis of the clause and clause structure in Acts is twofold. First, it is a functional study of the Greek clause as representation of a process, consisting of the elements of the process itself, participants and circumstances, and of how these relate to foregrounding. This is the primary focus of this volume. Secondly, it is an investigation of clause structure that applies to the Acts 2 narrative the method pioneered by Porter in his Philippians study.[24] The two approaches to the study of the clause are comple-

---

20. It is the pronoun τοῦτο at vv. 12 and 33 that forms an inclusio in the narrative, and not the words ἡμέραν...ἐπὶ τὸ αὐτό in vv. 1 and 47, as Mínguez has argued. See Mínguez, *Semiótica Narrativa*, p. 32.

21. For a recent discussion of chiasm see S.E. Porter and J.T. Reed, 'Philippians as a Macro-Chiasm and its Exegetical Significance', *NTS* 44 (1998), pp. 213-31.

22 Sloan, 'Signs and Wonders', p. 230.

23. Mínguez, *Semiótica Narrativa*, p. 48.

24. Porter, 'Word Order', p. 194.

mentary, the former being primarily functional and focusing on 'system', while the latter is primarily formal and centers on 'structure'. The terms system and structure, of fundamental importance in Halliday's functional grammar, have correlation with the Saussurean distinction between the paradigmatic and syntagmatic relations in language. Following Halliday and other functional grammarians, I place greater emphasis on paradigmatic relations, that is, those relations in virtue of which language is seen as a system, a large network of meaningful options available to language users for text creation.[25] Of these options, few, perhaps none, are more significant than those which emanate from the transitivity network. Consequently, in any discussion of the 'goings on' of the Pentecost episode, explicit reference to types of processes, participant relations and, to a lesser extent, attendant circumstances must play a prominent part.

(a) *Acts 2: Who Does What to Whom?*
Peter's audience (henceforth referred to as 'the Jews'[26]), God and Jesus stand out as the three most conspicuous participants in the Pentecost narrative. Indeed, when all of the references to the Jews, God and Jesus are considered, almost the entirety of Peter's speech is covered.

Of the three participants mentioned, both in terms of order of appearance and total number of references, 'the Jews' come first in Luke's plot. The 24 references to them are distributed as follows: In four instances, 'the Jews' appear as full explicit subjects, that is, as grammaticalized subjects of the clause in the form of a noun or a noun phrase: Ἰουδαῖοι (2.5), τὸ πλῆθος, 'the crowd' (2.6), οἱ μὲν οὖν ἀποδεξάμενοι τὸν λόγον, 'those who received the word' (2.41), and ὡσεὶ τρισχίλιαι 'about three thousand' (2.41b). In another six references, Peter's audience appears as abbreviated explicit subject, that is,

25. See Halliday, *Language as Social Semiotic*, pp. 40-42; and, more recently, Halliday, 'On Grammar and Grammatics', in R. Hasan, C. Cloran and D. Butt (eds.), *Functional Descriptions* (Amsterdam Studies in the Theory and History of Linguistic Science, 4.121; Amsterdam: John Benjamins, 1996), pp. 20-21.

26. I find no other convincing interpretation of the thrice-repeated Ἰουδαῖοι, nor do I accept Rius-Camps's deletion of the same word, against the best manuscript evidence, in v. 5. See my n. 13. Lake agrees on the alleged rightness of not including Ἰουδαῖοι in v. 5, yet bases his opinion largely on internal evidence. See Kirsopp Lake, 'The Gift of the Spirit on the Day of Pentecost', in F.G. Foakes Jackson and Kirsopp Lake (eds.), *The Beginnings of Christianity*. I. *The Acts of the Apostles*, V (London: Macmillan, 1933), p. 113.

as grammaticalized subject in the form of either a pronoun[27] or an adjective.[28] Thirdly, 'the Jews' also appear as non-explicit subjects on twelve occasions.[29] Lastly, this large group of individuals appears twice as non-subject participant, that is, occupying the complement (i.e. direct or indirect object) slot in two clauses which report their status as recipients of Peter's words.[30] Concerning the types of processes encoded in the clauses I have just referred to, mental and verbal processes predominate, as 'the Jews' hear, listen to, and are amazed and confounded at first, and later are 'cut to the heart' by Peter's words. Of the four material clauses in the episode,[31] two have both a participant performing an action and a second participant to whom the action is directed: τοῦτον...προσπήξαντες ἀνείλατε, 'it is this man whom you killed, having nailed him...' (2.23), and τοῦτον τὸν Ἰησοῦν ὃν ὑμεῖς ἐσταυρώσατε, 'this very Jesus whom you yourselves crucified' (2.36). In terms of high or low transitivity,[32] these two ergative clauses represent the high point of the Jews' participation in the plot of the Pentecost episode. When considered from this point of view, a certain crescendo is discernible in the 24 references to Peter's audience, beginning with mainly mental and verbal processes (i.e. low transitivity) in vv. 5-14, and moving to the two material processes encoded in ergative clauses in vv. 23 and 36 (i.e. high transitivity), the latter having an explicit subject. Conversely, once a significant section of 'the Jews' has accepted Peter's message, the transitivity co-efficient of clauses referring to 'the Jews' decreases significantly, as they appear four times as subjects of verbs in the passive voice,[33] the first two as addressees of imperatives issued by Peter.

27. ἡμεῖς ἀκούομεν (2.8); ἕτεροι δὲ διαχλευάζοντες ἔλεγον... (2.13); ὑμεῖς ὑπολαμβάνετε (2.15); ὃν ὑμεῖς ἐσταυρώσατε (2.36); βαπτισθήτω ἕκαστος ὑμῶν (2.38).

28. ἐξίσταντο δὲ πάντες καὶ διηπόρουν (2.12).

29. ἤκουον εἷς ἕκαστος (2.6); ἐξίσταντο δὲ καὶ ἐθαύμαζον (2.7); λέγοντες (2.7b); ἀκούομεν λαλούντων αὐτῶν (2.11); λέγοντες (2.12); τοῦτον...ἀνείλατε (2.23); ἀκούσαντες δὲ κατενύγησαν (2.37); εἶπόν τε (2.37b); τί ποιήσωμεν (2.37c); μετανοήσατε (2.38); σώθητε (2.40).

30. ἀπεφθέγξατο αὐτοῖς (2.14); παρεκάλει αὐτοὺς (2.40).

31. συνῆλθεν τὸ πλῆθος καὶ συνεχύθη (2.6); τοῦτον...προσπήξαντες ἀνείλατε (2.23) ὃν ὑμεῖς ἐσταυρώσατε (2.36); τί ποιήσωμεν (2.37).

32. See Hopper and Thompson, 'Transitivity in Grammar', pp. 251-99.

33. βαπτισθήτω ἕκαστος ὑμῶν (2.38); σώθητε (2.40); ἐβαπτίσθησαν (2.41a); προσετέθησαν (2.41b).

The *dramatis persona*, the initiator and agent par excellence in the Pentecost episode, is, not surprisingly, God. The 19 references to God as participant in the processes depicted in Acts 2 are distributed as follows. On eight occasions, that is, 42.1% of the total, God is the full explicit subject of the clause,[34] and never appears as abbreviated explicit subject. Throughout Peter's speech, God appears in 10 instances as non-explicit subject in clauses which follow closely after full explicit mentions of him as either God or the Lord.[35] Last of all, on one single occasion God occupies the complement slot of a clause in which David is said to have 'seen the Lord' (2.25). In all the above, material clauses predominate, that is, in a majority of instances, God is the subject who does something to someone or initiates an action which extends to someone or something.[36] Insofar as causation on the part of God as effective agent is involved, these are ergative clauses, at the highest point of Hopper and Thompson's transitivity scale.

Lastly, Jesus is introduced at v. 22, at the outset of the second section of Peter's address. The highly unusual manner in which Jesus is introduced, the structural significance of which I shall detail in the next section, is maintained throughout the rest of the speech. Indeed, the 'non-subject participant' mode (i.e. Jesus occupying the complement slot of the clause) is the most frequent mode of reference to Jesus in this episode (five instances). In the five clauses in question, Jesus appears on

34. λέγει ὁ θεός (2.17); οἷς ἐποίησεν δι᾽ αὐτοῦ ὁ θεός (2.22); ὃν ὁ θεὸς ἀνέστησεν (2.24); ὤμοσεν αὐτῷ ὁ θεός (2.30); τοῦτον τὸν Ἰησοῦν ἀνέστησεν ὁ θεός (2.32); εἶπεν [ὁ] κύριος τῷ κυρίῳ μου (2.34); καὶ κύριον αὐτὸν καὶ Χριστὸν ἐποίησεν ὁ θεός (2.36); ὅσους ἂν προσκαλέσηται κύριος ὁ θεός (2.39).

35. ἐκχεῶ (2.17); ἐκχεῶ (2.18); δώσω τέρατα ἐν τῷ οὐρανῷ ἄνω καὶ σημεῖα (2.19); λύσας τὰς ὠδῖνας τοῦ θανάτου (2.24); ἐκ δεξιῶν μού ἐστιν (2.25); οὐκ ἐγκαταλείψεις τὴν ψυχήν μου (2.27); οὐδὲ δώσεις τὸν ὅσιόν σου (2.27b); ἐγνώρισάς μοι ὁδοὺς ζωῆς (2.28); πληρώσεις με εὐφροσύνης (2.28b); θῶ τοὺς ἐχθρούς σου ὑποπόδιον (2.35).

36. δώσω τέρατα...καὶ σημεῖα (2.19); οἷς ἐποίησεν δι᾽ αὐτοῦ ὁ θεός (2.22); ὃν ὁ θεὸς ἀνέστησεν (2.24); λύσας τὰς ὠδῖνας (2.24b); οὐκ ἐγκαταλείψεις τὴν ψυχήν μου (2.27); οὐδὲ δώσεις τὸν ὅσιόν σου (2.27); πληρώσεις με εὐφροσύνης (2.28); τοῦτον τὸν Ἰησοῦν ἀνέστησεν ὁ θεός (2.32) ἕως ἂν θῶ τοὺς ἐχθρούς σου ὑποπόδιον (2.35); καὶ κύριον αὐτὸν καὶ Χριστὸν ἐποίησεν ὁ θεός (2.36). At least two of these clauses contain grammatical metaphors, namely 2.28b and 2.36, yet, for the purpose of clause structure analysis, they remain material processes. See Halliday, *Introduction to Functional Grammar*, p. 157.

the receiving end of actions initiated by the Jews (killing, nailing, etc.)[37] and by God (raising from the dead and 'making' him both Christ and Lord).[38] The rest of the references to Jesus in the speech are distributed as follows: There are no references as full explicit subject. There is one reference as abbreviated explicit subject of a verb in the passive voice, namely, κρατεῖσθαι αὐτὸν ὑπ᾽ αὐτου, 'for him to be grasped by [death]' (2.24). There are four references as non-explicit subject, of which two are passive verb forms.[39] The other two, together forming one single construction, are: (1) τήν τε ἐπαγγελίαν τοῦ πνεύματος τοῦ ἁγίου λαβὼν παρὰ τοῦ πατρὸς, 'having received the promise of the Holy Spirit from the Father...' and (2) ἐξέχεεν τοῦτο, 'He poured out this...' In summary, the total activity of Jesus in Peter's speech is limited to one single act: his pouring out the Holy Spirit ('this'), having himself received it from the Father. This single and qualified reference to Jesus as agent in an ergative clause stands within a succession of clauses depicting Jesus consistently as the victim/beneficiary of actions initiated by the Jews and God.

As I mentioned above, nearly at the end of Peter's speech, Luke connects the Pentecost event to Jesus by stating that it is Jesus who poured 'this' (τοῦτο) out which the audience had both seen and heard. Secondly, the peroratio-colophon and the response of the crowd center upon the person of Jesus, and Peter's instruction to those who receive the word is that they repent (of having rejected and murdered Jesus) and be baptized in Jesus' name. It would perhaps seem to many readers, therefore, both interesting and unusual that, although the entire episode turns out to be largely about Jesus, the mode of introduction of and reference to him is in fact by no means what one would expect of a narrative's protagonist.[40] Among the choices that Luke could have made (but did not) in order to highlight the importance of Jesus in the Pentecost episode are: first, full explicit references to him as subject, at least at the beginning of the christological kerygma (v. 22), or in the clause depicting his pouring out of the Spirit (v. 33). Secondly, notwithstanding

---

37. Ἰησοῦν τὸν Ναζωραῖον...τοῦτον...προσπήξαντες ἀνείλατε (2.22-23); τοῦτον τὸν Ἰησοῦν ὃν ὑμεῖς ἐσταυρώσατε (2.36).

38. ὃν ὁ θεὸς ἀνέστησεν (2.24); τοῦτον τὸν Ἰησοῦν ἀνέστησεν ὁ θεός (2.32); καὶ κύριον αὐτὸν καὶ Χριστὸν ἐποίησεν ὁ θεός (2.36).

39. οὔτε ἐγκατελείφθη εἰς ᾅδην (2.31); τῇ δεξιᾷ οὖν τοῦ θεοῦ ὑψωθεὶς (2.33).

40. See Porter, 'Word Order', pp. 193-94; Levinsohn, 'Participant Reference', pp. 31-44.

Luke's need to refer to Jesus as the sufferer of violent death, more references to him as initiator of processes of various types (e.g. he said, he healed, he rose [see more on this below]) would have contributed to making Jesus stand out as a key protagonist in the episode to a greater extent. The fact remains, however, that although the mentioned choices were, among many others, available to Luke for the depiction of processes and participants in his narrative, he has chosen to select the linguistic options discussed above, and not others. In a manner that defies imitation,[41] Luke has referred to Jesus 10 times over 14 verses of text, but in only one single instance as an agent who performs an action extending beyond himself.

(b) *Clause Structure and its Significance in Acts 2*
Given the comparatively overwhelming presence of God as an agent in this episode, Jesus' participation in it would appear only marginally significant to the reader, were it not for the striking choice of clause structure made by Luke at key points of the episode. In commenting on the structure of the various clauses in the Pentecost episode, Tannehill affirms that the accusatives referring to Jesus are placed 'in emphatic position at the beginning of a clause'.[42] The same point is made by Tannehill regarding first and second person pronouns, that is, they are placed first in the clause 'and thereby emphasized'.[43] As I have pointed out before, this is a fairly widespread opinion concerning the clause-initial position in the Greek clause.[44] Unfortunately, the ad hoc and unsystematic fashion in which these comments are made leaves many important questions unanswered: what exactly is meant by 'emphasis'? in relation to what are these items emphasized? And, most importantly, what is the frequency of the mentioned items in the initial position vis-à-vis other positions in the clause?

My findings in regard to clause structure for the Pentecost episode confirm the data gathered from my previous samplings of Acts chs. 27, 6–7, and 21–22. Subjects are not grammaticalized in a majority of instances (52% of independent clauses do not have explicit subjects, compared to 57% of dependent clauses), though they are grammatical-

41. See Mínguez, *Semiótica Narrativa*, p. 46.
42. Tannehill, *The Narrative Unity*, p. 36.
43. Tannehill, *The Narrative Unity*, p. 36 n. 27.
44. Similarly to Tannehill, see Barrett, *Acts*, p. 140.

ized more often than in non-narrative texts.[45] In independent clauses, the structures Pred.–Comp. and Pred. are equal in number of instances, whereas in dependent clauses the Pred. structure is three times more frequent than the Pred.–Comp. structure.[46] In both independent and dependent clauses, the most infrequent structure is Comp.–Pred., as in τοῦτον...προσπήξαντες ἀνείλατε ('having nailed this man [to the cross] you killed him'). If τίς τί questions are excluded from the Comp.–Pred. structure tally,[47] the unusualness of this clause type is highlighted even further, at just 9 per cent of the total in independent clauses, and 10 per cent in dependent clauses. When subjects are grammaticalized in the Pentecost episode, the subject occupies the initial position in 48 per cent of independent clauses and 44.5 per cent of dependent clauses, a fact that seems to dispute the hypothesis that subjects in the clause initial position are indicators of emphasis.[48] The difficulty inherent in making any such interpretive claims regarding the positioning of the explicit subject in the clause is further evidenced by the following example:

διὰ τοῦτο ηὐφράνθη **ἡ καρδία μου**
καὶ ἠγαλλιάσατο **ἡ γλῶσσά μου**,
ἔτι δὲ καὶ **ἡ σάρξ μου** κατασκηνώσει ἐπ᾽ ἐλπίδι (Acts 2.26)

On account of this, my heart rejoices and my tongue was gladdened and my flesh will dwell in hope.

45. See Porter, 'Word Order', pp. 194, 200.
46. Although when the data from all the Acts samples mentioned is considered, the structure Pred.–Comp. is predominant in independent clauses, while in dependent clauses Pred.–Comp. and Pred. structures are roughly equal in number of instances.
47. Both instances of Comp.–Pred. structure in the narrative section of Acts 2 are τί questions (2.12b and 2.37b). This is an example of a syntactical constraint imposed by the language system which significantly limits the meaningfulness of choice in this case.
48. The standard, most frequent or 'unmarked' clause structure must be determined first, and only then should the analyst put forth explanatory hypotheses regarding the non-standard, less frequent or 'marked' structures. Since in the Acts narrative, explicit subjects appear at initial and non initial positions of the clause in almost equal numbers, hypothesizing about the significance of either positioning becomes very difficult indeed. The facts concerning the positioning of the explicit subject appear to be different in non-narrative texts. See Porter, 'Word Order', pp. 194, 201.

where the positioning of the explicit subjects seems to be (as it is in the Hebrew original) a matter of stylistic effect, rather than a purposeful emphasis of 'my flesh' vis-à-vis 'my tongue' and 'my heart'.[49] It appears, therefore, that although Hellenistic Greek is clearly not a language with 'free' clause structure, there is, certainly insofar as narrative is concerned, significant room for variation of placement of the explicit subject within the clause. Further, as we have seen, although the Pred–Comp structure tends to occur with greater frequency than the Pred option throughout the Acts narrative, the difference is not significant. The fact remains, then, that by far the most infrequent choice of clause structure made by Luke in the Acts narrative is the Comp–Pred option. Yet, as I have pointed out before, mere figures tell us nothing about whether or not a particular syntactical pattern has 'value in the game', that is, whether or not it is significant as a purposeful authorial choice within the framework of the author's larger literary strategy. Further, as Halliday has noted, in order to show that an apparently prominent item of language is actually significant in relation to the text of which it is a part, the analyst must establish how that is so 'in virtue of and through the medium of [that item's] own value in the language—through the linguistic function from which its meaning is derived'.[50] In the case of the Pentecost episode, I am concerned to show how the 'complement-ness' of Ἰησοῦν τὸν Ναζωραῖον, τοῦτον τὸν Ἰησοῦν, and κύριον αὐτὸν καὶ Χριστὸν ('Jesus the Nazarene, this very Jesus, and both Lord and Christ'), a function of the transitivity network, made possible ultimately by the ideational function of language,[51] relates directly and powerfully to the larger narrative episode of which it is a part, an episode built primarily upon choices emanating from the transitivity network of Greek.

As I have shown above in this chapter, in the plot of the Pentecost episode the fundamental question of 'who does what to whom' appears to be central, and unfolds in rather explicit terms. In fact, Peter's speech

---

49. Similarly, Acts 2.17: προφητεύσουσιν οἱ υἱοὶ ὑμῶν καὶ αἱ θυγατέρες ὑμῶν, καὶ οἱ νεανίσκοι ὑμῶν ὁράσεις ὄψονται.

50. Halliday, *Explorations*, p. 112.

51. As has been stated before at various points, the ideational function of language is that function in virtue of which a speaker or writer expresses through language his experience of the world. Transitivity is, according to Halliday, the grammar of the clause in its ideational aspect. See Halliday, *Explorations*, p. 39.

may be aptly summarized along these lines: the Jews' malicious act against Jesus (i.e. murdering him) is overruled by God's more powerful act on his behalf (i.e. raising him from the dead). Jesus' single act as an agent in the entire episode, namely, his pouring out of the Spirit, is made possible by God's own consistent activity in Jesus' life, including God giving Jesus 'the promise of the Spirit' (2.33). Thus, the over-powering presence of God in the episode would necessarily relegate Jesus' comparatively passive participation to the background of the narrative, were it not for the strikingly unusual clause structure chosen by Luke to refer to Jesus at three key junctures of the speech. Of the three instances in which Jesus occupies the complement initial position I have referred to above,[52] the second possesses the greatest attention-drawing qualities. In this instance, to the unusualness of the clause structure is added the presence of the adjectival demonstrative pronoun, in a manner that is consistent throughout, as I have explained in Chapter 3 at some length. The same construction τοῦτον τὸν Ἰησοῦν is repeated in the colophon of v. 36 to construct an impacting summary statement. The remarkable similarities between this clause and another clause referring to Moses in Acts 7.35 are worth elucidating at this point:

Acts 2.36	Acts 7.35
καὶ κύριον αὐτὸν καὶ Χριστὸν ἐποί-ησεν ὁ θεός, **τοῦτον τὸν Ἰησοῦν ὃν ὑμεῖς ἐσταυρώσατε.**	**Τοῦτον τὸν Μωϋσῆν, ὃν ἠρνήσαντο** εἰπόντες…τοῦτον ὁ θεὸς [καὶ] ἄρχον-τα καὶ λυτρωτὴν ἀπέσταλκεν
God made him both lord and Christ, this very Jesus whom you yourselves crucified.	This very Moses whom they denied saying…even this man God sent as ruler and deliverer.

The comments I made regarding the clause in Acts 7.35 in my analysis of Stephen's speech are equally valid for the clause of Acts 2.36, particularly in light of the fact that, for Luke, Moses is a Christ-like figure

---

52. As indicated in the previous section, there are a total of five instances in which Jesus occupies the complement-initial position in the clause. The other two (2.24a and 2.36b), however, are complements in dependent clauses, a fact which tends to diminish the overall impact of the clause. On the issue of these relative clauses, see Haenchen, *The Acts of the Apostles*, pp. 139, 180, where Haenchen argues that these are 'ostensibly relative, but in reality main clauses to which Luke is addicted'.

in more ways than one.[53] In both instances, the complement–initial
position is occupied by a character who is central to the episode's plot,
yet who at the same time appears sidelined and incapacitated in light of
his own inactivity and the events initiated almost wholly by others. By
means of this most unusual clause structure, however, Luke draws
attention to their status as complements, as recipients of largely hostile
actions, who are finally vindicated by God's own all-powerful initiative. In the narrative of Acts 2 Jesus may be perceived as a passive victim of the actions performed by others. Yet, Luke does not allow the
reader to overlook him on this account. In fact, by highlighting his status as complement in particular, the writer is showing readers that, for
his present literary purposes, it is patients rather than agents that matter
most.[54] Indeed, it is while Jesus appears in a position of apparent helplessness that God's action on his behalf is shown to be all-conquering.
In terms of foregrounding scheme, it seems appropriate to describe the
three complement-initial clauses described above as the *frontground*[55]
of this narrative, with the ergative clauses having God and the Jews as
agents as the *foreground*, and all other material as the *background*. This
interpretation coheres with those I have offered of other episodes in
Acts, and represents a linguistic-literary substantiation of claims made
concerning the theme(s) of the Pentecost episode and/or Peter's speech
(see n. 9 above).

53. Compare, for example, Acts 7.20-22 with Luke's account of the birth and
childhood of Jesus in Lk. 2.

54. The significance of the complement-initial clauses may also be explained in
terms of thematic structure. The two elements in virtue of which a clause is structured as a message are known in functional grammar as theme and rheme. The
theme is the element that gives the clause its starting point, it is what the clause is
about. The remainder of the clause, the part where the theme is developed or com-
mented on, is the rheme. In the Greek of Acts (and probably in other narrative
texts), the standard is for the theme to be grammaticalized in a subject, whether
explicit or not, while the predicate and/or complement normally occupies the slot of
rheme, that is, it is that which is said about the theme. In the complement initial
instances I have pointed out, however, the order is reversed, and, e.g., Ἰησοῦν τὸν
Ναζωραῖον now occupies the theme slot, so that it may accurately be rendered as: it
is Jesus the Nazarene…whom you killed. See Halliday, *Introduction to Functional
Grammar*, pp. 38-39; Halliday and Hasan, 'Notes on Transitivity and Theme in
English', pp. 174-77.

55. This is Porter's term, used in *Verbal Aspect*, pp. 92-93.

4. *Christology and the Language of the Pentecost Episode*

In hypothesizing concerning the various traditions that Luke may have relied upon in the composition of the Pentecost narrative, it has been held by some scholars that the alleged undeveloped Christology of this episode is attributable to a very ancient source that Luke has chosen to leave untouched, his own unease with its content notwithstanding (see n. 6 above). For Barrett and Haenchen, this alleged primitive Christology is evident in Acts 2.36, where God is said to have made (ἐποίησεν) Jesus both Lord and Christ, a statement which—according to the two commentators—betrays an early form of adoptionism in Luke's source.[56] More significantly, however, Haenchen and others, especially Evans and Léon-Dufour, have seen further evidence of an early Christology in the transitive use of ἀνέστησεν with God as subject in v. 24 and throughout Acts.[57] In what follows, I shall attempt to answer primarily the latter claim, given its significance for the whole of Acts, and finally argue that the same explanation is equally applicable to the 2.36 text. The discussions by Léon-Dufour and Evans are a fitting springboard for my response for two main reasons. First, in the specific sections I am referring to, both writers give significant attention to both the language of resurrection and its theological interpretation. Secondly, both scholars provide chronologies of an alleged development of the understanding of Jesus' resurrection in the New Testament, based largely on the transitive or intransitive uses of the two relevant verbs. These chronologies are particularly open to evaluation and criticism.

Léon-Dufour's discussion begins by noting the diversity evident in the many New Testament texts which refer to Jesus' resurrection. Thus, some references state the fact of the resurrection in a straightforward

---

56. But see Witherington's response to this thesis in *Acts*, pp. 147-53.

57. See Haenchen, *The Acts of the Apostles*, pp. 91-92. I was first made aware of this issue through Petr Pokorny's 'Christologie et baptême à l'époque du christianisme primitif', *NTS* 27 (1980), pp. 368-80, where Pokorny refers to the use of ἀνέστησεν in v. 24 and argues that 'Pour la plupart, on parle de la résurrection de telle façon que l'impulsion exprimée ou tacite de cette action vient de Dieu même, aux termes de la dogmatique developpée de Dieu-Père' (p. 370). See also C.F. Evans, *Resurrection and the New Testament* (Studies in Biblical Theology, 2.12; London: SCM Press, 1970), pp. 20-22; Xavier Léon-Dufour, *Resurrection and the Message of Easter* (trans. G. Chapman; London: Geoffrey Chapman, 1974), pp. 5-14.

manner while others relate it to Jesus' death, highlighting the redemptive significance of both events. Secondly, the effective agent of Jesus' resurrection is in some instances God, while in others it is Jesus himself. After some further preliminary statements, Léon-Dufour raises a question which he attempts to answer throughout the remainder of his discussion: '...does the diversity in the [resurrection] formulas reflect an evolution in christology?'[58] For him, the answer is a resounding yes. Beginning with a discussion of the formula 'Christ has risen', which is in his view late and developed, Léon-Dufour cites two references: Lk. 24.34 and 1 Cor. 15.3-5, both of which use the verb ἐγείρειν. Focusing his analysis on the perfect form ἐγήγερται (1 Cor. 15.4), however, he concludes that since the form in question could be read as either passive or middle, it is not possible to ascertain who the agent is in this case.[59] Notwithstanding its 'more developed' nature, the writer concludes that the formula 'Christ has risen', is in fact, 'extremely ancient'.[60] Secondly, Léon-Dufour discusses what is in his view the more primitive formula, namely, 'God raised Jesus from the dead'. Surprisingly, in this case the author focuses his attention on the following two passages, both from 1 Thessalonians:

1 Thess. 4.14	1 Thess. 1.10
εἰ γὰρ πιστεύομεν ὅτι Ἰησοῦς ἀπέθανεν καὶ ἀνέστη	καὶ ἀναμένειν τὸν υἱὸν αὐτοῦ ἐκ τῶν οὐρανῶν, ὃν ἤγειρεν ἐκ [τῶν] νεκρῶν
If we believe that Jesus died and rose [again]	And to await expectantly his Son from heaven, whom he [God] raised from the dead.

Dismissing the 4.14 text as not being truly 'formulaic' (i.e. not having the form of a standardized confession) in its original form, Léon-Dufour goes on to argue that the 1.10 text contains a truly ancient for-

---

58. Léon-Dufour, *Resurrection and the Message*, p. 6.

59. What Léon-Dufour fails to mention explicitly is that ἐγείρειν, being a deponent verb, an active meaning is equally possible, not only in the perfect passive form he is discussing, but in aorist passive forms as well. Thus Moule: 'Whether one can find any substantial difference between Lk. 7.14 ἐγέρθητι (passive form), and 8.54 ἔγειρε (active form), is doubtful: they *appear* both to be simply intransitive in sense' (*Idiom Book*, p. 26). Likewise BDF, §78: 'The latter language preferred the aorist passive in the case of deponents (where a real passive meaning is at best a possibility)'. BDF offer, among other examples, the form ἐγερθείς.

60. Léon-Dufour, *Resurrection and the Message*, p. 11.

mula, preceding in time even the affirmation of 1 Cor. 15.4 he had discussed in the previous section.[61] The author's criterion for determining what is developed and undeveloped becomes clear in the chronology he suggests regarding the evolution of the subject in the New Testament writings:

1. 'Originally': God is the author of Christ's resurrection (Rom. 8.11; Gal. 1.1; Col. 2.12; Eph. 1.10)
2. In an 'intermediate stage': Christ is the passive subject (e.g. Christ has been raised)
3. In 'the language of tradition': Jesus takes up his own life again (Jn 2.19; 10.17)[62]

As it turns out, any New Testament clause that has God as the effective agent of Jesus' resurrection is necessarily primitive for Léon-Dufour, while, conversely, those clauses wherein Jesus is said to raise [himself] or rise from the dead are, evidently, the product of a late and developed Christology. The facts are, however, far more complex than this. To begin with, in the light of the author's statement concerning his inability to decide on the sense of ἐγείρειν, and given the fact that both of his two examples of 'developed Christology' contained forms of this verb, his concluding chronology seems hardly tenable. Secondly and more importantly, Léon-Dufour has failed to deal adequately with the use of ἀνίστημι in its resurrection sense in the New Testament. When the ἀνίστημι data are fully considered, Léon-Dufour's thesis becomes highly implausible, for, as is the case with ἐγείρειν in 1 Thessalonians, transitive and intransitive uses of ἀνίστημι are interspersed throughout the New Testament and other early Christian literature in a manner that defies chronological explanation. To wit, the intransitive use of ἀνίστημι when it means resurrection (as opposed to getting up, for example) and has Jesus as subject is exclusive in Mark, Luke and John,[63] while in Acts, five out of six instances of ἀνίστημι referring to Jesus' resurrection have God as subject,[64] with 17.3 being the exception.[65]

---

61. Léon-Dufour, *Resurrection and the Message*, pp. 12, 13.
62. Léon-Dufour, *Resurrection and the Message*, p. 16.
63. Mk 8.31; 9.9; 9.10; 9.32; 10.34; Lk. 18.33; 24.7; 24.46; Jn 20.9.
64. Acts 2.24; 2.32; 13.33; 13.34; 17.31.
65. τὸν χριστὸν ἔδει παθεῖν καὶ ἀναστῆναι ἐκ νεκρῶν. Although Christ is in this instance the subject of the intransitive ἀναστῆναι, the δει + infinitive construc-

The only other remaining instance of ἀνίστημι referring to Jesus in the New Testament is found in 1 Thess. 4.14, where it is used intransitively with Jesus as subject. However, as we have seen above, the same author earlier in the letter refers to the same event using ἐγείρειν, this time with God as the subject.

C.F. Evans's treatment of the subject is even more fraught with both omissions and inaccuracies than Léon-Dufour's. At the outset of his discussion, Evans affirms the following: 'that the two verbs [ἀνιστάναι and ἐγείρειν] are synonymous can be seen from their interchange in 1 Cor. 15'.[66] That the two verbs are partially synonymous is certain, but this may not be learned from a chapter where ἀνιστάναι does not at all appear![67] Further, unlike Léon-Dufour, Evans makes no reference to the deponent nature of ἐγείρειν, and assumes instead that 'the subject of ἐγείρειν is always God, or else the verb is used in the passive, which then always has the sense "raised by God"'.[68] Concerning the sense of ἀνιστάναι, Evans is equally confident and asserts that even when ἀνιστάναι is intransitive, it 'intends the sense "He was raised by God"'.[69] One cannot but be puzzled by Evans's bold yet unsubstantiated claims. As is also true of Léon-Dufour's discussion, the ultimate criterion behind Evans's theory becomes particularly clear when he provides a chronology of the alleged evolution of the concept of resurrection in the New Testament and later:

1.   God raised Jesus from the dead (Acts, Rom., Gal., etc.)
2.   Jesus is 'the raiser of his own body' (Jn 10.17 etc.)
3.   'A further step along': 'He truly raised himself...' (Ignatius, *Smyr.* 2.1)

tion, a common Lukan feature, reminds us that Jesus' rising from the dead is fulfillment of the all-encompassing divine necessity.

66.   Evans, *Resurrection and the New Testament*, p. 21.

67.   The noun ἀνάστασις does appear four times in 1 Cor. 15. However, Evans's discussion is centered on the meaning of the two verbs in question, particularly their transitive or intransitive meanings, for which reference to the noun is hardly relevant.

68.   Evans, *Resurrection and the New Testament*, p. 21.

69.   Evans, *Resurrection and the New Testament*, p. 21. Though he adds that the Son of Man predictions in Mark are 'not as clear', and that 'the only clear exceptions' are found in John, due to his 'advanced Christology'.

4. 'A very considerable further step': 'He transformed himself
    into an imperishable aeon and raised himself up (*Epistle to
    Rheginos* 45.17)[70]

This interpretation is familiar from Léon-Dufour's discussion, except
for the post-New Testament citations. Unfortunately, however, Evans
has ignored data that would dispute his thesis, as is evident in the case
of Ignatius. In his epistle to the Trallians, the second-century church
father writes concerning Christ:

> Κωφώθητε οὖν, ὅταν ὑμιν χωρὶς Ἰησοῦ Χριστοῦ λαλῇ τις...ὅς καὶ
> ἀληθῶς ἠγέρθη ἀπὸ νεκρῶν ἐγείραντος αὐτὸν τοῦ πατρὸς αὐτοῦ, ὅς
> καὶ κατὰ τὸ ὁμοίωμα ἡμᾶς τοὺς πιστεύοντας αὐτῷ οὕτως ἐγειρεῖ ὁ
> πατὴρ αὐτοῦ ἐν Χριστῷ Ἰησοῦ.

> Be deaf therefore, whenever anyone speaks to you apart from Jesus
> Christ...who was raised indeed from the dead when His Father raised
> Him, and who,—His Father that is—in the same manner will likewise
> also raise us in Christ Jesus who believe in Him.[71]

The strong and emphatic language used in this passage, and, particularly, the repetition of the subject in the last line, 'His Father', makes it
highly unlikely that Ignatius is here begrudgingly quoting an ancient
source in spite of his distaste for its primitive Christology. This point
highlights the fundamental problem in both of the above discussions.
Given the fact that both transitive and intransitive uses of ἀνιστάναι are
attested in writings of all periods up to the second century and beyond,
both writers are forced to base their chronologies on putative sources
and traditions no longer accessible to us outside of their own hypotheses. The discussions by Léon-Dufour and Evans are both stimulating
and incisive treatments of a subject of capital importance for both linguistic and theological study of the New Testament. Unfortunately, both
writers have rushed to conclusions of a theological/historical nature
without sufficient attention to the language of the texts they have
studied. More specifically, although both studies deal with the issue of
transitive and intransitive verbs and their significance, they are carried
out in isolation from and without any substantial reference to the transitivity network of Greek, or the set of choices made by individual New
Testament writers from that network. Had Léon-Dufour and Evans paid
closer attention to these choices in (for example) the Acts of the

70. Evans, *Resurrection and the New Testament*, p. 22.
71. Ignatius, *To the Trallians*, p. 9. My translation.

Apostles, they may have discovered that, particularly in the case of ἀνιστάναι clauses referring to Christ's resurrection, choices of subject and complement are often much more related to literary strategy than to putative sources or dogmatic development in the primitive church. In my view, the same holds true for the allegedly adoptionistic clause καὶ κύριον αὐτὸν καὶ Χριστὸν ἐποίησεν ὁ θεός, 'God made him both Lord and Christ' (2.36). When Barrett writes concerning this verse that 'Luke would not have chosen to express himself in this way',[72] he seems to be contemplating the clause in question as a self-contained theological pronouncement.[73] He fails to bring into his discussion, for example, the way in which in this episode Luke consistently opposes the actions of God and men, in both cases with Jesus as the object (see my summary above in this chapter), a feature, as I have pointed out, characteristic of Luke's presentation of key characters in other major episodes of Acts.

This last point may be further illustrated by reference to an insight from A.J. Greimas's narrative theory,[74] based ultimately on Vladímir Propp's ground-breaking *Morphology of the Folktale.*[75] Continuing with the work of Propp, Greimas proposed a metalanguage for the description of narrative participants and their actions. Though I do not accept Greimas's transformational generative framework,[76] his actantial

72. Barrett, *Acts*, p. 151. But, as I mentioned above, Barrett contradicts himself (see my n. 6).

73. The manner in which Barrett deals with this verse raises some important questions concerning the nature and aims of a commentary. Barrett's two-volume treatise on Acts, of which only the first tome has thus far been published, is an awe-inspiring display of historical, socio-cultural and literary knowledge of encyclopedic proportions. Yet, in dealing extensively with almost every single pericope of the book and relating his comments to almost every major differing view in previous scholarship, it seems to me, that Barrett fails to deal with Acts as a literary unit worthy of consistent, methodical analysis *for its own sake*. In discussing Acts 2.36, the question of sources and adoptionist Christology is raised immediately by Barrett, as it was in the works of Haenchen, Dibelius and others before them, without any substantial reference to the fundamental issue of 'who does what to whom', that is, the issue of transitivity as it unfolds throughout the episode.

74. See Greimas, *Sémantique structurale*, pp. 172-89.

75. Propp, *Morphology*.

76. Greimas's concern was to describe the logical structuring in the human imagination from which narrative plots, including actors and their actions, emanate. Thus, he writes: 'Cette permanence de la distribution d'un petit nombre de rôles, disions nous, ne peut être fortuite: nous avons vu que le nombre d'actants était

model seems useful regardless of one's larger theoretical persuasions. The essence of this model is the notion that in a narrative, most if not all of the actual participants (*acteurs*) are capable of being subsumed under generic categories (*actants/catégories actantielles*) expressed in pairs such as subject vs object, sender vs receiver, helper vs adversary, and so on. Unlike Greimas and his many followers, I am concerned to begin and end my analysis of narratives with the texts themselves, rather than a supposed semiotic square of pure logic and universal application. Yet, when the careful analysis of a specific text warrants it, Greimas's actantial model is a useful means of illustration and summary. Such is the case, I wish to argue, with the Acts narrative. In my analysis of the shipwreck narrative of Acts 27, Stephen's martyrdom in Acts 6–7, Paul's arrest and defense in Acts 21–22 and in the Pentecost episode, I have shown that the central participants all have in common their status as patients rather than agents, as those who are moved by rather than move events. At key points of each episode, however, God's actions on behalf of these individuals are shown (sometimes explicitly, sometimes rather covertly) to be decisive and all-powerful (Actant 1: the sufferer vindicated by God). At the same time, there are those who stand in the way and oppose, often with deadly force, the central characters. These individuals are introduced largely by means of ergative clauses, a fact which naturally creates the impression that it is they who are running things. Invariably, however, this natural expectation is subverted when the divine will, materialized in various forms, is introduced and sailors and soldiers (Acts 27), those who rejected Moses and Stephen (Acts 6–7), Paul the persecutor of Christians (Acts 22), and 'the Jews' who had Jesus murdered (Acts 2), are all shown to be ultimately ineffectual (Actant 2: the neutralized opponent). Regardless of what other agendas Luke may have in Acts, what I am here describing seems to be of fundamental importance to him. Indeed, I wish to argue that for Luke, the story of the early church is at the most primary level

déterminé par les conditions aprioriques de la perception de la signification'. These purely logical, deep level structures were then realized through a series of transformations, until they appear at the surface level of text in the form of actual participants and actual actions (*Sémantique structurale*, p. 173). For an introduction to Greimas, see Ronald Schleifer, *A.J. Greimas and the Nature of Meaning* (London: Croom Helm, 1987). For an application of Greimas's method to a biblical text, see Jean Calloud, *Structural Analysis of Narrative* (SBL Semeia Supplement, 4; Philadelphia: Fortress Press, 1976), pp. 47-102.

the story of 'who—in the final analysis—does what to whom?' It is at this level of literary/rhetorical strategy that Greimas's actantial model proves helpful. Besides providing a useful summary of the plot, it serves as a means of testing interpretations of individual passages or pericopes where key characters and/or their actions are involved. Those who see two particular clauses with Jesus as complement in Acts 2 as evidence of primitive Christology would do well to acquaint themselves with Jesus' role as participant throughout the Acts narrative, together with that of other key protagonists, from Stephen to Paul, of whom he is the ultimate archetype.

A legitimate complaint often heard from the ranks of more traditional New Testament scholars is that those who seek to introduce new methods of study often do so without showing how these methods are capable of shedding new light on old issues. Receptive to this criticism, in the foregoing pages I have attempted to provide a principled, linguistically-based interpretation of the Pentecost episode, yet one not written in isolation from previous discussion of this important passage of Acts.

CONCLUSION

'Luke's agenda was not ours.'
Ben Witherington III

Thus ends the first paragraph of Witherington's recent commentary on the Acts of the Apostles. Having warned his readers not to come to Acts seeking specific information on such subjects as baptism and church order, Witherington embarks upon his 800 page socio-rhetorical investigation of Luke's literary purpose in his 'second treatise'. What indeed is Luke's agenda in Acts? Contributing to answering this important question linguistically was one of my primary motivations in writing this thesis. The result, it is hoped, is a contribution to the analysis of New Testament Greek narrative which mirrors the work of 'linguistic criticism'[1] within non-biblical literary studies: It is an attempt at grounding what we say about narrative texts on principled, systematic

---

1.   See, for example, Carter, 'Introduction', pp. 1-17, in which, in response to what he considers unsystematic and capricious literary criticism, he writes, '…it is…a basic principle of a linguistic approach to literary study and criticism that without *analytic* knowledge of the rules and conventions of normal linguistic communication we cannot adequately validate [the] intuitive interpretations [of texts] either for ourselves or for others. In other words, I want to argue here for three main points of principle and practice:

(1)   That the greater our detailed knowledge of the workings of the language system, the greater our capacity for insightful awareness of the effects produced by literary texts;

(2)   That a principled analysis of language can be used to make our commentary on the effects produced in a literary work less impressionistic and subjective;

(3)   That because it will be rooted in a *systematic* awareness of language, bits of language will not be merely 'spotted' and evidence gathered in an essentially casual and haphazard manner. Statements will be made with recognition of the fact that analysis of one linguistic pattern requires reference to, or checking against, related patterns across the text… [emphasis original] (pp. 5-6).

and replicable analyses of the language of those texts.

As is to be expected, a significant narrowing down in scope took place from the initial stage of my research through to the commencement of writing. At the outset of my research in preparation for this volume, I sought to investigate foregrounding in Acts as a cluster concept including aspectual contrasts, clause structure, 'given' and 'new' elements, and other features of language. As I became immersed in the narrative, however, and complete analyses of clause structure and participant relations were produced for each major episode studied, I was confronted by the powerful effect of transitivity choices, as selected and arranged by Luke throughout each episode. The subsequent narrowing in focus to make this a study of transitivity-based foregrounding coincided with Halliday's primary emphasis within his functional grammar, and enabled me to fully utilize his theoretical framework, with various compatible refinements from several sources.

When I first began reading Halliday's work three years ago, the elements of his linguistic theory that attracted me the most were the ever present emphasis on function, the over-arching focus on text analysis, and the stress on relating the linguistic features of text to its situational context and vice-versa. In my largely theoretical first two chapters, I have attempted to show how these features, among others, make functional grammar ideally suited to the linguistically informed literary study of Greek narrative. Within the functional-grammatical framework, the network of transitivity has been shown to be of fundamental importance in tracing and interpreting, not only the basic narrative plot of Acts, but, even more importantly, the core of Luke's foregrounding scheme within his narrative. In the 'who does what to whom' set of questions is wrapped up the encoding of processes, participants and circumstances, that is, the elements which enable speakers/writers and hearers/readers to build a mental picture of reality and interpret their experience in a structured manner. A systematic study of transitivity-based foregrounding in Acts such as the one I have put forth is an important aid in separating that which is central from what is accessory in Luke's unique portrayal of events. In other words, it helps us to uncover the elements of the narrative by which the plot is moved forward.

In Chapter 2 I surveyed three major means of foregrounding which have been studied by scholars in recent times, to wit, aspectual contrast, the fronting of explicit subjects in the clause, and, finally, transitivity patterns. Though the placing of the explicit subject within the clause is, as I have shown, less relevant as an indicator of foregrounding in the Acts narrative than it may be in non-narrative texts, I argued that Porter's approach to clause structure analysis is both ground-breaking and extremely useful, and is, therefore, adopted throughout the present work. As I turned my attention to transitivity's role in foregrounding, reference to Hopper and Thompson's seminal essay 'Transitivity in Grammar and Discourse' (pp. 251-99) was obligatory. Hopper and Thompson's article provides a framework for the analysis of transitivity in discourse which is both fully compatible with, and adds precision to, Halliday's functional–grammatical approach to transitivity's role in foregrounding. Hopper and Thompson's fundamental thesis in their essay, namely, that a direct correlation exists between high transitivity and foregrounding has been shown to hold true for the Acts narrative. What makes Luke's foregrounding scheme in Acts both unique and powerful is that, contrary to expectation, the key protagonists, particularly Paul, whom Luke's readers naturally expect to be the movers and shakers in any account of the primitive church, appear, instead, consistently occupying the complement position of the clause, on the receiving end of processes initiated by others. The shipwreck episode of Acts 27 is perhaps the *locus classicus* of this theme. The stage upon which the action unfolds, the violently storm-tossed eastern Mediterranean, is an ideally suited setting for this story. Luke utilizes 24 inanimate participants, from the wind and waves to the ship itself, placing them often in the subject position of the clause, to underline the struggle for control in which the ship's passengers are enmeshed. While Paul and his companions ('we' in most instances) appear consistently as grammatically incapacitated,[2] the sailors and soldiers (most often referred to by means of the pronoun 'they') are introduced largely by means of ergative clauses, a fact which naturally creates the impression that it is they who are the 'igniters of events' in this story. This natural expectation is subverted, however, when the ceaseless and often frantic activity of the sailors and soldiers to sail in rough weather and, in the end, merely to save the ship are shown to be ultimately ineffectual. The foregrounding of the highly ergative 'they' subject, only to draw attention to the final futility of their actions, serves Luke's purpose of revealing to his readers the thoroughgoing and complete supremacy of the divine will, which Luke often refers to, somewhat obliquely, as

---

2. See my discussion in Chapter 2, where I show that this 'incapacitation' is not merely due to the prisoner status of Paul and his companions.

'what is necessary' (the impersonal verb δεῖν appears three times in Paul's short speech to the ship's crew in Acts 27.21-26).[3] The study of foregrounding in the Acts of the Apostles reveals that Luke's primary orientation in his 'second treatise' is neither political nor apologetic, but, rather, theological. More specifically, through his consistent choices from the transitivity network of Greek in key episodes of his narrative, Luke has sketched for his readers an artful and gripping outline of his theocentric philosophy of history.

What I offer in the present thesis is meant as an indicator of how functional grammar may be deployed in the linguistic analysis of foregrounding in Greek narrative. Among the possible avenues for further research, I wish to note these. First, there is the need for continued analysis of other Acts episodes along the lines I have proposed. The episode of Paul at Athens (Acts 17) could profitably be approached in this way, as it contains both narrative and speech, and has been the object of a large amount of scholarly work, especially from rhetorical critics. In subsequent study of this episode, I would like to seek to answer questions such as: Does Paul's Areopagus speech fit into the forensic or deliberative rhetorical genera? What does the use of personal pronouns throughout the speech reveal about the role of Paul vis-à-vis his audience? Is this a 'mission speech'? What does an analysis of transitivity in this episode reveal about how Paul is being portrayed by Luke? Is the structure of the clauses in this episode generally consistent with the data on clause structure I have gathered from other episodes in Acts, and what does this reveal concerning the cohesiveness of the episode?

Secondly, work should continue in the direction I have outlined in my Chapter 4, that is, the interpersonal function of language and the various rhetorical/literary uses that a writer may make of it, including, the management of distance between participants involved in discourse within the narrative. Porter's proposal that the interpersonal function of language is where 'rhetorical analysis' may primarily reside (my discussion in Chapter 4) is an interesting one, and needs further testing in both narrative and non-narrative texts. If indeed the determination of the specific rhetorical genus a speech belongs to is inseparably bound up with the role that the speaker adopts vis-à-vis his audience, one would expect rhetorical critics to pay increasing amounts of attention to this type of analysis.

---

3. See Cosgrove, 'The Divine DEI in Luke–Acts', pp. 168-90.

Thirdly, concerning clause structure analysis in the Greek of the New Testament, my findings concerning complement-initial clauses must be explored in other narrative texts. The Synoptics, starting with Luke's Gospel, seem to be the logical next locus for this investigation. As I have pointed out throughout this book, however, the investigation of grammatical or syntactical oddities must not be an end in itself, nor may the results of such investigations be considered necessarily meaningful in and of themselves, apart from larger literary and rhetorical considerations such as foregrounding. Once a comprehensive analysis of clause structure in narrative is achieved, the data obtained are likely to lead to further valuable findings in such key areas as cohesiveness and redaction criticism.

The above suggestions are examples of work that remains to be done to secure the place of modern linguistic research within the main stream of biblical studies. Yet, the future of modern linguistic analysis of the Greek New Testament is a bright one, as is evidenced by the growing number of scholars currently involved in research at various levels.[4] A basic assumption held in common by most if not all of these scholars is that, in Porter's words,

> The study of the New Testament is essentially a language-based discipline. That is, the primary body of data for examination is a text, or, better yet, a collection of many texts written in the hellenistic variety of the Greek language of the first century CE. Whatever else may be involved in the study of the New Testament…to remain a study of the New Testament it must always remain textually based, since the only direct access that we have into the world of the New Testament is through the text of the Greek New Testament.[5]

Though the choice of specific linguistic methods is a matter for debate, that linguistically informed analysis must play a central role in the study of the New Testament seems no longer to be in question. If the present work becomes a contribution to the advancement of this major shift in perspective, I shall consider my work to have been a success.

---

4.   See, for example, the work summarized in Professor Micheal W. Palmer's Greek Language and Linguistics Gateway at http://home.earthlink.net/~mwpalmer, or his online bibliography of recent Greek linguistics at http://home.earthlink.net/~mwpalmer/bibliographies.

5.   S.E. Porter, 'Discourse Analysis and New Testament Studies: An Introductory Survey', in Porter and Carson (eds.), *Discourse Analysis*, p. 1.

BIBLIOGRAPHY

Andrews, Edna, *Markedness Theory: The Union of Asymmetry and Semiosis in Language* (Durham: Duke University Press, 1990).

Argyle, A.W., 'The Greek of Luke–Acts', *NTS* 20 (1974), pp. 441-45.

Arnold, Bill T., 'Luke's Characterizing Use of the Old Testament in the Book of Acts', in Ben Witherington III (ed.), *History, Literature and Society in The Book of Acts* (Cambridge: Cambridge University Press, 1996), pp. 300-23.

Barrett, C.K., *The Acts of the Apostles*, I (ICC; Edinburgh: T. & T. Clark, 1994).

Basevi, Claudio, and Juan Chapa, 'Philippians 2.6-11: The Rhetorical Function of a Pauline Hymn', in Porter and Olbricht (eds.), *Rhetoric*, pp. 338-56.

Battistella, Edwin, *Markedness: The Evaluative Superstructure of Language* (Albany: State University of New York Press, 1990).

Bauckham, R., 'The Acts of Paul as a Sequel to Acts', in Bruce Winter and Andrew Clarke (eds.), *The Book of Acts in its Ancient Literary Setting* (A1CS, 1; Grand Rapids: Eerdmans; Carlisle: Paternoster Press, 1994), pp. 105-52.

Beardslee, W.A., *Literary Criticism of the New Testament* (Philadelphia: Fortress Press, 1970).

Beaugrande, Robert de, ' "Register" in Discourse Studies: A Concept in Search of a Theory', in Moshen Ghadessy (ed.), *Register Analysis: Theory and Practice* (London: Pinter, 1993), pp. 11-20.

Bergen, Robert D., 'Text as a Guide to Authorial Intention: an Introduction to Discourse Criticism', *JETS* 30.3 (1987), pp. 34-49.

Berger, Klaus, 'Rhetorical Criticism, New Form Criticism, and New Testament Hermeneutics', in Porter and Olbricht (eds.), *Rhetoric*, pp. 390-96.

Bergua, José (ed.), *Las mil mejores poesias de la lengua castellana* (Madrid: Ediciones Ibéricas, 30th edn, 1991).

Berry, Margaret, *Introduction to Systemic Linguistics. I. Structures and Systems* (London: Batsford, 1977).

Betz, Hans Dieter, *Galatians: A Commentary on Paul's Letter to the Churches in Galatia* (Philadelphia: Fortress Press, 1979).

Black, D.A., *et al.* (eds.), *Linguistics and New Testament Interpretation: Essays in Discourse Analysis* (Nashville: Broadman Press, 1992).

Blass, Friedrich, *Grammatik des neutestamentlichen Griechisch* (Göttingen: Vandenhoeck & Ruprecht, 1896).

Brawley, Robert L., 'Hermeneutical Voices of Scripture in Acts 2', in Brawley (ed.), *Text to Text Pours Forth Speech* (Bloomington, IN: Indiana University Press, 1995), pp. 75-90.

—'Paul in Acts: Lucan Apology and Conciliation', in Talbert (ed.), *Luke–Acts*, pp. 129-47.

Brooks, James A., and Carlon L. Winbery, *Syntax of New Testament Greek* (Lanham, MD: University Press of America, 1979).

Brown, Gillian, and George Yule, *The Acts of the Apostles* (London: Tyndale Press, 4th edn, 1956).

—*Discourse Analysis* (Cambridge Textbooks in Linguistics; Cambridge: Cambridge University Press, 1983).

Bruce, F.F., 'The Significance of the Speeches for Interpreting Acts', *Southwestern Journal of Theology* 33 (1990), pp. 20-28.

Burguière, Paul, *Histoire de l'infinitif en grec* (Etudes et Commentaires, 33; Paris: Librairie C. Klincksieck, 1960).

Butler, Christopher, *Systemic Linguistics: Theory and Applications* (London: Batsford, 1985).

Cadbury, Henry J., *The Making of Luke–Acts* (London: SPCK, 3rd British edn, 1968).

—'The Speeches in Acts', in F.J. Foakes Jackson and Kirsopp Lake (eds.), The Beginnings of Christianity I, V (London: Macmillan, 1933), pp. 402-427.

—'The Style and Literary Method of Luke. Part II: The Treatment of Sources in the Gospel of Luke', *HTS* 6 (1919), pp. 26-35.

Calloud, Jean, *Structural Analysis of Narrative* (SBL Semeia Supplement, 4; Philadelphia: Fortress Press, 1976).

Carter, Ronald, 'Introduction', in Carter (ed.), *Language and Literature* (London: George Allen & Unwin, 1982), pp. 1-17.

Centineo, Giulia, 'Tense Switching in Italian: the Alteration between *Passato Prossimo* and *Passato Remoto* in Oral Narratives', in Fleischmann and Waugh (eds.), *Discourse Pragmatics*, pp. 55-85.

Chamberlain, W.D., *An Exegetical Grammar of the Greek New Testament* (Grand Rapids: Baker Book House, 5th edn, 1988).

Chatman, Seymour, *Story and Discourse* (Ithaca, NY: Cornell University Press, 6th edn, 1993).

Classen, C. Joachim, 'St Paul's Epistles and Ancient Graeco-Roman Rhetoric', in Porter and Olbricht (eds.), *Rhetoric*, pp. 265-91.

Colmenero-Atienza, Javier, 'Hechos 7, 17-43 y las Corrientes Cristológicas Dentro de la Primitiva Comunidad Cristiana', *EstBíb* 33 (1974), pp. 31-62.

Comrie, Bernard, *Aspect* (Cambridge: Cambridge University Press, 1976).

—*Language Universals and Linguistic Typology: Syntax and Morphology* (Chicago: University of Chicago Press, 1981).

Conzelmann, Hans, *Acts of the Apostles* (trans. J. Limburg, A.T. Kraabel and D.H. Juel; Hermeneia; Philadelphia: Fortress Press, 1987).

Cosgrove, C.H., 'The Divine ΔΕΙ in Luke–Acts', *NovT* 26 (1984), pp. 168-90.

Cotterell, Peter, and Max Turner, *Linguistics and Biblical Interpretation* (Downers Grove, IL: IVP, 1989).

Countryman, L. William, *The New Testament is in Greek: A Short Course for Exegetes* (Grand Rapids: Eerdmans, 1993).

Crafton, J.A., 'The Dancing of an Attitude: Burkean Rhetorical Criticism and the Biblical Interpreter', in Porter and Olbricht (eds.), *Rhetoric*, pp. 429-42.

Dahl, Nils A., 'The Story of Abraham in Luke–Acts', in Leander E. Keck and J. Louis Martyn (eds.), *Studies in Luke–Acts* (London: SPCK, 1976), pp. 139-44.

Davison, M.E., 'New Testament Greek Word Order', *Literary and Linguistic Computing* 4 (1) (1989), pp. 19-28.

Derbyshire, Desmond C., and Geoffrey K. Pullum, 'Object Initial Languages', *International Journal of American Linguistics* 47.3 (1981), pp. 192-214.

De Waard, Jan, and Eugene Nida, *From one Language to Another* (Nashville, TN: Thomas Nelson, 1986).

Dibelius, Martin, *Studies in the Acts of the Apostles* (London: SCM Press, 1956), p. 205.

—'Style Criticism of the Book of Acts', in *idem, Studies in the Acts of the Apostles* (trans. Mary Ling; 1st Engl. edn; London: SCM Press, 1956), pp. 1-13.

Di Marco, Angelico-Salvatore, 'Rhetoric and Hermeneutic—On a Rhetorical Pattern: Chiasmus and Circularity', in Porter and Olbricht (eds.), *Rhetoric*, pp. 479-91.

Dos Passos, John, *The Big Money* (New York: Signet, 1979).

Dry, Helen, 'Foregrounding: An Assessment', in S.J.J. Hwang and W.R. Merrifield (eds.), *Language in Context: Essays for Robert E. Longacre* (Dallas: Summer Institute of Linguistics, 1992), pp. 435-50.

Du Bois, John W., 'The Discourse Basis of Ergativity', *Language* 63 (1987), pp. 805-55.

Dupont, J. 'La structure oratoire du discours d'Etienne [Actes 7]', *Bib* 66 (1985), pp. 153-67.

Elliott, J.K., (ed.), *Studies in New Testament Language and Text* (NovTSup, 14; Leiden: E.J. Brill, 1976).

Enkvist, Nils Erik, 'Text and Discourse Linguistics, Rhetoric, and Stylistics', in Teun A. Van Dijk (ed.), *Discourse and Literature* (Amsterdam: John Benjamins, 1985), pp. 1-16.

Epp, Eldon J., *The Theological Tendency of Codex Bezae Cantabrigiensis in Acts* (SNTSMS, 3; Cambridge: Cambridge University Press, 1966).

Erickson, Richard J., 'Linguistics and Biblical Language: A Wide Open Field', *JETS* 26.3 (1983), pp. 257-63.

Esler, Philip F., *Community and Gospel in Luke–Acts* (Cambridge: Cambridge University Press, 1987).

Evans, Craig A., 'The Prophetic Setting of the Pentecost Sermon', ZNW 74 (1983), pp. 148-50.

Evans, C.F., *Resurrection and the New Testament* (SBT, 2.12; London: SCM Press, 1970).

Fanning, Buist, *Verbal Aspect in New Testament Greek* (Oxford: Clarendon Press, 1990).

Fawcett, *Cognitive Linguistics and Social Interaction* (Heidelberg: Julius Groos Verlag, 1980).

Firth, John R., *Papers in Linguistics*, 1934–51 (London: Oxford University Press, 1957).

Fleischmann, Suzanne, 'Discourse Functions of Tense-Aspect Oppositions in Narrative: Toward a Theory of Grounding', *Linguistics* 23.6 (1985), pp. 851-82.

—*Tense and Narrativity* (Austin, TX: University of Texas Press, 1990).

Fleischmann, Suzanne, and Linda Waugh (eds.), *Discourse Pragmatics and the Verb* (London: Routledge, 1991).

Fowler, Roger, *Linguistics and the Novel* (London: Methuen, 1977).

García-Miguel, José M., *Transitividad y Complementación Preposicional en Español* (Verba, 40; Santiago: Universidade de Santiago de Compostela, 1995).

Gasque, Ward, *A History of the Criticism of the Acts of the Apostles* (Beitrage Zur Geschichte der Biblischen Exegese, 17; Tübingen: J.C.B. Mohr, 1975).

Ghadessy, Mohsen (ed.), 'The Language in Written Sports Commentary: Soccer—A Description', in Ghadessy, (ed.), *Registers of Written English*, pp. 19-24.

—*Register Analysis: Theory and Practice* (London: Pinter, 1993).

—*Registers of Written English* (London: Pinter, 1988).

Goldhagen, Daniel Jonah, *Hitler's Willing Executioners: Ordinary Germans and the Holocaust* (London: Abacus, 1996).

Goodenough, Edwin R., 'The Perspective of Acts', in Keck and Martyn (eds.), *Studies in Luke–Acts*, pp. 50-55.

Goodwin, W.W., *Syntax of the Moods and Tenses of the Greek Verb* (London: Macmillan, 1929).

Goodwin, W.W., and C.B. Gulick, *Greek Grammar* (Boston: Ginn & Co., 1930).

Greenberg, Joseph H., *Language Universals* (The Hague: Mouton, 1966).

—'Some Universals of Grammar, with Particular Reference to the Order of Meaningful Elements', in Greenberg (ed.), *Universals of Language* (Cambridge: MIT Press, 1963), pp. 49-57.

Gregory, Michael and Susanne Carroll, *Language and Situation: Language Varieties and their Social Context* (London: Routledge & Kegan Paul, 1978).

Greimas, A.J., *Les actants, les acteurs et les figures* (Paris: Librairie Larousse, 1973).

—*Sémantique structurale* (Paris: Librairie Larousse, 1966).

Grimes, Joseph E., 'Signals of Discourse Structure in Koine', in *idem* (ed.), *Society of Biblical Literature 1975 Seminar Papers*, I (Atlanta: Scholars Press, 1975), pp. 151-64.

Haenchen, Ernst, *The Acts of the Apostles* (trans. B. Noble and G. Shinn; Oxford: Basil Blackwell, 1971).

—' "We" in Acts and the Itinerary', *Journal for Theology and the Church* 1 (1965), pp. 65-99.

Hahne, Harry, 'Interpretive Implications of Using Bible-Search Software for New Testament Grammatical Analysis'. Paper presented at the annual meeting of the Evangelical Theological Society, 24 November 1994.

Halliday, M.A.K., *Explorations in the Function of Language* (London: Edwin Arnold, 1970).

—*An Introduction to Functional Grammar* (London: Edward Arnold, 1985).

—*Language as Social Semiotic* (London: Edward Arnold, 2nd edn 1979).

—*Learning How to Mean: Explorations in the Development of Language* (London: Edward Arnold, 1975).

—'Linguistic Function and Literary Style: An Inquiry into the Language of William Golding's The Inheritors', in Halliday, *Explorations in the Function of Language* (London: Edward Arnold, 1976), pp. 103-135.

—'On Grammar and Grammatics', in R. Hasan, C. Cloran and D. Butt (eds.), *Functional Descriptions* (Amsterdam Studies in the Theory and History of Linguistic Science, 4.121; Amsterdam: John Benjamins, 1996), pp. 20-21.

Halliday, M.A.K., and Ruqaiya Hasan, *Cohesion in English* (London: Longman, 6th edn, 1984).

—'Notes on Transitivity and Theme in English', *Journal of Linguistics* 3 (1967), p. 177.

—'Text and Context: Aspects of Language in a Social-Semiotic Perspective', *Sophia Linguistica* 6 (1980), pp. 4-91.

Harnack, Adolf von, *Luke the Physician* (trans. J.R. Wilkinson; London: Williams & Norgate, 2nd edn, 1909).

Harwood, Richard, 'The How and Why of it All', *The Washington Post*, Thursday, 14 August 1997, A21.

Hasan, Ruqaiya, 'Linguistics and the Study of Literary Texts', *Etudes de linguistique appliquée* 5 (1967), pp. 106-109.

—*Linguistics, Language and Verbal Art* (Oxford: Oxford University Press, 1985).

—'Rhyme and Reason in Literature', in Seymour Chatman (ed.), *Literary Style: A Symposium* (London: Oxford University Press, 1971), pp. 287-99.

Hasan, R., C. Cloran and D. Butt (eds.), *Functional Descriptions: Theory in Practice* (Amsterdam: John Benjamins, 1996).

Hatina, Thomas R., 'The Perfect Tense-Form in Recent Debate: Galatians as a Case Study', *FN* 8 (1995), pp. 3-22.

Hedrick, Charles W., 'Paul's Conversion/Call: A Comparative Analysis of the Three Reports in Acts', *JBL* 100.3 (1981), pp. 415-32.

Hellholm, David, 'Amplificatio in the Macro-Structure of Romans', in Porter and Olbricht (eds.), *Rhetoric*, pp. 123-51.

Hemer, Colin J., *The Book of Acts in the Setting of Hellenistic History* (ed. C. Gempf; WUNT, 44; Tübingen: J.C.B. Mohr, 1989).

—'First Person Narrative in Acts 27–28', *TynBul* 36 (1985), pp. 79-109.

Hengel, Martin, *Acts and the History of Earliest Christianity* (trans. John Bowden; London: SCM Press, 1979).

Hernández-Lara, Carlos, 'El Orden de las Palabras en Caritón de Afrodisias', *Myrtia* 2 (1987), pp. 83-89.

Hill, Craig C., 'Acts 6.1–8.4: Division or Diversity?', in Witherington (ed.), *History*, pp. 129-53.

Hopper, Paul J., and Sandra A. Thompson, 'Transitivity in Grammar and Discourse', *Language* 56.2 (1980), pp. 251-99.

Horsley, G.H.R., 'Speeches and Dialogue in Acts', *NTS* 32 (1986), pp. 609-14.

Hubbard, Benjamin J., 'The Role of Commissioning Accounts in Acts', in Talbert (ed.), *Perspectives on Luke–Acts*, pp. 187-98.

Hughes, Frank, 'The Parable of the Rich Man and Lazarus (Luke 16.19-31) and Graeco-Roman Rhetoric', in Porter and Olbricht (eds.), *Rhetoric*, pp. 29-41.

Jackson, Foakes, *The Acts of the Apostles* (London: Hodder & Stoughton, 1945).

Jacquier, E., *Les actes des Apôtres* (Paris: Librairie Victor Lecoffre, 2nd edn, 1926).

Jakobson, Roman, 'Linguistics and Poetics', in Thomas A. Sebeok (ed.), *Style in Language* (Cambridge, MA: MIT Press, 1960), pp. 350-68.

—'Shifters, Verbal Categories and the Russian Verb', in S. Rudy (ed.), *Roman Jakobson: Selected Writings*, II (10 vols.; The Hague: Mouton, 1971), pp. 130-47.

Jervell, Jacob, *Luke and the People of God* (Minneapolis: Augsburg, 1972).

—'The Future of the Past', in Witherington (ed.), *History*, pp. 104-26.

—*The Theology of the Acts of the Apostles* (New Testament Theology; Cambridge: Cambridge University Press, 1996).

Jeska, Joachim, 'Lukanische Summarien der Geschichte Israels (Act 7 und 13) im Kontext frühjüdischer Geschichtssummarien' (PhD dissertation in progress [1998] at University of Münster, Germany).

Katz, J.J., and J.A. Fodor, 'The Structure of a Semantic Theory', *Language* 36 (1963), pp. 170-210.

Kennedy, George, *The Art of Rhetoric in the Roman World* (Princeton, NJ: Princeton University Press, 1972).

—*New Testament Interpretation through Rhetorical Criticism* (Chapel Hill: University of North Carolina Press, 1984).

Kilgallen, John, 'Acts: Literary and Theological Turning Points', *Bulletin de théologie biblique* 7 (1977), pp. 177-80.

—*The Stephen Speech: A Literary and Redactional Study of Acts* 7:2-53 (AnBib, 67; Rome: Biblical Institute Press, 1976).

Klijn, A.F.J., 'Stephen's Speech—Acts VII. 2-53', *NTS* 4 (1957–58), pp. 25-31.

Labov, William, 'Some Further Steps in Narrative Analysis', available online at: http://ling.upenn.edu/~labov/sfs.html.

Lake, Kirsopp, 'The Gift of the Spirit on the Day of Pentecost', in Foakes Jackson and Kirsopp Lake (eds.), *The Beginnings of Christianity*. I. *The Acts of the Apostles*,V (London: Macmillan, 1933).

Langendoen, Terence, *The London School of Linguistics: A Study of the Linguistic Theories of B. Malinowski and J.R. Firth* (Research monograph, 46; Cambridge, MA: MIT Press, 1968).

Larsen, Iver, 'Word Order and Relative Prominence in New Testament Greek', *Notes on Translation* 5(1) (1991), pp. 29-34.

Laso-De La Vega, José S., *Sintaxis Griega* I (Enclopedia Clásica, 6; Madrid: Consejo Superior de Investigaciones Científicas, 1968).

Leech, Geoffrey N., 'Foregrounding and Interpretation', in *idem*, *A Linguistic Guide to English Poetry* (London: Longman, 1969), pp. 62-87.

—'Linguistics and the Figures of Rhetoric', in Roger Fowler (ed.), *Essays on Style and Language* (London: Routledge & Kegan Paul, 1970), pp. 135-56.

—*Principles of Pragmatics* (London: Longman, 1983).

Lentz, John C., *Luke's Portrait of Paul* (SNTMS, 77; Cambridge: Cambridge University Press, 1993).

Léon-Dufour, Xavier, *Resurrection and the Message of Easter* (trans. G. Chapman; London: Geoffrey Chapman, 1974).

Levinsohn, Stephen H., *Textual Connections in Acts* (SBLMS, 31; Atlanta, GA: Scholars Press, 1987).

Levinson, Stephen, *Pragmatics* (CTL; Cambridge: Cambridge University Press, 1983).

Levinskaya, Irina, *Diaspora Setting* (A1CS, 5; Grand Rapids: Eerdmans; Carlisle: Paternoster Press, 1996).

—'Participant Reference in Koine Greek Narrative', in D.A. Black *et al.* (eds.), *Linguistics and New Testament Interpretation: Essays in Discourse Analysis* (Nashville: Broadman Press, 1992), pp. 31-44.

Lohfink, Gerhard, *Paulus vor Damaskus* (Stuttgarter Bibelstudien 4; Stuttgart: Verlag Katholisches Bibelwerk, 1967).

Longacre, Robert E., *The Grammar of Discourse* (New York: Plennum, 1983).

Louw, J.P., 'Verbal Aspect in the First Letter of John', *Neot* 9 (1980), pp. 98-104.

Lunn, Patricia, and Thomas Cravens, 'A Contextual Reconsideration of the Spanish -ra "Indicative" ', in Fleischmann and Waugh (eds.), *Discourse Pragmatics*, pp. 147-78.

Lyons, John, *Language, Meaning and Context* (Suffolk: Fontana, 1981).

Machen, J.G., *New Testament Greek for Beginners* (Toronto: Macmillan, 60th edn, 1989).

Maddox, Robert, *The Purpose of Luke–Acts* (Studies in the New Testament and its World; Edinburgh: T. & T. Clark, 2nd edn, 1985).

Malherbes, A.J.,*Ancient Epistolary Theorists* (SBLSBS, 19; Atlanta: Scholars Press, 1988).

Malinowsky, Bronislav, *Argonauts of the Western Pacific* (London: Routledge, 1922).

—'Classificatory Particles in the Language or Kiriwina', *BSOS* 1, part 4 (1920), pp. 33-78.

—*Coral Gardens and their Magic* (New York: American Book Co., 1935).

—'The Problem of Meaning in Primitive Languages', supplement to O.K. Odgen and I.A. Richards, *The Meaning of Meaning* (New York: Harcourt, 1923), pp. 296-336.

Mandilaras, Basil G., *The Verb in the Greek Non-Literary Papyri* (Athens: Hellenic Ministry of Culture and Sciences, 1973).

Marguerat, Daniel, 'The End of Acts (28.16-31) and the Rhetoric of Silence', in Porter and Olbricht (eds.), *Rhetoric*, pp. 74-89.

—Saul's Conversion (Acts 9, 22, 26) and the Multiplication of Narrative in Acts', in C.M. Tuckett (ed.), *Luke's Literary Achievement* (JSNTSup, 116; Sheffield: Sheffield Academic Press, 1995), pp. 127-55.

Marshall, John W., 'Paul's Ethical Appeal in Philippians', in Porter and Olbricht (eds.), *Rhetoric*, pp. 357-74.

Martín-Asensio, G., 'Review of Wilhelm Egger, "How to Read the New Testament: An Introduction to Linguistic and Historical-Critical Methodology" ', *Themelios* 23.2 (1998), pp. 61-62.

Matthiessen, Christian, 'Register in the Round: Diversified in a Unified Theory of Register Analysis', in Ghadessy (ed.), *Register Analysis*, pp. 221-92.

Matthiessen, Christian, and Christopher Nesbitt, 'On the Idea of Theory-Neutral Descriptions', in R. Hasan, C. Cloran and D. Butt (eds.), *Functional Descriptions* (Amsterdam: John Benjamins, 1996), pp. 39-83.

Mattill Jr, A.J., 'The Value of Acts as a Source for the Study of Paul', in Charles H. Talbert (ed.), *Perspectives on Luke–Acts* (Danville, VA; Association of Baptist Professors of Religion, 1978), pp. 76-98.

McCoy, W.F., 'In the Shadow of Thucydides', in Witherington (ed.), *History*, pp. 3-32.

McDonald, J. Ian H., 'Rhetorical Issue and Rhetorical Strategy in Luke 10.25-37 and Acts 10.1–11.18', in Porter and Olbricht (eds.), *Rhetoric*, pp. 59-73.

McKay, K.L., *A New Syntax of the Verb in New Testament Greek* (SBG, 5; New York: Peter Lang, 1994).

Milne, Pamela, *Vladimir Propp and the Study of Structure in Hebrew Biblical Narrative* (Sheffield: Almond/Sheffield Academic Press, 1988).

Minguez, Dionisio, *Pentecostes: Ensayo de Semiotica Narrativa en Hechos 2* (Rome: Biblical Institute Press, 1976).

Moessner, David P., 'The "Script" of the Scriptures in Acts', in Witherington (ed.), *History*, pp. 233-41.

Monaghan, James, *The Neo-Firthian Tradition and it Contribution to General Linguistics* (Linguistische Arbeiten, 73; Tübingen: Max Niemeyer, 1979).

Monro, D.B., *Homeric Grammar* (Oxford: Clarendon Press, 1891).

Moule, C.F.D., 'The Christology of Acts', in Keck and Martyn (eds.), *Studies in Luke–Acts* (London: SPCK, 1976), pp. 159-85.

—*An Idiom Book of New Testament Greek* (Cambridge: Cambridge University Press, 1953).

Moulton, J.H., *A Grammar of New Testament Greek*. I. *Prolegomena* (Edinburgh: T. & T. Clark, 1988).

Mukarovsky, Jan, 'Standard Language and Poetic Language', in Paul R. Garvin (ed.), *A Prague School Reader on Esthetic, Literary Structure and Style* (Washington DC: Georgetown University Press, 1964), pp. 17-30.

Mullins, T.Y., 'New Testament Commission Forms, Especially in Luke–Acts', *JBL* 96 (1976), pp. 603-14.

Munck, Johannes, *The Book of Acts* (AB; Garden City, NY: Doubleday, 10th edn, 1981).

—'La vocation de l'Apôtre Paul', *ST* 1 (1947), pp. 130-45.

Mussies, Gerhard, 'Variation in the Book of Acts' Part 2 *FN* 8 (1995), pp. 23-61.

Neyrey, Jerome H., 'The Forensic Defense Speech and Paul's Trial Speeches in Acts 22–
   26: Form and Function', in Charles Talbert (ed.), *Luke–Acts: New Perspectives from
   the SBL Seminar* (New York: Crossroad, 1984), pp. 210-24.
—'Luke's Social Location of Paul: Cultural Anthropology and the Status of Paul in Acts',
   in Witherington (ed.), *History*, pp. 251-79.
Neyrey, Jerome H., and Bruce J. Malina, *Portraits of Paul* (Louisville, KY: John Knox
   Press, 1996).
Nida, E., J. Louw, A.P. Snyman and W.V. Cronje (eds.), *Style and Discourse* (Cape Town:
   Bible Society of South Africa, 1983).
North, Helen. F., 'Rhetoric and Historiography', *Quarterly Journal of Speech* 42 (1956),
   pp. 234-42.
O'Toole, Robert F., 'Acts 2:30 and the Davidic Covenant of Pentecost', *JBL* 102.2 (1983),
   pp. 245-58.
—*The Unity of Luke's Theology* (Wilmington, DE: Michael Glazier, 1984), pp. 63-67.
Palmer, F.R., *Semantics: A New Outline* (Cambridge: Cambridge University Press, 1976).
Parks, E. Patrick, *The Roman Rhetorical Schools as a Preparation for the Courts under the
   Early Empire* (The Johns Hopkins University Studies in Historical and Political
   Science, 83.2; Baltimore: The Johns Hopkins University Press, 1945).
Parsons, M., and Richard I. Pervo, *Rethinking the Unity of Luke–Acts* (Minneapolis: Fort-
   ress Press, 1990).
Pearson, B.W.R., and S.E. Porter, 'The Genres of the New Testament', in Porter (ed.),
   Handbook to Exegesis of the New Testament (NTTS, 26; Leiden: E.J. Brill, 1997),
   pp. 131-66.
Peer van, Willie, *Stylistics and Psychology: Investigations of Foregrounding* (Croom Helm
   Linguistics Series; London: Croom Helm, 1986).
Pervo, Richard I., 'On Perilous Things: A Response to Beverly Gaventa', in Mikeal Par-
   sons and Joseph Tyson, *Cadbury, Knox and Talbert: American Contributions to the
   Study of Acts* (SBL Centennial Publications; Atlanta: Scholars Press, 1992), pp. 30-
   41.
—*Profit with Delight: The Literary Genre of the Acts of the Apostles* (Philadelphia: Fort-
   ress Press, 1987).
Pokorny, Petr, 'Christologie et baptême à l'époque du Christianisme primitif', *NTS* 27
   (1980), pp. 368-80.
Porter, S.E., 'Dialect and Register in the Greek of the New Testament: Theory', in M.
   Daniel Carroll R. (ed.), *Rethinking Contexts, Rereading Texts: Contributions from
   the Social Sciences to Biblical Interpretation* (Sheffield: Sheffield Academic Press,
   2000), pp. 190-208.
—*Idioms of the Greek New Testament* (Sheffield: Sheffield Academic Press, 1992).
—*The Paul of Acts: Essays in Literary Criticism, Rhetoric and Theology* (WUNT, 115;
   Tübingen: J.C.B. Mohr [Paul Siebeck], 1999).
—'Register in the of Greek of the New Testament: Application with Reference to Mark's
   Gospel', in M. Daniel Carroll R. (ed.), *Rethinking Contexts, Rereading Texts: Con-
   tributions from the Social Sciences to Biblical Interpretation* (Sheffield: Sheffield
   Academic Press, 2000), pp. 209-29.
—'Studying Ancient Languages from a Modern Linguistics Perspective', *FN* 2 (1989),
   pp. 147-72.
—Thucydides 1.22.1 and Speeches in Acts: Is there a Thucydidean View?', *NovT* 32
   (1990), pp. 121-42.

—*Verbal Aspect in the Greek of the New Testament, With Reference to Tense and Mood* (New York: Peter Lang, 1989).

—'The "We" Passages', in D. Gill and C. Gempf (eds.), *The Book of Acts in its Graeco-Roman Setting* (A1CS, 2; Grand Rapids: Eerdmans; Carlisle: Paternoster Press, 1994), pp. 545-74.

—'Word Order and Clause Structure in New Testament Greek', *FN* 6 (1993), pp. 177-206.

Porter, S.E. (ed.), *Handbook to Exegesis of the New Testament* (NTTS, 26; Leiden: E.J. Brill, 1997), pp. 131-66.

Porter, S.E., and D.A. Carson (eds.), *Biblical Greek Language and Linguistics: Open Questions in Current Research* (JSNTSup, 80; Sheffield: JSOT Press, 1993).

—*Discourse Analysis and Other Topics in Biblical Greek* (JSNTSup, 113; Sheffield: Sheffield Academic Press, 1995).

Porter, S.E., and J.T. Reed, 'Greek Grammar Since BDF: A Retrospective and Prospective Analysis', *FN* 4 (1991), pp. 143-64.

—'Philippians as a Macro-Chiasm and its Exegetical Significance', *NTS* 44 (1998), pp. 213-31.

Porter, S.E., and T.H. Olbricht (eds.), *Rhetoric and the New Testament: Essays from the 1992 Heidelberg Conference* (JSNTSup, 90; Sheffield: JSOT Press, 1993).

Porter, S.E., and D.L. Stamps (eds.), *The Rhetorical Interpretation of Scripture: Essays from the 1996 Malibu Conference* (JSNTSup, 180; Sheffield: Sheffield Academic Press, 1999).

Powell, Mark A.,*What are they Saying about Acts?* (Mahwah, NJ: Paulist Press, 1991).

Propp, Vladimir, *Morphology of the Folktale* (trans. L. Scott; Austin, TX: University of Texas Press, 1990).

—*Theory and History of Folklore* (trans. Ariadna Martin; Minneapolis: University of Minnesota Press, 1984).

Ramsay, William, *Saint Paul the Traveller and the Roman Citizen* (London: Hodder & Stoughton, 1896).

Rapske, Brian, 'Acts, Travel and Shipwreck', in D. Gill and C. Gempf (eds.), *The Book of Acts in its Graeco-Roman Setting* (A1CS, 2; Grand Rapids: Eerdmans; Carlisle: Paternoster Press), pp. 23-34.

Reed, Jeffrey T., *A Discourse Analysis of Philippians: Method and Rhetoric in the Debate over Literary Integrity* (JSNTSup, 136; Sheffield: Sheffield Academic Press, 1997).

—'Identifying Theme in the New Testament: Insights from Discourse Analysis', in S.E. Porter and D.A. Carson (eds.), *Discourse Analysis and Other Topics in Biblical Greek* (JSNTSup, 113; Sheffield: Sheffield Academic Press, 1995), pp. 75-101.

—'Using Ancient Rhetorical Categories to Interpret Paul's Letters: A Question of Genre', in Porter and Olbricht (eds.), *Rhetoric*, pp. 292-324.

Reid, T.B.W., 'Linguistics, Structuralism and Philology', *Archivum Linguisticum* 8.2 (1956), pp. 28-37.

Richard, Earl, *Acts 6:1–8:4, The Author's Method of Composition* (SBLDS, 41; Missoula, MT: Scholars Press, 1978).

—'The Polemical Character of the Joseph Episode in Acts 7', *JBL* 98.2 (1979), pp. 255-67.

Rius-Camps, José, 'Pentecostés versus Babel: Estudio Crítico de Hechos 2', *FN* 1 (1988), pp. 35-61.

—'Las variantes de la recensión occidental de los hechos de los apóstoles (V): Hch 2.14-40', *FN* 15 (1995), pp. 63-78.

Robbins, Vernon K., 'By Land and by Sea: the We-Passages and Ancient Sea-Voyages', in Talbert (ed.), *Perspectives*, pp. 215-42.

Robertson, A.T., *A Grammar of the Greek New Testament in the Light of Historical Research* (Nashville: Broadman Press, 1934).

Romero-Figueroa, Andrés, 'OSV as the Basic Word Order in Warao', *Linguistics* 23.1 (1985), pp. 105-21.

Sanders, J.T., *The Jews in Luke–Acts* (London: SCM Press, 1987).

Satterthwaite, Philip E., 'Acts against the Background of Classical Rhetoric', in Winter and Clarke (eds.), *The Book of Acts in its Ancient Literary Setting*, pp. 337-79.

Schiffrin, Deborah, *Approaches to Discourse* (Oxford: Basil Blackwell, 1994).

Schleifer, Ronald, *A.J. Greimas and the Nature of Meaning* (London: Croom Helm, 1987).

Schmidt, Daryl, 'Verbal Aspects in Greek: Two Approaches', in Porter and Carson (eds.), *Biblical Greek Language and Linguistics*, pp. 63-73.

Schoeni, Marc, 'The Hyperbolic Sublime as a Master Trope in Romans', in Porter and Olbricht (eds.), *Rhetoric*, pp. 171-91.

Schubert, Paul, 'The Final Cycle of Speeches in the Book of Acts', *JBL* 87.1 (1968), pp. 1-16.

— 'The Place of the Areopagus Speech in the Composition of Acts', in J.C. Rylaarsdam (ed.), *Transitions in Biblical Scholarship* (Essays in Divinity, 6; Chicago: University of Chicago Press, 1968), pp. 235-61.

Schweizer, Edward, 'Concerning the Speeches in Acts', in L. Keck and J. Martyn (eds.), *Studies in Luke–Acts* (London: SPCK, 3rd edn, 1978), pp. 208-16.

Sheeley, Stephen M., *Narrative Asides in Luke–Acts* (JSNTSup, 72; Sheffield: Sheffield Academic Press, 1992).

Siegert, Folker, 'Mass Communication and Prose Rhythm in Luke–Acts', in Porter and Olbricht (eds.), *Rhetoric*, pp. 42-58.

Sloan, Robert B., 'Signs and Wonders: a Rhetorical Clue to the Pentecost Discourse', *EvQ* 63 (1991), pp. 225-40.

Smit, Joop, 'Argument and Genre of 1 Corinthians 12–14', in Porter and Olbricht (eds.), *Rhetoric*, pp. 211-30.

Snyman, A.H., 'Persuasion in Philippians 41-20', in Porter and Olbricht (eds.), *Rhetoric*, pp. 325-37.

Soards, Marion L., *The Speeches in Acts* (Louisville: Westminster/John Knox Press, 1994).

Spencer, F. Scott., 'Acts and Modern Literary Approaches', in Bruce Winter and Andrew Clarke (eds.), *The Book of Acts in its Ancient Literary Setting* (A1CS, 1; Grand Rapids: Eerdmans; Carlisle: Paternoster Press, 1994), pp. 381-414.

Squires, John T., *The Plan of God in Luke–Acts* (SNTSMS, 76; Cambridge: Cambridge University Press, 1993).

Stamps, Dennis, 'Rethinking the Rhetorical Situation: the Entextualization of the Situation in New Testament Epistles', in Porter and Olbricht (eds.), *Rhetoric*, pp. 193-210.

Steyn, Gert J., *Septuagint Quotations in the Context of the Petrine and Pauline Speeches of the Acta Apostolorum* (Contributions to Biblical Exegesis and Theology, 12; Kampen: Kok, 1995).

Steyn, Jacques, 'Some Psycholinguistic Factors Involved in the Discourse Analysis of Ancient Texts', *Theologia Evangelica* 17.2 (1984), pp. 51-65.

Strauss, Mark L., *The Davidic Messiah in Luke–Acts* (JSNTSup, 110; Sheffield: Sheffield Academic Press, 1995), pp. 131-47.

Sylva, Dennis D., 'The Meaning and Function of Acts 7: 46-50', *JBL* 106.2 (1987), pp. 261-75.

Talbert, Charles H., *Literary Patterns, Theological Themes, and the Genre of Luke–Acts* (SBLMS, 20; Missoula: Scholars Press, 1974).

—'Martyrdom in Luke–Acts and the Lucan Social Ethic', in Richard Cassidy and Philip Scharper (eds.), *Political Issues in Luke–Acts* (Maryknoll, NY: Orbis Books, 1983), pp. 99-110.

Tannehill, Robert C., *The Narrative Unity of Luke–Acts: A Literary Interpretation* (2 vols.; Minneapolis: Fortress Press, 1990).

Thurén, Lauri, 'On Studying Ethical Argumentation and Persuasion in the New Testament', in Porter and Olbricht (eds.), *Rhetoric*, pp. 464-78.

Toolan, Michael J., *Narrative, a Critical Linguistic Introduction* (London: Routledge, 1988).

Tuckett, C.M. (ed.), *Luke's Literary Achievement* (JSNTSup, 116; Sheffield: Sheffield Academic Press, 1995).

Turner, Nigel, *Grammar of New Testament Greek*. III. *Syntax* (Edinburgh: T. & T. Clark, 1963).

—'The Quality of the Greek of Luke–Acts', in J.K. Elliott (ed.), *Studies in New Testament Language and Text* (NovTSup, 44; Leiden: E.J. Brill, 1976), pp. 387-400.

Ure, Jean, and Jeffrey Ellis, 'Register in Descriptive Linguistics and Linguistic Sociology', in Uribe-Villegas (ed.), *Issues in Sociolinguistics* (The Hague: Mouton, 1974), pp. 42-59.

Uribe-Villegas, Oscar, 'Introduction: Sociolinguistics in Search of a Place among the Academic Disciplines', in *idem*, (ed.), *Issues in Sociolinguistics* (Contributions to the Sociology of Language, 15; The Hague: Mouton, 1977), pp. 21-35.

—'On the Social in Language and the Linguistic in Society', in Oscar Uribe-Villegas (ed.), *Issues in Sociolinguistics* (The Hague: Mouton, 1977), pp. 60-85.

Van Dijk, Teun A., *Text and Context* (London: Longman, 1977).

Veltman, Fred, 'The Defense Speeches of Paul in Acts', in Talbert (ed.), *New Perspectives*, pp. 243-59.

Vielhauer, Philip, 'On the Paulinism of Acts', in Keck and Martyn (eds.), *Studies in Luke–Acts* (London: SPCK, 1976), pp. 33-48.

Vorster, Johannes, 'Strategies of Persuasion in Romans 1.16-17', in Porter and Olbricht (eds.), *Rhetoric*, pp. 152-70.

Walaskay, Paul W., *And so we Came to Rome: The Political Perspective of St Luke* (SNTSMS, 49; Cambridge: Cambridge University Press, 1983).

Wallace, Stephen, 'Figure and Ground: The Interrelationships of Linguistic Categories', in Paul J. Hopper (ed.), *Tense-Aspect: Between Semantics and Pragmatics* (Amsterdam: John Benjamins, 1982), pp. 201-223.

Watson, Duane, 'Paul's Rhetorical Strategy in 1 Corinthians 15', in Porter and Olbricht (eds.), *Rhetoric*, pp. 231-49.

Wedderburn, A.J.M., 'Tradition and Redaction in Acts 2:1-13', *JSNT* 55 (1994), pp. 27-54.

Wilcox, Max, 'A Foreword to the Study of the Speeches in Acts', *Studies in Judaism in Late Antiquity* 12.1 (1975), pp. 206-24.

Witherington III, Ben, 'Editing the Good News: Some Synoptic Lessons for the Study of Acts', in Witherington (ed.), *History*, pp. 324-47.

Witherington III, Ben (ed.), *The Acts of the Apostles: A Socio-Rhetorical Commentary* (Grand Rapids: Eerdmans, 1998).

—*History, Literature and Society in the Book of Acts* (Cambridge: Cambridge University Press, 1996).

Wuellner, Wilhelm 'Biblical Exegesis in the Light of the History and Historicity of Rhetoric and the Nature of the Rhetoric of Religion', in Porter and Olbricht (eds.), *Rhetoric*, pp. 492-513.

Yule, G.U., *The Statistical Study of Literary Vocabulary* (Cambridge: Cambridge University Press, 1944).

Zehnle, Richard F., *Peter's Pentecost Discourse* (SBLMS, 15; Nashville: Abingdon Press, 1971).

Zerhusen, Bob, 'An Overlooked Judean Diglossia in Acts 2?', *BTB* 25 (1995), pp. 118-30.

INDEXES

INDEX OF REFERENCES

OLD TESTAMENT

Deuteronomy		*1 Samuel*		*Isaiah*	
29	121	13.14 LXX	114	44.28	114
				45.7	114
Joshua		*Psalms*			
14.1	114	28.3 LXX	97	*Jeremiah*	
		29.3	97	7.4-5	102
		105	121		

NEW TESTAMENT

Matthew		8.54	166	2 (cont.)	160, 161,
8.23	142	9.59	143		164, 171,
14.6	142	14.1	139		172
		15.30	107	2.1-4	153
Mark		16.22	139	2.1-3	152
2.23	139, 140	18.33	167	2.1	155
5.7-10	62	22.49	136	2.3	152
5.15	62	24.7	167	2.4-5	152
5.18-19	62	24.34	166	2.5-14	157
8.31	167	24.46	167	2.5	153, 156
9.9	167			2.6	156, 157
9.10	167	*John*		2.7	157
9.32	167	2.19	167	2.8	157
10.34	167	6.64	136	2.11	157
		10.17	167, 168	2.12-21	154
Luke		20.9	167	2.12-13	152
1.1-4	90			2.12	152, 155,
1.3	143	*Acts*			157, 161
1.59	139	1	108, 115	2.13	152, 154,
2	100, 164	1.1	90		157
3.21	139	1.11	106	2.14-21	150
6.1	139	1.24	106	2.14-16	153
6.6	139	2	115, 149-	2.14	153, 157
6.12	139		51, 155,	2.15-21	152
7.14	166		156, 158,	2.15	105, 157

Index of References 193

22.25-29 | 133
22.26 | 106
23 | 131
23.6-9 | 153
23.9 | 106
23.11 | 75, 76
23.12-35 | 75
23.17 | 106
23.18 | 106
23.27 | 106
24 | 130, 131
24.1-26 | 75
24.5 | 106
24.11 | 136
24.17 | 136
25.1-12 | 75
25.13–26.32 | 75
26 | 129-31
26.31 | 106
26.32 | 106
27 | 17, 50, 60, 61, 63, 64, 66, 67, 69, 71, 77-79, 82, 83, 89, 108, 109, 115, 146, 151, 160, 171, 175
27.1 | 60, 71
27.2 | 71, 74
27.3 | 66, 71, 73, 74
27.4 | 71, 74
27.5 | 71
27.6 | 71, 74
27.7 | 71, 74, 75
27.8 | 71
27.9-10 | 75
27.9 | 74
27.10 | 66, 72, 74, 75, 77
27.11 | 73, 74
27.12 | 72, 74
27.13-17 | 72
27.13 | 72-74, 78, 85
27.14 | 74

27.15-16 | 64
27.15 | 71, 73, 74
27.16 | 71, 72, 85
27.17 | 66, 73, 85, 86
27.18 | 66, 71-73, 83, 84
27.19 | 72, 73, 84
27.20 | 71, 74
27.21-26 | 75-77, 176
27.21-25 | 78
27.21 | 66, 74, 75
27.22 | 74-76
27.23 | 76
27.24 | 76
27.25 | 66, 75, 76
27.26 | 76
27.27 | 71, 74, 78, 83, 84
27.28 | 73
27.29 | 71, 73, 84
27.30 | 72, 73
27.31 | 75
27.32 | 73
27.33-34 | 75
27.33 | 66, 74, 75
27.34 | 75
27.35 | 75
27.36 | 73
27.37 | 71, 72
27.38 | 72, 73
27.39 | 72, 74
27.41 | 73, 74
27.42 | 66, 74, 85
27.43-44 | 73
27.43 | 73, 74
27.44 | 60, 140
28.4 | 106
28.8 | 140, 141
28.17 | 140
28.24 | 153

Romans
8.11 | 167

1 Corinthians
14 | 150

14.4 | 150
14.6-13 | 150
14.33-36 | 24
15 | 25, 168
15.3-5 | 166
15.4 | 166, 167
15.37 | 136

Galatians
1.1 | 167

Ephesians
1–3 | 44
1 | 45
1.4 | 45
1.7 | 45
1.10 | 167
1.11 | 45
1.12 | 45
1.14 | 45
1.16 | 45
1.17 | 45
1.23 | 45
2 | 45
2.11 | 44, 45
2.19 | 45
2.20 | 46
2.21 | 46
2.22 | 46
3 | 46
3.6 | 46
3.12 | 46
3.13 | 46
3.20 | 46
4–6 | 44
4 | 46
4.25 | 44
5–6 | 46

Philippians
2 | 25, 68
3 | 25
3.4 | 65
3.13 | 68
3.18 | 66

Colossians
2.12 | 167

INDEX OF MODERN AUTHORS